THE DOOMSDAY MOTHER

Also by John Glatt

Golden Boy
The Perfect Father
The Family Next Door
My Sweet Angel
The Lost Girls
The Prince of Paradise
Love Her to Death
Lost and Found
Playing with Fire
Secrets in the Cellar
To Have and to Kill
Forgive Me, Father
The Doctor's Wife
One Deadly Night
Depraved
Cries in the Desert
For I Have Sinned
Evil Twins
Cradle of Death
Blind Passion
Deadly American Beauty
Never Leave Me
Twisted

THE
DOOMSDAY
MOTHER

Lori Vallow, Chad Daybell,
and the End of an American Family

JOHN GLATT

ST. MARTIN'S PRESS
NEW YORK

First published in the United States by St. Martin's Press,
an imprint of St. Martin's Publishing Group

www.stmartins.com

Library of Congress Cataloging-in-Publication Data

Names: Glatt, John, author.
Title: The doomsday mother : Lori Vallow, Chad Daybell, and the end of
    an American family / John Glatt.
Description: First edition. | New York, NY : St. Martin's Press, 2022.
Identifiers: LCCN 2021044957 | ISBN 9781250276674 (hardcover) |
    ISBN 9781250276681 (ebook)
Subjects: LCSH: Daybell, Chad, 1968- | Vallow, Lori, 1973- | Filicide—
    United States—Case studies. | Murder—Investigation—United States—
    Case studies.
Classification: LCC HV6542 .G59 2022 | DDC 364.152/30973—dc23
LC record available at https://lccn.loc.gov/2021044957

Our books may be purchased in bulk for promotional, educational, or business use.
Please contact your local bookseller or the Macmillan Corporate and Premium Sales
Department at 1-800-221-7945, extension 5442, or by email at
MacmillanSpecialMarkets@macmillan.com.

First Edition: 2022

10 9 8 7 6 5 4 3 2 1

For my wife and soul mate
Gail Freund

CONTENTS

Prologue   1

PART ONE: LORI

PART TWO: CHAD DAYBELL

PART THREE: GASOLINE AND FIRE

PART FOUR: END-TIMES

PROLOGUE

Sunday, January 26, 2020

Newlyweds Chad and Lori Daybell didn't appear to have a care in the world as they left their luxurious rented condo for an afternoon at the beach. They were honeymooning on the beautiful Hawaiian island of Kauai and enjoying another perfect day in paradise.

Lori, a strikingly beautiful forty-six-year-old blonde, wore large sunglasses, a blue swimsuit, and a beige cover-up. Chad, five years older, sported a baggy blue T-shirt, beach shorts, and flip-flops. They were an odd-looking couple, with Lori appearing somewhat out of place with her dumpy new husband.

It was a twenty-five-mile drive to the ritzy Kauai Beach Resort, where they had spent most afternoons sunbathing and swimming. They were almost there when a Kauai police car with flashing lights pulled over their rented black Ford Explorer on Kuhio Highway. They were escorted into the resort's parking lot, where more than a dozen armed police and detectives were waiting.

"Step out," ordered a Kauai police sergeant. "We have a search warrant for you guys, your car, and your belongings."

Lori calmly stepped out of the car, unfazed, as the officer handed her two search warrants. Chad looked visibly nervous. He was ordered to sit in a police SUV while their vehicle was searched. Lori took her time, though, reading the search warrants for their rental car and condo, before being escorted into the back of a separate police car.

A few minutes later, as they sat across from each other in parallel police vehicles, Chad mournfully stared at his new wife, put his hand on the window, and mouthed, "I love you."

That day in the parking lot was the culmination of a massive nationwide search for Lori and Chad Daybell. Two months earlier, they had gone on the run after lying to police in Rexburg, Idaho, about the whereabouts of Lori's seven-year-old autistic son, J.J., and teenage daughter, Tylee. The children had literally disappeared off the face of the earth the previous September and police feared for their safety.

"It is astonishing that rather than work with law enforcement to help us locate her own children," read a Rexburg police press release from December 30, 2019, "Lori Vallow has chosen instead to leave the state with her new husband."

In the couple's wake, they'd left behind a trail of highly suspicious deaths: their respective former spouses—Charles Vallow and Tammy Daybell—as well as Lori's brother Alex and third husband, Joe Ryan.

The story of the missing children made global headlines, with J.J.'s and Tylee's faces appearing everywhere. No one could believe that a mother could possibly be so coldly indifferent about her children's welfare.

Then came the strange revelations that Chad and Lori believed they were gods, leading an army of chosen ones to survive the end of the world. They were also on a divine mission to rid the world of evil zombies, constantly being revealed to Chad by his spirit guides on the other side.

A prodigious author of more than two dozen books on what he claimed was the fast-approaching doomsday, Chad was viewed as a gifted prophet by his legion of followers.

"I don't fictionalize any of the events portrayed," he wrote in his 2017 autobiography, *Living on the Edge of Heaven*. "My torn veil allows information to be downloaded into my brain from the other side. The scenes I am shown are real events that will happen."

Lori, a five-times married devout Mormon and mother of three, had been an avid fan of Chad's books for years. When she finally met him at a 2018 Preppers (preparing for the end-times) conference, he informed her that they had been married many times before in previous lives. That they had been anointed by God to gather the 144,000 people who would survive the Armageddon that Chad forecast would happen on July 22, 2020.

The day before police pulled them over in Hawaii, Lori had been served with an order from an Idaho court, compelling her to produce J.J. and Tylee within five days or face arrest. Now, as police searched their SUV, half a dozen reporters, including a team from NBC's *Dateline,* were on the edge of the parking lot videoing the proceedings.

At around 3:30 P.M., police winched the couple's rental SUV to a tow truck and informed them they were free to leave. Lori was allowed to take away some personal belongings, including a plastic Ziploc bag containing thousands of dollars in cash.

East Idaho News reporter Nate Eaton, on assignment from Rexburg, Idaho, approached the couple, holding a large microphone as his colleague Eric Grossarth shot video.

"Lori," shouted Eaton. "Can you tell me where your kids are? Where are your kids?"

"No comment," replied Lori glibly as she grabbed Chad's hand and led him away.

"They've been missing for four months," Eaton continued. "You have nothing to say? You're over here in Hawaii."

Receiving no answer from Lori, Eaton turned his attention to Chad, who was anxiously clenching his jaw.

"Chad, where are Lori's kids? What happened to [your wife] Tammy? Why have you guys been in Hawaii so long? There are people around the country *praying* for your children, *praying* for you guys. Why don't you just give us answers?"

"That's great," quipped Lori, nonchalantly flashing a cold smile as the couple headed into the resort.

PART ONE

LORI

ONE

THE CHEERLEADER

Lori Norene Cox was born on June 26, 1973, in Rialto, California, the fifth child of Barry and Janis Cox. Their eldest, Stacey Lynn, had been born seven years earlier, followed by two sons, Alexander Lamar in 1968 and Adam Lane a year later. A daughter, Laura Lee, was born on August 7, 1971, but tragically died at the age of six weeks. Four years later, Janis gave birth to Summer Nouvelle, completing the family.

The Cox family had deep roots in Rialto, named after the bridge in Venice and just fifty-six miles east of Los Angeles. Barry was a successful life insurance underwriter with political aspirations. In March 1974 he actively campaigned for a vacant seat on the Rialto City Council.

"I would like to see more long-range city planning," read his campaign statement. "I support programs that benefit the needs of the youth and the elderly and want to reduce all unnecessary spending."

Prior to the election, Cox, then thirty-three, was profiled in the *San Bernardino County Sun,* which highlighted his Mormon credentials. A lifelong member of the Church of Jesus Christ of Latter-day Saints (LDS), he served as a missionary in England in the early 1960s.

Although he failed to win a seat on the city council, Barry was appointed the 1974 Beneficial Life Insurance man of the year for selling over a million dollars of insurance. He won the award again the following year, and his bosses took out an advertisement in the *San Bernardino County Sun* to publicly congratulate him.

* * *

In 1980, seven-year-old Lori, known by the family as Lolo, started at Trapp Elementary School. She was slightly overweight with blond hair and blue eyes, her natural charm and affability drawing people to her like a magnet.

In third grade she became best friends with Rose Vaughan (not her real name), whose parents knew Barry and Janis Cox. The two girls soon became inseparable, and Rose was always at the Coxes' house in Sycamore Avenue, where she got to know Lori's parents and siblings well.

"We were together all the time," said Rose. "Lori was always very, very sweet. She was kind and cared about everybody."

The Cox family lived in a large house on the ultraexclusive El Rancho Verde Country Club, across from the eighteen-hole golf course. Lori and her four siblings were raised in affluence and always had the best of everything.

"Lori grew up spoiled," said Rose. "Her parents were well-off and bought the kids everything they wanted."

The Coxes attended the Redlands California Temple in Redlands, where Lori and her siblings were all active in the children's program. But Rose, who was not Mormon, noticed that the Coxes were far more flamboyant than other big LDS families in Rialto, and not particularly religious.

"Her family did not act Mormon," Rose explained. "They went to church occasionally, but it wasn't like they were superdevout."

Rose's mother was a teacher and strict, so nothing had prepared her for Lori's unconventional parents. Janis favored high heels, tight leopard-skin pants, short tight tops, bleached-blond hair, and freshly done nails.

"They would leave all the kids alone and go to Hawaii for the weekend," said Rose. "They were not present."

Lori's parents also did not believe in taxes and would battle the IRS for decades. In 2019, Barry self-published a manifesto entitled *How the American Public Can Dismantle the IRS,* dedicating it to all freedom-loving USA citizens.

"The reader will learn the American public has been brainwashed or indoctrinated by IRS propaganda," wrote Cox, "which is used as a weapon of FEAR to scare the hell out of every American."

Outspoken at social gatherings, Barry Cox would often argue that taxes were illegal and that the IRS was a criminal organization.

"He was very vocal," said Rose. "My father hated him because he refused to pay taxes."

As Rose got to know the Cox family better, she tried to avoid Lori's older brother Alex. The tall, gangly teenager never had a girlfriend and seemed fixated on his younger sister Lori.

"Alex just gave me the creeps," said Rose. "When Lori and I were in the pool, he was always watching us and I didn't like that."

Lori Cox was a popular student who always got good grades without trying too hard. In May 1984, the fifth grader won the Trapp Elementary School spelling bee and was singled out in a local newspaper report.

While Lori was in middle school, Barry and Janis started frequenting the Santa Anita racetrack, often taking Lori along for good luck.

"Her parents pulled Lori out of school a lot to go to the track," remembered Rose. "I think her father was a gambler."

Lori's brother Adam once won a bet with his father about who would win the Kentucky Derby, and Barry paid up by building a basketball court in their front driveway.

According to Rose, Barry and Janis would also go to Hawaii for weeks at a time, leaving the children alone in the house. They gave sixteen-year-old Alex blank checks to buy food for the siblings, putting him in charge of Lori and Summer.

Alex would cash the checks, spending most of the money on himself. He would also order pizza and throw parties for his friends.

"Alex was supposed to look after Summer," said Rose, "but he was always doing something bad, so Lori had to."

Several times Barry and Janis brought Lori to Hawaii, where she fell in love with the magical islands, which would draw her back again and again throughout her life.

Every Friday night, Lori would go over to Rose's house for dinner and spent holidays with her family. Looking back, Rose believes that Lori craved the security of a stable family and looked to Rose's parents to provide what she lacked at home.

"I had more of a really centered family," Rose explained. "My mom and dad were always around and cooked dinner every night. Lori really liked that, and she used to like coming over to my house. Her mom just didn't act like a mother."

When Lori was in sixth grade, Janis decided Lori should lose weight and put her on a strict diet. Lori was not happy, but her mother insisted that Lori had to stick to it so she could become a cheerleader. Janis also enlisted her daughter to join her church softball team, which Janis loved coaching. And she would ridicule Lori in front of her friends if Janis caught her eating chips or something else Janis considered fattening.

One night while they were in seventh grade, Lori tearfully confided to Rose that Alex wanted to have sex with her. They were sitting on the floor in Lori's bedroom when she suddenly burst into tears, blurting out that her older brother had been making sexual moves on her.

"We grew up together so we talked about everything," said Rose. "Suddenly Lori was crying and emotional and she just said, 'Alex is trying to have sex with me. What can I do?'"

The two girls fell into each other's arms and hugged and cried. Finally Rose told Lori that she had no idea what to do. Lori never brought it up again and Rose never pursued it. Now, in hindsight, Rose wishes that she had told her parents at the time.

"I had a really good relationship with my mom," she said, "but I just got scared and didn't follow up. And I regret it because what if that could have changed the course of history?"

In fall 1988, Lori and Rose moved up to Eisenhower High School. The previous year Lori's older sister, Stacey, had married a Home Depot executive named Steve Cope and left home.

Under her mother's supervision, Lori had now slimmed down and was in great shape. She joined the Eisenhower cheerleading squad as a flier, the member thrown up in the air to the cheers of the crowd.

"She was popular [and] had a lot of friends," said her older brother Adam. "There's a lot of what Lori has that attracts people to her."

Lori soon became close to another member of the cheerleading squad, Bernadette Flores-Lopez, who remembers them clicking immediately. Although Bernadette came from a less affluent part of town, she was soon a regular visitor to the Coxes' Sycamore Avenue house along with the rest of the cheer squad. They would hang out and swim in the Coxes' pool. The cheer squad's favorite routine was to the Sly and the Family Stone 1960s hit "Dance to the Music," which they regularly rehearsed at the Cox house.

"I thought she was just a Barbie doll," said Bernadette. "She was just really, really friendly, not overly friendly, but she was just really sweet. I was just so excited to get to know her."

Bernadette remembers Lori as being a devout Mormon who attended religious-seminary classes before school every morning.

"In her house there was a giant copy of the Book of Mormon," said Bernadette.

In her senior year, Lori started dating another Eisenhower student named Nelson Yanes. She was smitten from the start.

"We grew up right around the corner from each other," said Nelson. "I was her first boyfriend."

Nelson, who came from a wealthy family but was not Mormon, soon met Lori's unconventional parents and remembers them as "a different type of family."

Almost overnight, Lori Cox had transformed from a plain chunky girl into a miniature version of her flashy mother.

She embarked on a new social life revolving around the cheerleading squad, making her something of a celebrity at Eisenhower High School. She even went on a cheerleading trip to Six Flags Magic Mountain, where they did an impromptu performance.

"She bleached her hair and started wearing skimpy clothes," recalled Rose. "She started getting her nails done and wore red lipstick. . . . She was all about her social circle with flashy cars and flashy clothes. That just wasn't the Lori that I grew up with."

Rose also didn't approve of Lori's new boyfriend, Nelson, and thought he was a "hothead." Rose remembers him as having a temper and yelling at Lori in the school hallways, where she would cower and never stand up for herself.

"The more Lori started to be around Nelson," said Rose, "the less I started to be around."

Lori now adored being the center of attention and loved people telling her how beautiful she was, after losing so much weight. Rose had never before seen this narcissistic streak. She wondered if Lori was trying to impress her older brother Alex and whether he was still pursuing her sexually.

"And I don't know if it was because she grew up chunky," said Rose, "and then all of a sudden got really thin. Or if it had anything to do with Alex and what Lori had told me in the seventh grade."

On April 24, 1989, Lori's sister Stacey gave birth to a daughter she named Melani. Over the years Lori would become a second mother to her niece. They would become close and Melani would adopt her aunt's extreme religious beliefs.

"Lori used to carry me around as a little baby," said Melani, "and pretend that I was hers when she was sixteen."

The following year Stacey, now living in Washington State, was diagnosed with type 1 diabetes and put on an insulin program. She was told by her doctor to regularly inject insulin and closely monitor her blood sugar. Stacey would refuse to adhere to this life-or-death regimen.

On July 6, 1990, sixteen-year-old Stacey Gilliam, who was in the same year as Lori Cox at Eisenhower High School, was brutally murdered by her boyfriend, Mark Barros. The two were in his van celebrating his seventeenth birthday eating pizza and cake and discussing religion in a Winchell's parking lot in San Bernardino. Barros suddenly asked if she was afraid to die, and Stacey said she was not. He then took out a knife and repeatedly slashed her throat before stabbing her in the chest.

The following morning Barros went to a police station and surrendered, telling police he had been thinking about murdering Stacey for a year.

Lori Cox knew Stacey and was, like everyone else at Eisenhower High, shocked by the murder.

"It was absolutely horrible," remembers Rose Vaughan.

Years later there would be rumors that Lori had been in the car, too, when her friend had been murdered.

"Lori was not there that night Stacey was murdered," Rose says.

Barros pleaded guilty to second-degree murder and served twenty-eight years in prison before being granted parole in February 2018.

Lori Cox graduated from Eisenhower High School on June 12, 1991. Her yearbook graduation photo shows a sophisticated young lady with long blond hair in California-style beachy waves. She has a wide smile and is wearing a dark bustier top and glam gloves with zippers.

According to Lori's Eisenhower alumni page, her favorite school memory was a 1989 cheerleading pep rally before a big football game, when all eyes were on her.

TWO

"A PSYCHOLOGICAL HORNET'S NEST"

Soon after graduating, eighteen-year-old Lori Cox left home and moved in with her high school sweetheart, Nelson Yanes. When Lori informed her parents that she and Nelson wanted to marry, they were against it.

"He wasn't my favorite and we didn't have a close relationship," Janis would later say. "She left home and we asked Lori to wait a year."

But in 1992, against her parents' wishes, Lori eloped to Las Vegas with Nelson. None of the Cox family nor any of Lori's friends attended the wedding.

The marriage was short-lived; when Rose Vaughan ran into Lori a year later at a grocery store, Lori told her she was planning to divorce Nelson. She invited Rose over to the house she was renting in Rialto with Nelson, who was out at the time.

"We chatted on her couch for an hour," said Rose. "She said she was going to get a divorce from Nelson and that she was moving, but she didn't know where to. She claimed Nelson was beating her up, but I don't know if that was true or not."

After her divorce, Lori moved to Austin, Texas, where she enrolled at the Baldwin Beauty Schools and found a job as a hairstylist in a local salon. Her brother Adam was already living in Austin, making a name for himself as a shock-jock radio DJ under the moniker Bo Nasty.

Adam's fiancée, Nicole Meier, met Lori in Austin soon after she arrived. Nicole found her future sister-in-law beautiful, outgoing, but constantly craving attention.

"She probably looked in the mirror more than anyone I know," said

Nicole, "and it was a running joke in the family. She loved to look at herself . . . [and] always had drama in her life."

Soon after arriving in Austin, Lori started dating William LaGiola, who was a year older than her. It was a tempestuous relationship, and for the next couple of years they periodically lived together, as Lori tried unsuccessfully to convert him to the Mormon religion. The relationship turned violent, with Lori calling the police to their Bluff Springs Road house on several occasions.

On July 16, 1995, Travis County deputy sheriff Michael Mancias met with Lori, who claimed that William had hit her in the mouth and thrown her on the bed, injuring her.

"[We] did observe an injury to Lori Cox," he wrote in his report. "Her upper lip did have a small cut on the inside of the mouth."

LaGiola was charged with assault, but the case was later dismissed because the victim, Lori, failed to show up for court.

Meanwhile, in Washington State, Lori's sister Stacey was in a bitter custody battle for her six-year-old daughter, Melani. Her father, Steve Cope, claimed that Stacey, now dangerously ill with type 1 diabetes, was refusing to take her insulin shots and her "obsessive" behavior was "irreparably damaging" Lori's beloved little niece.

In an August 1995 motion for custody of Melani, filed with the Superior Court of King County, Cope outlined his wife's tragic physical and mental decline. In his seventeen-page sworn declaration, Cope blamed Barry and Janis Cox for many of Stacey's problems.

"Stacey has always admitted to me, and others, that her family was a psychological hornet's nest," he wrote. "Her mother Janis Cox is obsessed with issues of weight, physical appearance and feminine bodies."

By mid-1994, he wrote, Stacey viewed "all food as poison," fearing sugar and some vegetables. She was also germophobic, washing her hands at least four times an hour. He also claimed his wife was suicidal and refused to take her insulin injections.

Instead of seeking hospital attention, he wrote, Stacey had insisted on vacationing in Hawaii, saying it was the only place that would make her happy.

At the end of December 1994, Stacey weighed just seventy-six pounds and was hospitalized three times, where she had to be fed intravenously.

Cope was especially concerned about the effect Stacey's behavior was having on Melani's welfare. Her mother refused to let her attend kindergarten because of germs, as well as drawing up a list of "forbidden foods" for Melani, including milk.

"Melani's last two lower teeth came in without enamel," he wrote, "due to a lack of calcium at the time they were growing in. Melani now fears the dentist."

Cope wrote that he tried hard to keep the kitchen stocked with healthy food, but Stacey would return it to the store while he was out at work.

"Melani has become the caretaker for her mother," he wrote, "believing she is responsible [and] sacrifices her own childhood to caring for her mother."

He stated that Stacey now rarely left the house and had only gone to church once in the last eight months, leaving Melani with a lack of religious instruction.

In late March 1995, Cope went on a business trip to Atlanta. He returned to find Stacey had gone to stay with her parents in California without telling him and had taken Melani with her. For the next few months they lived with Barry and Janis Cox.

"I spent a lot of time in the Cox home," remembered Melani in 2020. "Barry and Janis, my grandparents, lived in California, and I lived with them for a while. My mom was sick and I remember my dad traveling a lot for his job."

On July 1, Cope flew to California to attend Lori's brother Adam Cox's wedding to Nicole Meier. Lori also attended the sealing service—a ritual performed in LDS temples to establish the existence of family relationships throughout eternity—held at the Jesus Christ of Latter-day Saints temple in La Jolla.

A couple of days later, Cope brought Stacey and Melani back to Washington with him. The three months Melani had lived in her grandparents' house had changed her beyond recognition. She now believed she was a three-year-old boy and had cut her hair short with scissors and started wearing baseball hats like her uncle Alex.

"Something weird has happened to Melani," wrote her father. "She insists she's a boy and upon meeting new people will insist, 'Call me A.J., Alex, or Bobby and I am 3 years old.' When she does that she begins talking in a different pitch, as if she were 3 years old."

On July 28, Cope became so concerned about Melani's welfare that he decided to remove her from her mother. He packed up her clothes and told her they were going on a fishing trip. Then he drove her to his brother and sister-in-law's house.

"In order that Melani and I can return to the house," he wrote, "I am asking that Stacey be required to vacate it. I have arranged for my mother to come and be with Melani while I work."

On August 14, Barry Cox filed his own sworn declaration on behalf of his daughter, demanding permanent custody of Melani. Cox accused his son-in-law of being an absent father who put work above his family. Cox said he had tried unsuccessfully to steer Cope to the right path.

"I loved Steve and I wanted to help him," wrote Cox. "Accordingly, I warned Steve at one point that his absence and estranged attitude for his wife and child would lead to problems. I told him that a wife was like a delicate flower and needed to have tender love and care. He was indifferent to my suggestions."

Cox described his son-in-law as "a construction worker type" with no appreciation for "things of delicacy or of a sensitive emotional nature."

Cox also labeled Steve's allegations against him and Janis "false," writing that he was shocked by Steve's "malicious" statements.

"Steve abducted Melanie [sic] in the middle of the night," he wrote, "and left Stacey alone in the house . . . to die. He ran away like a thief in the night."

The court awarded custody of Melani to her father, Steve Cope, who eventually divorced Stacey and remarried.

On October 22, 1995, Lori, now twenty-two, married William LaGiola after becoming pregnant. None of Lori's family attended the wedding. From the beginning there was constant drama in the marriage, with Lori frequently dialing 911 to summon the police.

On February 21, 1996, Lori, still using her maiden name, Cox, swore out an affidavit against her new husband. She accused him of mentally and physically abusing her over the last three years and stated that William had threatened to kill her and their unborn child if she dared call the police on him again.

"William has beat me up," claimed Lori, "hitting and pushing me and holding the phone away from me so that I could not call 911."

She added that William had warned her that if he went to jail, he would find her and kill her, no matter how long it took.

Once again the case against LaGiola was dismissed by an Austin court.

On April 8, 1996, Lori gave birth to a baby boy she named Colby. By this time, the couple had separated and William had moved back to his parents' house in Brackettville, Texas. After Colby was born, William finally agreed to convert to Mormonism, so the couple could be reunited and bring up their new baby together.

A few months later, Lori swore out a bizarre criminal complaint against William LaGiola, explaining that she had agreed to give him one last chance after Colby was born. In mid-July, she had driven her three-month-old baby two hundred miles west to Brackettville to attend William's Mormon baptism.

"During our relationship I prayed that he would accept my religion," wrote Lori. "Repent of his carnal, selfish and sensual behavior and become a Christian."

According to Lori, she arrived in Brackettville to find William had been living with another woman. Nevertheless, she agreed to move into his parents' house after William apologized and promised to support her and Colby.

"He said he wanted and needed his wife and baby," wrote Lori. "He took advantage of my good faith, my charity and my vulnerable situation."

According to Lori's affidavit, William then took her car keys and allegedly "imprisoned" her and Colby at his parents' house for the next several months. In early November, she claimed, while William was passed out drunk after a one-night stand with a new girlfriend, Lori sneaked out with Colby at 4:00 A.M. and drove to her parents, now living in San Antonio, Texas.

For the next two weeks, she alleged William called her every day, begging her to come back to him with Colby. She finally relented and agreed to give him one last chance.

"I was desperate for help," she explained. "I also wanted to return to Brackettville to get my clothes . . . and needed my belonging [sic] for me and the baby that were in his possession."

Once again, according to Lori, things didn't work out. When she tried to leave with Colby, William and his father, Vito LaGiola, told her she was free to go, but Colby must remain with them. Lori agreed to stay.

A couple of weeks later they spent a family Thanksgiving at Barry and Janis Cox's home, so Lori could earn some extra money cutting relatives' hair. The plan was for William to drive her car back to Brackettville, then return it to San Antonio with all their belongings.

"William did not keep his word to return my car or my belongings," wrote Lori. "William also used my baby's welfare card (LoneStar) for his own personal expenses."

As Lori told it, she then had her father and the Brackettville sheriff escort her to Vito LaGiola's house to collect her car. They arrived to find all her belongings lying in the street, and she had to call a repo company to get her car back.

"William is void of any light and intelligence to know the difference between right and wrong," wrote Lori. "They believe they can lie and cheat and conspire to do evil . . . without any consequences. Obviously I am filing for divorce immediately! I also plan to file civil charges."

THREE

JOE RYAN

For the next several years Lori and Colby were constantly on the move, living in numerous places, as Lori struggled to survive as a hairstylist. Lori drifted from job to job in a rootless existence. She doted on her little son, who represented the only permanence in her life.

In the late 1990s Lori was living in Westlake, Texas, where she became friends with a young woman named Tami Joyce. Lori always had her adorable toddler son, Colby, with her, and Tami remembers what good care Lori took of him. Tami was also impressed by how Lori kept in shape by running twice a day and avoiding alcohol.

Lori told Tami how madly in love she had been with the boy's father, and how she had wanted a life with him. She blamed LaGiola for not wanting one, too, claiming it led to their divorce.

Later Colby would remember his early days with his mother as she floundered. He had to grow up fast and became used to packing up his things and moving at the drop of a hat. He always felt protective of Lori, who treated him more as a best friend than a son.

"It was always like we were trying to get away," he said. "She's trying to provide for me, trying to figure out what she wanted to do. I just remember our situation always being very hard."

In May 1998, Barry and Janis Cox took Lori, her sister Summer, and Colby on a family vacation to Hawaii. Alex had stayed behind at the Coxes' house in San Antonio to look after his ailing sister, Stacey, now divorced. Over the past year, her health had deteriorated further and she was very sick.

The day the group arrived in Hawaii, Alex called with the bad news that he had gone to check on Stacey and found her unconscious.

"He was very upset," said Summer. "He called an ambulance and they took her to the hospital."

The group spent the rest of the trip on the phone getting updates on Stacey's condition and flew home early when Stacey lapsed into a coma and was moved to a hospice.

Lori called her nine-year-old niece, Melani, to break the devastating news that her mother was not going to make it.

"I don't think I would have wanted to have that phone call by anybody else," said Melani. "I remember flying up with my dad, who took me to see my mom [for the] last time in hospice."

Stacey Cope died on May 21, 1998, age thirty-one, and was buried in San Antonio.

On May 3, 1999, Lori's father, Barry Cox, was sentenced to a year and a day in prison and ordered to pay almost a quarter of a million dollars in restitution to the IRS. He had not paid any federal income taxes in 1988, 1989, and 1990.

On his release from prison, Cox sued the United States, the IRS, the US Department of Justice, and the probation service for personal injury damages.

"Time and again [I] personally confronted the IRS cabal with the FACTS," Cox later wrote in his autobiography, "showing that it is an illegal and criminal organization."

All four of his suits were dismissed, with the district court noting that Cox's true intention was to "collaterally attack his criminal conviction."

Cox appealed that decision, and the US Court of Appeals dismissed it as "frivolous."

Over the next few years Barry Cox would refuse to pay any of his back taxes, as the interest continued to accrue. He kept appealing all the decisions against him, leading to years of litigation.

In 2001, Lori and Colby moved to Driftwood, Texas, twenty-four miles west of Austin. She had recently started dating a forty-three-year-old, successful business analyst named Joe Ryan, whom she'd met at the hair salon where she worked. For Lori, who had been struggling to find her footing for years, the tall, handsome Ryan offered a lifeline for her and Colby to finally get some stability.

Joe Ryan had been brought up in foster care and wanted to start a family, immediately falling in love with the beautiful blonde, who wielded her charm on him. For Colby, now five, the new man in his mother's life was not a welcome addition, and he would later claim that Ryan was abusive.

In early 2002, Ryan proposed and Lori immediately accepted, on the understanding that he would convert to Mormonism. At Lori's suggestion they flew to Maui to get married on a beach.

In a beautiful ceremony, Joe gave his new bride an expensive diamond wedding ring. Once again, none of the Cox family were there for the wedding, Lori's third.

After their honeymoon they moved into a big house on Island Oaks Lane in Driftwood, Texas, and Lori soon became pregnant again.

"A lot of things changed quickly," Colby said. "All of a sudden she was having my sister [Tylee]."

Soon after they were married, Joe flew his sister, Annie Cushing, to Texas to meet his new bride. She was impressed with Lori and found her delightful.

"They were madly in love," Annie remembered. "They were just this incredibly beautiful couple [and] like celebrities wherever we went. They were both extroverts. They were larger-than-life."

During the visit Lori was charming and magnanimous. Annie was happy that her brother had found someone so perfect to start a family with.

"They were just like this little whirlwind of generosity and love," she said.

Tylee Ashlyn Ryan was born on September 24, 2002, and was a beautiful baby. Lori was delighted to have a daughter, and Colby immediately bonded with his new sister.

But although Lori and Joe looked like the perfect couple in photographs, things fell apart fast. Joe had a bad temper and could explode at the least provocation. He seemed to enjoy spanking Colby and giving him little hits on the head as punishment.

"He thought it was funny," said Colby. "He was pretty physically abusive."

After getting married, Lori had quit her job as a hairstylist. Joe built her a hair salon in the house so she could do her old clients' hair. One day Joe flew into a rage and destroyed the salon with a baseball bat.

"He was very explosive," said Colby, who was scared of his stepfather and always tried to keep out of his way.

In the summer of 2003, Ryan flew Annie Cushing and her children out to Texas for a second visit. He wanted them to meet his baby daughter, Tylee, and see his lavish new forty-four-hundred-square-foot house. After his miserable childhood in foster care, he desperately wanted Colby, Tylee, and his sister's children to grow up as cousins, giving him the family he had never known.

"They had built this absolutely amazing home," remembered Cushing. "It was spare no expense [and] he had designed everything."

Lori was her usual charming self, and all the kids loved her as she fussed over them. One morning Lori pulled out some chemicals and hair dye and brought Tylee into her newly built hair salon to have her hair dyed blond. Annie was astonished.

"That was really weird," she remembered. "I thought Tylee's baby hairs were blond and they were just growing in dark, but she had roots. And while she was talking to my oldest daughter and me, [Lori] just started putting highlights in Tylee's hair [and] she wasn't even one year old."

Soon after arriving, Annie saw trouble in the marriage.

One day, Annie's six-year-old daughter was getting out of Joe's SUV when she accidentally bumped the horn. He started yelling at the little girl, who burst into tears. As a furious Joe came toward her, Annie stepped between them to de-escalate the situation.

A couple of days later, she was shocked to see Joe pulling Colby across the room by his hand, which Joe had bent back sharply. Then he took off his belt and spanked the seven-year-old.

"What the hell are you doing?" asked Annie. Joe just ignored her and carried on beating the boy.

"It was . . . an unnecessary use of force," said Annie. "The guy had very little experience with kids. And he had this rage issue."

Later Annie spoke to Lori about the incident, explaining she didn't think it was a good idea to discipline Colby by pulling his hand so far back and using a belt. Lori seemed unconcerned and said she would talk to Joe about it.

"She was very chill about it," said Annie. "She had no issue with the belt, [so] they had clearly agreed on that."

For the rest of the trip Annie felt as if she were walking on eggshells. One day there was a bad rainstorm and the ceiling of the new living room started to leak. Suddenly Joe exploded, punching the wall and dropping f-bombs. Then he started throwing things. All the children froze, including Tylee in her little walker.

After that, Annie and her kids flew home, and she never saw her brother again.

"That was the end of our relationship," she said. "I was very angry."

FOUR

A TICKING TIME BOMB

As Lori's marriage fell apart, the thirty-year-old mother of two threw herself into her Mormon religion. She had always been a strong believer, but as she became more and more disillusioned with Joe Ryan, she sought refuge in LDS teachings.

She regularly took Colby and Tylee to church and had started dancing by herself at night in an empty room filled with mirrors to religious music and her favorite eighties love songs. It was her form of meditation and getting closer to God.

Lori now believed that Tylee was the reincarnation of her dead sister, Stacey, and that spirits from behind the veil (the unknown state of being after death) were giving Lori instructions on every aspect of her life. Since marrying Joe Ryan, she had moved away from mainstream Mormon beliefs into her own uncharted territory.

In 2003, Lori auditioned for *Wheel of Fortune,* as God had told her that she would win big on the popular TV game show. The former spelling bee champion aced her audition and then made the fourteen-hundred-mile trip to Sony Pictures Studios in Culver City, California, to appear on the show.

She wore a sexy tight-fitted pink top exposing white shirt cuffs, her long blond hair cascading past her shoulders. Millions watched as Lori spun the wheel. She shrieked with delight when she won $17,500 by completing the blanks making the phrases "Gopher," "Doc," "Isaac," and "Captain Stubing" (from *The Love Boat*). Lori was ecstatic as the audience applauded.

Host Pat Sajak had introduced her as a hairstylist from Austin.

"How's the hair in Austin?" he asked.

"It's good," gushed Lori. "Austin's a happening place."

"Probably thanks to you," quipped Sajak, before asking Lori a little about herself.

"I have a wonderful husband, Joseph, at home, who is watching our two beautiful children, Colby, who's seven, and Tylee, who is one."

"And what do you guys like to do for fun?"

"We like to play all kinds of sports on our three acres."

"Okay, it sounds like you have a nice life there. Congratulations."

"Thank you."

They went to commercials.

A few months later, Lori entered the Mrs. Hays County beauty pageant and won. In pictures taken afterward, she and Joe look like the perfect married couple. Lori is proudly wearing the Mrs. Hays County sash with a smiling Joe Ryan wrapping his arms around her waist.

"I don't know what really prompted her to want to do the pageant," said her sister Summer, "other than it gave her kind of an outlet and she thought it might help her marriage at the time."

As the new Mrs. Hays County, Lori automatically qualified for the Mrs. Texas beauty pageant. The winner of that state pageant would go on to compete for the coveted title of Mrs. America. Lori devoted herself to getting into the best possible shape by running and working out. The mission to become Mrs. America now dominated her life.

The 2004 Mrs. Texas pageant was held in June in Grapevine, Texas. According to the official Mrs. Texas website, the competition "celebrates the achievements, poise, and personality of today's married women." Lori got breast implants to improve her chances of winning.

The official pageant brochure contained a large photograph of Lori, alongside her personal adage: Love, Faith, Service. A picture of the whole Ryan family showed Lori, a grinning Colby, and Joe Ryan proudly holding little Tylee. The caption read:

From Lori, Joe, Colby and Tylee. We would like to thank all sponsors and fanatical supporters:

Janis and Barry Cox—San Antonio
Alex Cox—Phoenix

Lori arrived in Grapevine on a Friday morning for the two-day contest to meet the other twenty-seven contestants. They were then treated to a beauty seminar, followed by lunch. After an afternoon of rehearsal, Lori, with Joe, joined the other competitors and their husbands for a party.

On Saturday afternoon the official pageant began with all the competitors performing a line dance dressed in miniskirts, matching red cowboy hats, and boots.

"Now we have contestant number thirteen, Lori Ryan," intoned the announcer, as Lori confidently strutted to the front of the stage, waving her cowboy hat at the crowd. "She is Mrs. Hays County. She is thirty years old and she stands at five feet, six inches tall. She has blond hair and blue eyes. Her favorite thing is anything with chocolate."

Lori made the cut to the top fifteen semifinalists for the swimsuit part of the competition. She then took the stage to great applause, wearing a skimpy teal-colored bikini that showed off her well-toned body to full advantage.

For the evening-gown portion, Lori looked radiant in a white sparkly gown, as she waltzed onto the stage and winked at the audience.

"[Lori] is Mrs. Hays County," said the announcer. "Her husband's name is Joe. They've been married three and a half years and they have two children, eight and one-year-old. She was just recently on the *Wheel of Fortune* and won over seventeen thousand dollars. She's also involved with a wonderful group of twelve women and they're writing a book to help encourage other women. Contestant number thirteen, Lori Ryan."

Lori was then questioned by the pageant judges before they made their decision.

"Tell us what you are," asked a judge. "What makes you tick?"

"Being a good mom is very important to me, and a good wife and a good worker," replied Lori. "And being all those things together is not easy. So, I'm basically a ticking time bomb."

She would not make the top five.

A few days later, Lori started divorce proceedings against Joe Ryan, who then moved out of the house. She sold her wedding ring to a San Antonio jeweler for $4,300 and tried to move on with her life.

Colby was relieved that his abusive stepfather was out of his life: "When he left, it was definitely [a] relief. I felt safer."

Lori flew her fifteen-year-old niece, Melani, out to Texas to be a nanny for Tylee. In this period Lori became close to Melani, who began to see her as a surrogate mom.

"Lori's just a fun mom," Melani later told *Dateline*. "I loved taking Tylee to do everything and Colby, too. We'd go out on the boat on the lake."

In August 2004, Lori moved Colby and Tylee into her parents' home at 502 Roble Vista in San Antonio while she negotiated a divorce settlement with Joe Ryan. She also found a job as a hairstylist at the Wildflower Salon in nearby Austin, Texas.

Once again the family were uprooted, and Colby had to change schools and find a new set of friends.

"For me it was just normal," he said.

Barry and Janis Cox were still busy fighting the IRS, which was now demanding $335,518 in unpaid taxes. Alex had joined his parents in their legal battle against the US government.

In April 2005, the US District Court San Antonio Division denied a motion by Barry, Janis, and Alex Cox labeling the government's case against them as "irrelevant" and "a waste of time." The court found the Coxes' objections to having to pay their back taxes were "without merit." It also attached a tax lien to their property at 502 Roble Vista, where Lori and her children now lived, ruling that any money they received for the sale of it should go toward paying their back taxes.

Barry, Janis, and Alex Cox immediately appealed the decision, and their quixotic fight against the US government continued.

*   *   *

On May 6, 2005, Lori and Joe Ryan were officially divorced on the grounds of insupportability. Under Texas family law it was a no-fault divorce, meaning "discord or conflict of personalities," preventing "any reasonable expectation of reconciliation."

Under the final divorce decree, Lori and Ryan shared custody of two-year-old Tylee as joint managing conservators. It also laid out a detailed schedule for which parent would have Tylee during summer vacations and holidays.

Joe Ryan was ordered to pay Lori $1,500 a month in child support, as well as to provide medical care until Tylee was eighteen. The divorce court also ordered Ryan to take out a life insurance policy for himself, naming Lori the prime beneficiary, who would receive no less than $350,000 as Tylee's trustee in the event of his death.

On August 30, fresh off her divorce, Lori Ryan filed for bankruptcy, owing almost $724,000 to creditors. She told a Texas bankruptcy court that she needed at least $6,200 a month for basic living expenses, including $500 for food.

According to her filing, she was now paying $1,900 a month for a newly rented apartment in Austin, Texas, where she was living with Colby and Tylee. She and Joe Ryan jointly owed nearly $100,000 in federal and county taxes, with Lori running up more than $17,000 in credit card debt.

Lori reported earning just $41,000 as a self-employed hairstylist between 2003 and 2005 and listed the sale of her wedding ring in February 2004 for $4,300.

FIVE

CHARLES VALLOW

In late 2005, Lori was cutting hair in the Austin salon where she now worked when forty-nine-year-old Charles Vallow walked in for a haircut. The tall, strikingly handsome financial planner wore an expensively tailored suit and was in great shape, having been a college baseball player once drafted by the Houston Astros. Originally from Louisiana, Vallow was the archetypal Southern gentleman with an accent to match.

He asked the beautiful blond thirty-two-year-old hairstylist out on a date, and before long they were talking marriage.

"He was smitten right away," said Charles's sister Kay Woodcock. "They looked like they were made to be together."

Charles was also coming off a bitter divorce, from Cheryl, and had two young sons, Cole, eleven, and Zach, eight. Charles and Lori were both looking for a new relationship, and Lori saw Charles Vallow, who earned around a quarter of a million dollars a year, as her knight in shining armor who would rescue her from debt.

"My mom has always looked for stability," said Colby. "Someone to take care of her. He was really sweet and he really cared about her from the beginning."

On February 24, 2006, Lori married Charles Vallow in Las Vegas. It was her fourth wedding, and once again none of her family were present, but when they finally met him, they agreed he was her best choice so far.

"Charles Vallow to me was the best of Lori's husbands," said Janis Cox. "We all liked him."

The first time Charles's ex-wife, Cheryl, met Lori, Cheryl was charmed.

She had moved on with her life after the divorce and was delighted that Charles had found someone.

"I was happy to see him find his next spouse," she explained. "I really was, because I thought [she's a] beautiful woman, she's got two kids, and she's very religious. This is going to be wonderful."

At Lori's son's baseball game, soon after they met, Lori suddenly asked Cheryl if she thought Lori was an idiot for marrying Cheryl's ex-husband.

"I found that very funny," said Cheryl. "But that was the only pleasant moment we ever had in all these years."

When Kay Woodcock, fifty-one, first chatted with her new sister-in-law, the subject of previous marriages soon came up.

"I asked her, 'Well, have you been married before?' And she said, 'Yeah.' I said, 'How many times have you been married?' And she said, 'Three.' And I said, 'You're thirty-two, girl, better hope this one sticks.'"

A few months earlier, Lori's brother Adam had been questioned by the police for causing the death of a young woman. The shock jock was hosting his *Morning Rave* show on the Sacramento radio station KDND-FM when he introduced a new on-air water-drinking contest called "Hold Your Wee for a Wii." Listeners would drink as much water as they could in the studio, then hold it in without going to the bathroom. Whoever held out the longest won a Nintendo Wii.

According to the Toxicology Education Foundation, drinking huge amounts of water in a short time can be fatal, as was the case with mother-of-three Jennifer Lea Strange, twenty-eight, one of eighteen contestants that morning.

During the on-air contest a nurse called in to the show to warn it was dangerous, but Adam Cox and his sidekick laughed it off. They even joked that Jennifer's distended stomach made her look pregnant.

A few hours after the contest Adam Cox learned that Jennifer, who had come in second, had gone home and then died of acute water intoxication.

"I think I went into shock," he wrote in his 2019 book, *My Crazy Radio Life.* "I had the worst feeling come over me. I believe it was the saddest day that I can remember except for the day that I got a call . . . that my older sister Stacey had passed away."

Cox, along with nine other employees, was fired from the station and investigated by the Sacramento attorney general for possible criminal charges of aiding and participating in Strange's wrongful death. None were ever brought, but Strange's family was awarded $16.5 million in damages from the radio station.

After being fired, Cox was blacklisted and struggled to find another job in radio.

"Nobody was going to hire a DJ with a reputation as a killer," he explained in his book. "I was branded with a cruel and false charge."

Charles and Lori settled down in a big house with a pool near Austin, Texas. His two young sons would spend weekends, summers, and alternating holidays with him and Lori, and the rest of the time with their mother. The new blended family worked well, and everyone seemed to get along.

Although brought up Catholic, Charles enthusiastically converted to the Church of Jesus Christ of Latter-day Saints at Lori's request and became active in the church.

"Every Sunday Charles would go to church with Lori and the kids," said Kay. "He went in at full force. He was very happy in it."

Colby started in fifth grade at Cedar Creek Elementary School, and Tylee was enrolled in the Children's Center of Austin Daycare. They were both delighted to finally have some stability in their lives.

Lori loved the lavish new lifestyle Charles provided. There were big cars, the best designer clothes, and expensive vacations; all the things that Lori had grown up with and then lost.

And Charles ensured that Lori had a special dancing room with mirrors as her own personal refuge to convene with the spirits.

On August 8, 2006, Lori called the Hays County Sheriff's Office to report that Joe Ryan had sexually abused Colby and Tylee during their marriage. Detective Jeri Skrocki was assigned to investigate, arranging for Lori and both children to be interviewed at Roxanne's House, a nonprofit child-advocacy center that helps abused children. Skrocki videotaped Tylee's interview with social worker Melissa Rodriguez.

The three-year-old was first asked about her visits with her father and what they did. Tylee replied that she slept with him and they had snacks. After identifying her female body parts as "boobies," "potz," and "butt," she denied her father had ever looked at or touched hers or that she had ever said otherwise. Tylee told the social worker that she slept with her father because she was scared of monsters and wore his "jammies."

Tylee said she liked visiting him but admitted saying she did not. She was "scared of Daddy," although she could not explain why.

At the end of the twenty-eight-minute interview Rodriguez asked again if Tylee was scared of Joe Ryan, and this time she said no.

The social worker then interviewed Colby, who claimed his stepfather had sexually molested him when he was eight. He graphically described what happened, admitting that he had only told his mother about it two days earlier. To this day Colby maintains he was molested.

Finally, Detective Skrocki interviewed Lori and Charles Vallow about the allegations. Lori told the detective that her sister-in-law Annie Cushing had warned her to get Colby away from her brother because of the rough treatment she had witnessed when she visited the family.

"Ms. Ryan stated that she discovered 100's of gay porn sites on his computer when they were married," read the subsequent police report. "She stated that she had no idea that her husband was 'gay' and preferred men. She confronted him about his habits and she left him shortly after that."

Lori then wrote out a seven-page statement detailing her allegations against Joe Ryan, initialing each page. She said she was currently staying with her parents in San Antonio and provided their phone number.

Later that day Detective Skrocki called Joe Ryan to make an appointment for him to be interviewed. He said he wanted to speak to his attorney first.

Six weeks later, Joe Ryan filed a motion in Hays County District Court to have Lori imprisoned for eighteen months for refusing him access to Tylee. He also accused her of violating their custody agreement by not living within one hundred miles of him. He asked the court to order Lori to pay all his legal costs.

Lori's brother Alex was now living in suburban Phoenix, Arizona, where he'd found a job emptying Porta Potties. Now thirty-eight and balding, Alex had started performing stand-up comedy at local clubs. His ten-minute act consisted of zany impressions of cartoon characters such as Daffy Duck and Homer Simpson, as well as Hannibal Lecter, the fictional cannibal serial killer in *Silence of the Lambs.*

"I'm Alex," he would begin, "and I'm going to be Looney Tunes."

Comedian Mary Tracy first met Alex at Chilly Bombers Comedy Club in Phoenix, where they were both on the program. They instantly bonded and began writing jokes together.

"Alex was great at impressions," said Mary. "He was a genuinely funny guy [and] becoming known on the smaller-club scale. He was completely inappropriate sometimes, but we just had a great time. I thought of Alex as my little brother."

Around the same time Alex also met Australian-born stand-up comic Tim Bateman at an open mike in a small club called the Hidden House. Bateman was struck that Alex never drank liquor, although he loved hanging out with the other comics after shows.

"Alex was an odd kind of guy," said Bateman. "He was friendly and talkative [and] his impersonations were good. I really liked him."

Comedian Don Steinmetz, who by day was a detective in the Phoenix Police Department, also befriended Alex. Don urged him to work his Porta Potties job into his comedy routine.

"He cleaned them out," said Steinmetz, "and I kept telling him, 'You should write material about that,' and he would do a little bit."

Steinmetz believes that Alex used stand-up to make friends and genuinely loved the comedy environment, although he had no ambitions to turn professional.

"He enjoyed the camaraderie and being accepted," Steinmetz explained, "and he took on this different persona as a stand-up comic."

Steinmetz often wondered why he never saw Alex with a girlfriend, but put it down to his strict Mormon beliefs he often talked about.

Although they were never romantically involved, Alex and Mary Tracy—whom he affectionately nicknamed Mir—often socialized together, grabbing a burger or going to a movie. He often spoke about his sister Lori, although Mary sensed he felt conflicted about her.

"Lori was almost like an annoyance to him," said Mary, "but whatever she needed, he took care of."

After Lori reported Joe Ryan for sexually molesting Colby and Tylee, officers from the Hays County Sheriff's Office descended on his house, seizing his mattress, sheets, and clothes to be forensically examined for DNA traces. He was also ordered to undergo a sexual-offender assessment test.

"He went and took a polygraph and psychosexual test and they all came back negative," said his attorney, Keith Taniguchi. "They also couldn't find any DNA, and that supported his innocence. And in the meantime they denied him access to Tylee. Lori condoned all this activity. In fact she encouraged it."

On March 31, 2007, Tylee was interviewed by a Roxanne's House therapist in the presence of Lori. The four-and-a-half-year-old was asked if she knew who "Joe" was, and she replied, "He's my old daddy. My new daddy is Charles."

Under the examiner's questioning, Tylee said that Joe had never hurt her or touched her inappropriately. She was then asked if anyone had ever told her to complain about him for doing bad things. Tylee replied that Colby and Charles had. At that point the interview abruptly ended.

"When the child made these statements," read the official court-ordered report, "the mother's jaw dropped, eyes widened, and [she] appeared shocked. She did not seem fearful that she was in trouble. Rather, she seemed in disbelief and shock."

A subsequent report, prepared by psychologist Vivian Lewis, the clinical director of the Orion Treatment Center in Austin, was sharply critical of Lori as a mother. It noted that Lori had told therapists that she spoke with her dead sister, Stacey, who she believed had been reincarnated as Tylee. She also consulted with a dead lawyer whose spirit visited her at night.

"Ms. Vallow is deeply religious and seems genuinely so," wrote Lewis. "She also mentions other ghost conversations and directives from her God."

A month later, therapist Susan Shinsky, who had been seeing Tylee since she was three, caught Lori coaching her daughter to make damaging accusations against her ex-husband. Shinsky warned Lori not to "push" Tylee, but Lori had refused, rendering all counseling counterproductive.

"Tylee has almost bottled up due to being pushed so much," read Shinsky's report. "Tylee almost 'spilled' the beans during one session, but then closed up. Ms. Vallow is very anxious and is tied up in multiple legal situations. This anxiousness appears to be affecting Tylee."

The therapist wrote that Lori "genuinely believes" Tylee was in danger, noting that her belief system was "riddled with ghosts" and "fanatical religious dogma."

SIX

"I'M GOING TO KILL YOU!"

On May 23, 2007, Lori Vallow and Joe Ryan were at the Travis County Courthouse for a custody hearing. Ryan had not seen his daughter, Tylee, for months and desperately sought visitation rights. During a court recess Lori was in the busy cafeteria when her ex-husband walked past her. She suddenly screamed out that he'd hit her, and Ryan was immediately arrested for assault with injury.

Attorney Keith Taniguchi, who was also in the cafeteria and witnessed the incident, said Lori had maliciously made it up to get back at Ryan.

"He was just in there getting a drink or something," said Taniguchi, "and all of a sudden he's being arrested for assaulting her."

Charles Vallow was also in a heated custody dispute with his ex-wife, Cheryl, and they had the same judge, who eventually combined the two cases. Cheryl often saw Lori at hearings and noticed how she enjoyed being the center of all the court drama.

"She loved it," Cheryl later told the *East Idaho News*. "I saw her more in court than I did out of the courthouse. I saw an instability and I didn't want her around my boys."

At the end of July, psychologist Vivian Lewis prepared a confidential Sex Offender Assessment on Joe Ryan. She found that he posed no danger to Tylee and should be reintroduced into her life as soon as possible. A grand jury had also declined to indict Joe Ryan on charges of indecency with a child by sexual contact, so he had a spotless record.

The psychologist's July 24 report observed that although Ryan had admitted to "rape and dominance fantasies," he had never acted on them nonconsensually.

"He does state that the mother of the child in question," read Lewis's report, "enjoyed these kinds of games and Ms. Vallow would initiate, at times, these types of sex play and behavior. He adamantly feels that she was not forced and scared entering into their sexual activities and mutual enjoyment."

Lewis noted that these kind of sexual fantasies and games were common between consenting adults.

"[Joe Ryan] has verbalized great frustration," wrote Lewis, "during this [sic] past four years of accusations, multiple investigations and now 12 months of his daughter not knowing her biological father."

The psychologist also expressed grave concern about how Lori would react to her findings that Tylee should restart visitations with her father.

"Ms. Vallow is a devout Mormon," Lewis wrote, "who has mentioned to me that death would be an option before giving Tylee to her father . . . even for a visit. These are real and serious concerns. I have no way of knowing if Ms. Vallow was serious."

As Lewis suspected, Lori did not take the psychologist's findings well and called her brother Alex for help. For months she had been feeding him ludicrous stories of how Joe Ryan was molesting Colby and Tylee. Now she asked Alex to go on a family crusade and come to Austin to sort out the Joe Ryan problem once and for all.

"He was obsessed that Joe Ryan was molesting Tylee," said Alex's friend Mary Tracy. "And there was no question about it in his mind."

Alex had even asked Mary to report Lori's ex-husband to the police for having child pornography. But she refused, saying no one would believe it as she had never even met him.

"The next thing I know, Alex is in Texas for some family matter," said Mary. "Well of course the family matter was assaulting Joe."

At 11:05 A.M. on Sunday, August 5, 2007, Joe Ryan left home for his much-anticipated visit with Tylee. It was the first time he would see his daughter in more than a year, and he dreamed of rekindling their relationship. He immediately noticed a silver Pontiac Grand Prix with its headlights on parked three doors away. As he drove past, the car pulled out going the opposite way, as the driver yanked his baseball cap down to hide his face. Ryan was suspicious and called a neighbor to watch his house.

When Joe arrived at the Kids Exchange facility at Collinfield Drive for the scheduled noon visitation, he went into the meeting room where Lori was waiting with Tylee.

The two-hour meeting went well. At 2:00 P.M., Ryan said goodbye to Tylee and had to wait fifteen minutes to give Lori enough time to leave the premises with their daughter.

At 2:15 P.M., Joe Ryan signed out and walked into the parking lot to his car and began putting things in the trunk. Suddenly Alex Cox, who had been waiting at a nearby picnic table, approached.

"Do you remember me?" he asked menacingly. "I'm Alex."

"What do you want?"

"We need to talk."

Frightened, Joe Ryan asked a woman standing nearby, Carrie Pernice, to witness whatever happened next.

"What's wrong?" she asked.

"Alex Cox is my ex-wife's brother," Ryan told her as Cox came nearer.

"We are going to talk right now," Alex said sternly.

"We have nothing to talk about," said Ryan, starting to walk away.

"Yes, we do," snapped Cox, "and *this* is for what you did to my nephew."

Alex reached into his pants and pulled out a Taser, lunging at Ryan and pushing it hard into his chest. Thinking it was a real gun, Ryan attempted to run away before feeling a sharp electric shock to his shoulder, followed by a second one in his back. He hit the asphalt face-first and thought he'd been shot.

Ryan got up and made a run for it, as Alex chased him with his stun gun, shouting, "I'm going to kill you!"

Another witness was leaving Kids Exchange when he saw Alex Cox brandishing the weapon and Ryan running for his life .

"I yelled [for him] to call 911," Ryan later told police. "I said, 'This is Alex Cox and he is trying to kill me.'"

As the witness started punching 911 into his cell phone, Alex ran over to his Pontiac parked across the street and sped away.

"I yelled for Alex to come back," said Ryan. "Alex just flipped the bird back towards us."

Later, Tylee would reveal that she and Lori had been sitting in Alex's car, watching the entire incident, which Lori had orchestrated.

Joe Ryan was treated at the scene by EMS, and he and the two witnesses were interviewed by Austin police. The following afternoon Joe showed up at an emergency room with severe chest pains and was admitted overnight for observation. He was found to have a fractured right wrist.

For the rest of his life Ryan would suffer heart problems he believed to be a direct result of Alex Cox's Taser attack. His health would never be the same and he started drinking heavily.

In early January 2008, Lori and Tylee failed to show up for Joe Ryan's next scheduled supervised visitation. But a month later one did take place—with dire consequences.

Ryan collected his daughter with a supervisor in tow, and as they were leaving Kids Exchange, two pickup trucks started following them. Ryan called 911 and was instructed to go to a public place and wait for a police officer to meet him. He did, and the two trucks parked a short distance away.

After police noted their license plate numbers, Ryan was instructed to return to his house with Tylee and the supervisor and lock the doors. A police sergeant later arrived at his house to escort them back to the Kids Exchange, noting the same two trucks now parked a few doors away.

Later that night, after dropping Tylee back with her mother, Ryan received a threatening phone message warning him against any further visitations.

Ten days later, Tylee's newly appointed guardian ad litem, Mary Fogel, reported her concerns about the long-term effects and "collateral damage" all this drama was having on Tylee.

"There are many disturbing events in this case," wrote Fogel, "that included a tasering incident at Kids Exchange after the first supervised visit, and an alleged assault in the courthouse cafeteria after a hearing. Given the information . . . I am concerned that there is a heightened potential for violence and physical endangerment in this situation that could potentially involve Tylee."

Fogel was particularly disturbed by Tylee's flat reaction after they had been chased by two trucks during the last visitation and the police had had to intervene.

"Her father was visibly shaken," Fogel observed. "Tylee had no emotional reaction at all. It was as if nothing was happening."

Tylee's psychological profile, Fogel noted, indicated that she suffered from "a high level of repressed anxiety," endangering her emotional and mental health. "Tylee has grown accustomed to adults who are highly upset and accustomed to police officers and bodyguards at the age of five."

On December 4, 2007, Alex Cox was indicted by a Travis County grand jury for aggravated assault with a deadly weapon on Joe Ryan and causing him serious bodily injury.

"Alexander L. Cox," read the indictment, "intentionally, knowingly, or recklessly caused serious bodily injury to Joe Anthony Ryan, Jr. by using a taser . . . and causing him to fall and break his wrist."

On February 28, 2008, Alex was arrested at work and placed in Maricopa County jail before being extradited to Austin, Texas. Mary Tracy visited him there.

"Alex thought he was a frigging hero and he should have a cape," she recalled. "He was like, 'I'd totally do it again,' and he didn't care when he went to jail."

On March 31, 2008, Cox pleaded guilty to the second-degree felony and was sentenced to ninety days imprisonment in Travis State Jail.

He spent his three months' incarceration in maximum security, writing jokes and reading the Bible. He exchanged a stream of letters with Mary Tracy, who was his only visitor. He was also in constant contact with Lori, who was still feeding his obsession that Joe Ryan was molesting her kids. He often discussed it with his fellow inmates, whom he was busy recruiting for another attack on his former brother-in-law.

On May 27, he wrote to Mary Tracy asking her to call his mother to help him find Joe Ryan.

"Mir, would you do me a favor," he wrote. "Call Janis and ask her to put Joe's address on a postcard & his license plate #. I think it will be popular in here. No name just address & plate #. Thanks."

A month later, on June 24, he asked Mary to call Lori and get a photograph of Joe Ryan to give to an inmate who would soon be getting out.

"The world is coming undone," he told Mary. "The pedafile [sic] is unpunished [and] I'm in jail. . . . I guess it's time for the apocalypse. Can you get a picture from Lori of one of her ex-husbands and send it to me? Some of the guys would like to hang out with him. Alex."

In his letters, Alex urged Mary to convert to Mormonism. He wanted her to read Romans, chapter 13, "to cause a little repentance for your horny granny ass."

He told her, "Summer has a copy of the Book of Mormon for you. I have spent the last three days reading the Old Testament."

At the beginning of July, Alex was released from jail and went straight back to the Phoenix comedy stand-up circuit with brand-new material. The highlight of his new routine was his vicious Taser attack on Joe Ryan.

"Have you ever had something that you knew was the right thing to do?" he asked the audience. "But it turns out that later on it was a felony? This is a true story. I found out that my ex-brother-in-law was a pedophile, so took a stun gun and I discharged it right in his nut sack. And in Texas that's a felony."

As the audience applauded, Alex told them he had expected to receive a medal but got three months behind bars instead.

Fellow comedian and Don Steinmetz, who by day was a detective in the Phoenix Police Department, did not find the new bit funny and tried to get his wayward friend back on track. He warned Alex to let law enforcement do its job and get over his obsession with Joe Ryan.

"We talked about it," said Steinmetz. "I said maybe that's not the way you want to resolve things in the future [or] you could wind up with more severe problems."

SEVEN

SETTLING DOWN

Soon after being released from jail, Alex brought Mary Tracy to a Cox family gathering at Janis and Barry's new house in Queen Creek, Arizona. Mary was intrigued. Alex had often talked about Lori and his parents, and she was puzzled by their unusual relationship.

"They were a family unit," said Mary. "Alex didn't have respect for his mom and dad, but when they said, 'Jump!,' he'd say, 'How high?'"

Mary and Alex arrived on a hot Sunday afternoon, and Lori was wearing a skimpy bikini, parading around the house with Colby and Tylee in her wake.

"I just thought that was so odd," said Mary. "She looked great, but I've never actually been around someone who walked around the house in a bikini. I remember feeling that Lori was high-maintenance."

Alex had previously told Mary that in a long-standing Cox family tradition every Sunday, no matter where they were, the siblings would call their mother with their football picks for that day.

"And it was their weekly connection that they all had together," said Mary. "I thought it was kind of cool."

During the afternoon, Barry Cox invited Mary into his office, saying he had something important to tell her. She already knew from Alex about his father's ongoing battle with the IRS and the time he'd spent in jail.

Then Barry sat her down and said he wanted to talk about a particular passage in the Bible and began quoting Matthew 25:35–40.

For when I was hungry and you gave me something to eat, I was thirsty and you gave me something to drink, I was a stranger and you invited me in, I needed clothes and you clothed me, I was sick and you looked after me, I was in prison and you came to visit me.

"And he said, 'I want to thank you for visiting my son,'" Mary recalled. "I just thought that was just so sweet of him, to care so much about Alex like that."

A few months later, Alex flew to Colombia for a sex trip. Now forty and working as a long-distance truck driver, he met women online. Socially awkward in one-on-one situations, he often made the opposite sex feel uncomfortable, so he took to the internet to find intimate partners.

He often complained to Mary Tracy about his problems finding girl-friends, usually in late-night calls when he was driving his truck.

"Nobody worked out for him," she said. "But he did like to go on these online things with the girls in South America. He just liked that type of woman."

Alex booked the "Romance Tour" through a Colombian dating site that arranged flights and hotels as well as providing prospective sex partners. He excitedly told Mary about his upcoming trip, hoping this time the girls would actually last.

He flew to Medellín and checked into the hotel for the weeklong romantic vacation. On the first night he attended a party to meet young Colombian girls. He dressed casually in a short-sleeve sky-blue shirt and light brown dress pants.

Maria Escobel (not her real name) was one of the girls hired for the event and introduced herself to Alex, offering to be his interpreter during his trip.

"My name is Alex. Alex Cox," he told her, James Bond–style, flashing a big smile.

Alex told Maria he drove trucks for a living, did comedy on the side, and was a certified massage specialist.

"He met a few girls that night, maybe three or four," said Maria, "[and] at the end of the night he left with one of them."

The following afternoon Maria met Alex in his hotel lobby, as she had agreed to show him around town. She took him to her favorite Chinese restaurant for lunch, where Alex charmed her with his jokes.

Although Alex had a different girl every night, he spent his days with Maria. On Sunday they went to the beach and Alex invited her up to his hotel room, where they kissed. The next day Alex promised her the best massage of her life.

"He was absolutely right," she said. "His hands were strong and soft."

Then Alex invited her to stay the night and they had sex.

"He got on his knees, he kissed me," Maria recalled. "He gently pushed me on the bed, and the next I knew was he was taking off my pants. Everything happened so fast."

After they finished, Alex talked about being raised a Mormon, saying he was now excommunicated. When Maria asked why, Alex replied that he liked sex too much and refused to wait until marriage. "He told me also about a few sexual experiences he'd had."

They spent the rest of his trip together, and Alex proposed marriage. He even took her to a jewelry store in a local mall to buy an engagement ring, but she said she needed more time before she could make a lifetime commitment.

"Everything was happening so fast," Maria explained. "I found it odd."

Something strange about Alex frightened her, and she sensed he was a disturbed person. "The second time we had sex, he had such a glare in those green eyes. Such lust. His eyes were shining in an evil way, and that made me feel uncomfortable [and] scared."

At the end of his trip, Maria saw Alex off at the airport. He promised to keep in touch and did call several times before he stopped. Over the next few years Alex would send a stream of money transfers to women he had met in Colombia on sex visits.

For the next few months, Joe Ryan's supervised visitations with Tylee were fraught with tension. The five-year-old now regularly saw therapists, who began to notice inconsistencies in her accounts of whether her birth father was molesting her. Once again, they suspected Tylee was being coached by her mother.

On June 30, 2008, Tylee said she didn't want to stay overnight with her dad because he'd molested her and Colby. Two weeks later she said she didn't want to confront him about being molested. When asked why, Tylee burst into tears, saying he might be "mad" because "maybe it wasn't true."

Her guardian ad litem, Mary Fogel, reported that at a July meeting, Tylee had said she was now happy to visit her father.

"Tylee added, 'I'm scared about overnights,'" wrote Fogel in her subsequent report. "When questioned about this, she said something like, 'because Joe molested me and Colby.' When Tylee's mother came into the session toward the end, Tylee looked at her mother and said, 'I told her.'"

The first week of August, Tylee had her first supervised overnight visit with her father. It had been agreed that throughout August, Tylee would visit her father from Saturday morning at 10:00 A.M. to the same time Sunday morning. The exchanges would take place at Kids Exchange and be unsupervised until Saturday at 8:00 P.M., when a social worker would arrive at Ryan's house to spend the night.

After the first overnight visitation, the supervisor reported that Tylee had taken photographs all over the house, explaining her mom had asked her to. The supervisor later checked Tylee's overnight bag, packed by Lori, finding two toy guns, a diaper, and a baby blanket.

"This is very confusing," wrote Fogel, "given the mother's keen sense of Tylee's age, size, developmental stage, and interests."

In September 2008, Lori and Charles Vallow moved their family to Chandler, Arizona. Known as the Community of Innovation, the Phoenix suburb was voted one of the best places to live in Arizona, with Intel and other high-tech companies based there.

Charles's finance business was thriving and he spent at least three days a week away on business. Lori had no need to work, so she could enjoy a life of leisure. And Alex lived just a few miles down the road.

Lori and Charles joined the local Mormon temple and attended services every Sunday with their children. They seemed like a happy, successful family and soon became a respected part of the community.

"They were just this bustling busy family," Charles's sister Kay told *Dateline*. "Their life was built around the church."

Twelve-year-old Colby finally had a stable home life and didn't have to worry about being constantly on the move.

"We stayed in one house," he said. "We had all our family around us [and] they all came over for parties. There wasn't court drama [and] everybody was just calm."

However, Lori's move to Arizona meant Joe Ryan now had to make a two-thousand-mile round-trip journey to visit Tylee, recently diagnosed with a serious pancreatic condition and hospitalized twice. He already paid Lori $1,500 a month in child support, and the added travel and hotel expenses were financially crippling. He was struggling to afford his scheduled visitations.

So Ryan's attorney, Keith Taniguchi, filed a series of custody motions to force Lori to return with Tylee to Austin, Texas.

"His job was becoming more tenuous," explained Taniguchi. "He was running into real problems."

A Travis County, Texas, court dispatched a social worker at Joe Ryan's expense to Phoenix to inspect Tylee's new living conditions. Lori charmed her.

"And she came back with glowing reviews," remembered Taniguchi. "That Lori was perfect, the house was all nice [and] they even had a swimming pool."

After moving to Chandler, Lori enrolled Tylee in a small charter school called the Learning Foundation and Performing Arts (LFPA) in nearby Gilbert. The school specialized in a variety of performing arts programs, and Lori was eager to develop her daughter's natural talent for singing and dancing.

"A student can attend rigorous academic tutoring one day," read the prospectus, "and hip-hop the next."

Tylee soon became best friends with another girl in her class, Vaisia Itaaehau. The two girls became inseparable and their mothers also became close.

"Lori was the mom I wanted to be," said Echo Itaaehau. "She was awesome. We loved her and thought she was great."

Vaisia was Tylee's first close friend, and Tylee began confiding in her about her real father, Joe Ryan, and how confused she was about him after all her years of therapy.

"When she was really young," said Vaisia, "she used to have complete meltdowns once it was time to go to her dad's. He may have abused her . . . but she couldn't remember."

Since moving to Arizona, Tylee said her life was much improved.

"She was only really going to his house because it was court ordered," said Vaisia. "Once she was old enough, she didn't want to see him again."

Echo and Vaisia rarely saw Charles Vallow when they visited Lori's house, as he was usually away on business, but when they did, he was always friendly.

"Charles was a go-getter," said Echo. "A dynamic-type person, and they lived well. They were always doing fun things and [taking] vacations."

On July 26, 2009, Joe Ryan got into a heated argument with Lori at a visitation handover inside a Barnes & Noble bookstore in Gilbert, Arizona, and called the police.

"Respondent [Lori Vallow] disturbed the peace of the child by causing a confrontation in the presence of the child," read Ryan's motion of contempt filed by his attorney, Keith Taniguchi. "It so alarmed the movant [Joe Ryan] that he had to call the police for assistance."

A week later, Lori failed to bring Tylee to another scheduled exchange, leaving Ryan to fly back to Austin without seeing his daughter. That year alone Lori would be found guilty of seven different counts of civil contempt.

"She was now on a full-fledged campaign to deny him access to Tylee," said Taniguchi. "Chandler Police [has] multiple police reports about all the run-ins that they had."

In late December, Joe Ryan flew to Phoenix to see Tylee perform in her school's Christmas play. After it finished, Lori whisked her away, denying Joe his scheduled holiday visit.

Eventually Ryan would relocate to Phoenix to be nearer Tylee, even though it meant a 40 percent cut in his salary. But Lori stubbornly continued her fight to keep him out of his daughter's life. They constantly argued about money, with each side claiming the other owed thousands of dollars in child support.

Finally, Ryan appealed to his ex-wife to bury the hatchet for Tylee's sake.

"I would think . . . Tylee would be your first obligation," he emailed her in August 2011. "Tylee is worth everything. She is smart and talented and beautiful and I'm not sure what your intentions are. You really are only hurting Tylee and I hope you will find it in you to sacrifice for your daughter and do the right thing."

Over the next two summers, Lori Vallow helped run a youth summer camp at the Chandler Center for the Arts. Tylee and Vaisia performed in several plays Lori directed, including *Broadway Kids*.

"Every summer they do a kid's summer camp," said Echo, "and Lori was one of the directors who helped put it together."

Tylee and Vaisia performed several song-and-dance routines under Lori's enthusiastic direction. The girls had just five days of camp to learn the show, which was then performed on a Friday night from the stage of the Chandler Center for the Arts.

"Lori helped direct *Broadway Kids*," said Vaisia. "Lori was very charismatic and energetic, so kids took her direction pretty well."

Lori was close to Vaisia and always listened to what she had to say. They would have long talks about the Mormon religion, and although Lori espoused mainstream beliefs, she enjoyed talking about the end-times.

"They were all within the normal," said Echo, who was also brought up LDS. "Vaisia would share them with me. They were what normal LDS families would talk about, because we all talk about scriptures and the last days and so forth."

EIGHT

J.J.

On May 25, 2012, Charles Vallow's nephew's girlfriend, Mandy Leger, gave birth to a little boy the couple named Canaan Trahan. He was born ten weeks premature, weighing under three pounds, with drugs in his system. He almost died.

Dennis Trahan, twenty-six, and Mandy, thirty-eight, were both drug addicts and unable to care for Canaan, so he became a ward of the state. Doctors managed to save his life, slowly weaning him off the drugs.

At seven weeks he was ready to leave the hospital, and Social Services asked his grandparents Larry and Kay Woodcock if they would adopt him. They agreed immediately and brought him back to their home in Lake Charles, Louisiana, renaming him Joshua Jaxon or J.J.

Larry, sixty-five, bonded with J.J. on the first night he came home. The fragile baby was restless, as he was still dependent on drugs, and Larry opened his robe and tenderly laid him on his chest and put his tiny head by his heart to calm him down.

"And I remember laying him there," said Larry, "and I wrapped him in my robe and I got him good and tight. And from that moment on, I just absolutely fell in love with that little boy."

Larry and Kay now devoted themselves to taking care of J.J. They ran a thriving transportation company, working 24-7, so bringing up a needy baby presented a huge challenge.

"We had many discussions about this," said Larry. "I'd be in my seventies by the time he got into school."

A few months later, Charles and Lori Vallow offered to adopt J.J. The Woodcocks gratefully accepted, believing it to be the perfect solution and called it the "easiest-hardest decision" they ever had to make.

"They wanted their own child together, and J.J. was it," said Larry. "He was our little boy, but we knew in the future it would be best for J.J. Especially when we could see him or have him anytime we wanted."

On February 14, 2013, Charles and Lori collected nine-month-old J.J. and began the official adoption process with the State of Louisiana. When they brought him home to Chandler to meet his new siblings, Colby and Tylee, there was some initial wariness about bringing a new baby into the family.

"I remember the conversation of them telling us they wanted to adopt him," said Colby. "We're all grown. You're really going to bring a baby into a grown house?"

But as soon as J.J. arrived, Colby and Tylee fell in love with the adorable baby boy, and he instantly became part of the Vallow family.

"He was already a miracle baby," said Colby. "He barely made it out of being born, so he just came into our lives and we fell in love with him so easily."

As J.J. got older, he was diagnosed with autism and needed special care and medication. Lori rose to the occasion, teaching Colby and Tylee how to prepare his bottles and help him go to sleep when he was restless. Tylee also took on a protective mothering role, forming a deep bond with the little boy.

A few months later Kay and Larry flew to Arizona to visit J.J. in his new home. They were delighted at how well he was doing. Lori was on her best behavior and charmed the Woodcocks, who were overjoyed that J.J., with all his special needs, now had such a loving and attentive mother.

"I thought she was a wonderful woman," said Kay. "A wonderful mother. A devout Christian. I thought she had it all."

There was absolutely no hint of Lori's manic dark side, and she played the role of perfect mother and loving wife. The Lori the Woodcocks saw was the polar opposite of the controlling, paranoid woman who talked to her dead sister and other spirits, who had so alarmed Tylee's social workers back in Texas.

* * *

On September 24, 2013, Tylee spent her eleventh birthday in Phoenix Children's Hospital with pancreatitis. It was the latest in a series of hospitalizations she had endured for the debilitating disease.

Since the move to Arizona, Tylee had come into her own and developed a sassy character. Although she worshipped her mother and they were close, Tylee had an undercurrent of disapproval, too, for her mother and would call her out on things. Tylee's relationship with her stepfather, Charles, was also complicated. They constantly bickered as Tylee began to assert herself.

"[Tylee] and Charles didn't get along too well," said Vaisia. "She was very outspoken and [had] a strong sense of self, which caused a lot of friction between the two."

The two best friends now did everything together. They went to the mall, swam in Charles's pool, watched movies, and went on photography expeditions.

"Just anything that we thought would be fun," said Vaisia. "We mostly enjoyed talking. She was just so funny and entertaining."

And little J.J., who called his adoring sister TyTy, would often join them.

"I loved being around J.J. and Tylee," said Vaisia. "Tylee was really protective over J.J. and she was kind of another mama to him. I just loved how she would play with him and just always have a really good time with him."

In early 2014, Lori and Charles Vallow decided to move to the Hawaiian island of Kauai after Colby graduated from high school and J.J.'s official adoption papers were signed. Since first going as a child, Lori had always wanted to live in Kauai. She had persuaded Charles that the island offered great business opportunities, and her parents also planned to move there at the same time. An added bonus would be that Joe Ryan would finally be out of Tylee's life.

In early April, Lori, her mother, Janis, Charles, and Tylee all flew to Kauai on a reconnaissance mission, meeting a Realtor to view houses in the Kapaa district. On their return Lori swore everyone to secrecy, in case Ryan found out and made trouble. Eventually he learned about the plan through one of Tylee's school friends and was furious, vowing to stop his daughter going at all costs.

On April 22, he emailed Lori demanding to know what was going on:

"I want to make sure we address the rumors of you moving to Hawaii and issues I see right now. From the rumor mill, it's my understanding once the adoption of the 2nd special needs baby is completed, you plan to move. I want to be very clear we will use the court process to oppose the move."

He warned Lori that making Tylee keep secrets, with all the scheming involved, could trigger her pancreatitis.

"She and her friends are upset she will be moving," he wrote, "and possibly not see each other again. As you may know, this is very dramatic for children."

He wrote that it would be "most upsetting" not being able to see his daughter regularly. "She has been experiencing this for the past nine years, and now she is in the middle again. Please take all this into consideration before involving Tylee again."

Five weeks later, Lori's newly appointed attorney, H. Lee Dove, replied directly to Joe Ryan's attorney, Leslie I. Tennen, laying out his client's position:

"Mrs. Vallow's husband, Charles, has accepted a job offer in Hawaii. The Vallows will need to relocate this summer. Please explain to Mr. Ryan that he cannot stop Mr. and Mrs. Vallow from moving; he can only ask the Court to prohibit Tylee from relocating with them."

On June 12, Lori tried to calm the waters by emailing Ryan directly. She suggested they meet in person to negotiate visiting arrangements for Tylee after the Hawaii move.

"Hi Joe, I am happy to tell you what's going on," she began. "Charles did accept a job in Hawaii. It is a great opportunity for us to get to live in paradise and learn the culture there. We are moving by August 1st."

Lori wrote that there were only two options for Tylee: either she went to Hawaii or she stayed in Phoenix with him and vacationed in Hawaii. Lori added that she had already approached two schools on Kauai and talked to GI specialists and pediatricians to make them aware of Tylee's pancreatic condition.

"It is an island," Lori told Ryan, "but it is still in the US and very modern in every way."

A few minutes later Ryan replied with a third option of Charles moving to Hawaii and Lori and Tylee remaining in Arizona:

"It's easier for him to commute back and forth than Tylee commuting. Why does Tylee loose [*sic*] parenting time when it's Charles that wants to work in Hawaii? If you want to move to Hawaii, I cannot stop you. I will oppose Tylee moving to Hawaii."

The next day Lori replied saying she understood Ryan was upset, again offering to meet to talk things out: "Do you want to agree on a visitation schedule that Tylee is happy with? Or do you want the attorneys to handle it?"

Ryan wrote back straight after receiving her email, reminding her that she either needed his written consent or a court order for Tylee to move to Hawaii.

"I am not giving you written consent," he told her angrily.

NINE

KAUAI

The first week of August 2014, the Vallow family moved to Kauai, closely followed by Lori's parents and aged grandmother. A week earlier the State of Louisiana had issued a Final Decree for Adoption for J.J., making Charles and Lori Vallow his legal parents. They now officially changed his name on his birth certificate from Canaan Trahan to Joshua Jaxon Vallow.

Charles and Lori moved into a large house on Aloalii Drive in the exclusive Princeville area, while her parents rented a condo nearby at an upscale new development called Kaiulai. Lori enrolled Tylee in a local traditional Hawaiian school and hired a nanny for J.J., buying him a Pomeranian named Crushie.

They left before Joe Ryan had time to take legal action to stop Tylee's moving to Hawaii, and he soon gave up his fight and resigned himself to losing his daughter.

On their first weekend there, Lori and Charles attended the Church of Jesus Christ of Latter-day Saints in nearby Hanalei. After the service they introduced themselves to their new congregation at a sacrament meeting. Then they met with members individually to tell them about themselves.

"I was amazed how Lori's story was so similar to mine," said April Raymond. "So here's another Mormon woman who's been divorced and been through what I've been through. We were also both fitness instructors, so we connected on that level, too. I felt very understood by her."

They exchanged phone numbers, and a week later Lori invited April to lunch, soon winning her over with her boundless energy, positivity, and enthusiasm.

"We became fast friends," said April. "Everyone just fell in love with her right away."

April was instantly sucked into Lori's life, feeling that some "divine design" was at work. April was soon visiting Lori's home several times a week for pool parties, BBQs, and dinners. Her two boys played with Tylee and J.J. on the beach, and Charles would babysit when April and Lori went on temple trips to the neighboring island of Oahu.

"When she came to Kauai, she would always cut and color my hair," said April, "while Charles would grab all the kids and take them to lunch."

April thought Lori and Charles had the perfect marriage, with a healthy combination of friendship and camaraderie. April aspired to have such a good relationship one day. But she also saw how Lori was in charge and called all the shots. It seemed to suit them both, though, and they seemed like the perfect family.

"Lori was an exceptional mother," said April. "She was really good with J.J., who needed to be around her constantly. Tylee was the typical teenager, with a bit of angst towards her mom, but always with her at the same time. Nothing seemed unusual there."

Lori would often become emotional when she opened up to April about her disastrous marriage to Joe Ryan and her remorse for what he'd done to her kids.

"She would cry when she told the story," remembered April, "and how much guilt she felt that she had married this man."

Colby, who was now eighteen, loved his new life in Kauai and bonded with his stepfather, Charles, who went out of his way to teach Colby things. After a lifetime of drama and uncertainty, Colby felt the family had landed in paradise.

"It's the most beautiful place you've ever seen," he told *Dateline*. "Charles was superhappy, my mom was superhappy. [We] got paddleboards and just found the active things that [we] liked."

Lori enthusiastically threw herself into church activities and was soon appointed president of the Primary, a program for children from six to twelve. She regularly taught a group of twenty children the gospel of Jesus Christ and how to live it. Every Sunday, after the main sacrament, Lori gathered her pupils for several hours of music and storytelling.

Her parents were also active in their new congregation. Janis ran the church music programs and played the piano, while Barry taught an adult class in Gospel doctrine. They also organized Christmas parties and other special social events.

"They were very involved," said April. "I found Barry to be very intelligent, charming, and likable. But I found Janis very cold and not very engaged as a mother or a grandmother."

Lori and Charles soon became friends with Wade and Frankie English, who were also active in the Kauai LDS church. As Charles and Wade were both from Louisiana, they immediately hit it off.

"I was part of the Sunday school programs," said Frankie. "[Lori] had a beautiful voice. She could really sing. She was always happy, bubbly, and was great . . . teaching the kids music."

Lori recruited April Raymond to run the Young Woman's Program, and twelve-year-old Tylee was in her group for the weekly church activities.

"It gave me an opportunity to really get to know Tylee individually," said April. "She was always very diligent . . . so we spent a lot of time together."

On their daylong temple trips to Oahu, which required a short flight to the neighboring island, Lori often spoke about her conservative Mormon beliefs.

"Her beliefs were pretty mainstream," said April. "I know she had a preoccupation with near-death experiences, but it wasn't the focal point of our conversations. It didn't seem like it was that prominent in her belief system at that time."

But she often complained that Charles was not her spiritual equal. She looked down on him as a convert to Mormonism, feeling that he did not really understand the LDS culture and was holding her back.

As Charles was often away on business, he set Lori up with a juice business on Kealia Beach to give her something to do. She named it Juice Island

and hired a young man from California to help run it from an old food truck. She was rarely there and only came to collect the weekly takings.

In early 2015, Lori's brother Alex arrived to stay for a while. He was struggling in Arizona and wanted to move to Kauai to be nearer to Lori and his parents. Lori brought him to the church to meet the congregation and introduced him to April.

Earlier Lori had told April how Alex had tried to kill her ex-husband on her behalf and gone to jail for it. She said she felt responsible for him.

April did not know what to think. She'd heard about Lori's contentious relationship with Joe Ryan, but it was the first time she'd heard anything about an attempted murder.

"Alex admitted to trying to kill him," said April. "That's when I started feeling, like, this is something very wrong. He was very loyal to Lori and would do anything she asked him to."

On the few occasions April met Alex during his brief stay, she tried to avoid him. "He was a little off and lacked social skills or maybe just really didn't connect with people."

Alex seemed fascinated at how April, who was also blond, and his sister looked so alike that people often confused them. He would ask April intimate questions to see how she physically measured up against Lori.

"Alex seemed to have a very strange preoccupation with Lori," explained April. "And he would want to know things, like how much I weighed or what my ring size was or my shoe size, and then compare it to Lori. And that just made me feel very uncomfortable."

Charles Vallow often flew Vaisia Itaaehau over to Kauai for the holidays to spend time with Tylee. The girls loved playing together on the beach, paddleboarding and zip-lining, and just having fun.

"Being in Hawaii with Tylee was a dream," said Vaisia. "I just loved being around her and J.J. so much."

Charles had bought Tylee a GoPro video camera, so she and Vaisia would spend hours shooting zany videos of themselves on the beach, then post them online for their friends back in Phoenix.

"Tylee liked to take pictures and make videos," said Vaisia's mother, Echo. "She took all this cool video in Hawaii and was really sarcastic and joking a lot of the time and sassy and funny."

Lori often joined in the girls' activities and would discuss her Mormon beliefs with Vaisia. Lori recommended some new LDS authors, singling out a novelist and podcaster from Idaho named Chad Daybell, who wrote a series of novels about the end-times. Lori seemed obsessed with his books and was reading all of them.

Lori was also reading another Mormon author named Julie Rowe, after attending one of her conferences about near-death experiences. Lori started listening to Rowe's podcasts and would often talk about what she'd learned from them.

"And that ignited her interest," said April.

In summer 2015, nineteen-year-old Colby left Hawaii to return to the mainland for an LDS mission in Idaho. It didn't work out, and he soon returned to Kauai. April recalls that Lori was embarrassed, as cutting a mission short was considered dishonorable in her small Mormon congregation, and it caused much gossip.

"Colby was having some emotional trauma and wanted to leave the mission," remembered April. "I know that Lori felt a lot of pressure and felt judged."

On Colby's return to Kauai his stepfather gave him an ultimatum: either get a job or move out of the family house. Colby had two short-lived jobs at Ace Hardware and Foodland, but when they didn't work out, he went back to Arizona and started college.

Tylee was doing well at her school. Now in eighth grade, she studied traditional Hawaiian culture and loved participating in local dance performances. She had a natural gift for dancing, singing, and entertaining.

On May 25, 2016, Lori threw a fourth birthday party for J.J. and invited all his friends. Larry and Kay Woodcock flew over and were delighted by how well everything seemed to be going with their grandson. The Vallows seemed like the perfect, loving family, and there was no hint of any trouble in paradise.

* * *

Tylee was active in social media and had an Instagram account under the name typicaltylee. One posting read, "In this world you either crank that soulja boy or it cranks you."

On Mother's Day 2017, Tylee posted a poignant picture of herself and Lori together on the beach.

"My love for my mom grows everyday. She is truly the best person for the job. Through everything we have been through as a family and as individuals her faith just gets stronger. She's the best example of how I want to be a mother someday. Happy Mother's Day."

Then in her more private Finsta [Fake Instagram] account, shared only with close friends, Tylee wrote, "We're here for a good time not a long time;))."

After Tylee moved to Hawaii, Joe Ryan's life fell apart. He began drinking heavily and got three DUIs, losing his job and then his house. One day he turned up at his former attorney Keith Taniguchi's house, destitute and asking for a place to stay.

"Joe was depressed losing Tylee and it led him to drink," said Taniguchi. "He was broke and he stayed at my house . . . for several months, attempting to make some money so he could move on. He was about ready to sell his car, which was the only thing he had worth anything."

After staying for a few weeks, Taniguchi lent him enough money to go to New York and see his sister Annie Cushing to try to get back on his feet. But, according to Annie, he never made it there.

Even though Barry and Janis Cox were now living in Hawaii, they could not avoid the IRS and the back taxes they owed. On June 1, 2016, the IRS issued a Notice of Levy on Janis Cox's Social Security income, claiming she now had almost $425,000 in unpaid income taxes from 2001 to 2010.

Six months later, on January 3, 2017, Janis filed an eighty-page complaint against the United States of America. She alleged that the entire IRS tax assessment and collection system was "illegal" and she was "immune" from paying taxes. She also claimed that the IRS had "fraudulently confiscated" $60,000 from her, as well as seizing her San Antonio house in February 2008, which was subsequently sold at an IRS auction for $249,000.

Janis demanded that the IRS revoke the levy and pay her damages of $10,000 for "pain and suffering," plus another $10,000 for her court costs and legal research.

On May 31, 2017, the US District Court for the District of Hawaii denied Janis's case out of hand.

"The Plaintiff's claims," wrote chief US district judge J. Michael Seabright, "based on the frivolous premise that Plaintiff is immune from paying taxes are DISMISSED without leave to amend."

Soon after the court decision, Barry and Janis Cox suddenly left Kauai and moved back to the mainland. They were followed by Lori, Charles, and their children.

"She told us on a Monday that this was going to be her last week on Kauai," said April Raymond. "It was very abrupt and seemed very unplanned and rushed, like everything in Lori's life."

TEN

"THE WORLD IS A BETTER PLACE WITHOUT JOE RYAN"

In the summer of 2017, Charles Vallow moved the family back to Chandler, Arizona. He rented a beautiful house in the San Tan Valley at Lori's behest, just an hour away from Alex. Now Lori began to distance herself from Charles, feeling more and more alienated from him on a religious level.

She started immersing herself in radical offshoots of the Mormon religion, plunging deeper into Chad Daybell's books and doing her own research online. She discovered the AVOW (Another Voice of Warning) website, which teaches that the end-times are imminent and how to prepare for them. Its motto is "If ye are prepared, ye shall not fear."

She also learned about the concept of multiple probations: continual reincarnation until achieving perfection. She started going to the Mormon temple for hours every day to pray and hear the spirit voices from beyond the veil that were now guiding her. She believed that God had chosen her as one of the sacred 144,000 who would survive the end-times and be there to witness the Second Coming of Jesus Christ.

Every night Lori went into the new mirrored dancing room Charles had thoughtfully provided her, ecstatically dancing to her favorite Christian music.

On a more physical plane, she enrolled five-year-old J.J. at the Lauren's Institute for Education (L.I.F.E.), which catered for special needs children. But the severely autistic child was a handful and had to be constantly watched. He suffered from insomnia and would in the small hours sneak out the front door for a walk. Charles had to secure the entire house with dead bolts and alarms to prevent J.J. from escaping.

Charles decided to get his son a service dog and called Dog Training Elite in Phoenix. Trainer Neal Mestas came to the Vallow home with his own service dog, Bailey, to demonstrate all the necessary training involved.

"When J.J. met her," recalled Mestas, "he said, 'I want a Bailey.' So that's why they named their service dog Bailey as well."

Charles signed up for the eight months of in-home training, costing around $7,000, needed to officially certify the black goldendoodle.

"The first night that Bailey stayed with him," said Mestas, "was one of the first nights that J.J. slept through the night and didn't get out of bed."

As the training progressed, Mestas took Bailey and J.J. out to nearby shops and restaurants to adapt to public places. Lori was supportive.

"We also did training sessions at the airport," said Mestas, "as they were going back and forth to Hawaii, where Charles still had a home."

The trainer was impressed by what a close family the Vallows appeared to be, and how attentive Lori always was to J.J. and all his needs.

"I thought, 'What a great family,'" Mestas remembered. "They cared about their son and they seemed definitely in love and supportive of each other."

At college Colby had met a young girl named Kelsee and they got engaged. But when he introduced her to his mother, things became uncomfortable. Lori was jealous, viewing Kelsee, who was not Mormon, as her rival. She began treating Colby more like a boyfriend than a son.

"It just became a competition," Colby later explained. "And [Kelsee] was saying, 'Do you see how she challenges me on that?'"

Colby became frustrated as he just wanted his mother and fiancée to get on well.

"There was just that disconnect," said Colby, "like [Kelsee] took me away from her and . . . that just made this huge dynamic."

In January 2018, Colby married Kelsee in the backyard of Lori and Charles's new house. It was the first time the entire Cox family had been together since Lori and Charles's return from Kauai, and it was a great success.

"We were excited," Colby told Fox 10's Justin Lum. "Everybody was together [and] we had a big guest list of our family there."

Unfortunately, Tylee came late and missed being in the official wedding pictures.

Two months later, Charles Vallow's eighty-five-year-old mother, Tilda, died. Affectionately known as Miss Tilly, his entire family went to the beloved matriarch's funeral in Lake Charles, Louisiana. Lori refused to go, saying she was too busy, so Charles went by himself.

It was then that Larry and Kay Woodcock first noticed that something had changed in the marriage.

"I could tell there was something going on," said Larry. "[When] one of the spouses no longer wants to be there and . . . visit with other people, then there's an issue."

Larry believed that Charles was so blindly in love with Lori that he refused to accept their relationship had changed, even though the writing was on the wall.

"And I think that was simply his downfall to his death," said Larry.

On April 3, 2018, Joe Ryan's badly decomposed body was found in his Phoenix apartment, three weeks after he had died. When his neighbor Roy Zlinga's pet dog kept scratching at Ryan's front door, Roy went to investigate and smelled a pungent odor and saw flies everywhere. Zlinga immediately called the leasing office, who summoned the police.

They arrived to find the front door dead-bolted from the inside, so they accessed the apartment through an open back window.

"Joseph was found on his bed in his bedroom," read the police report, "in advanced stages of decomposition. He was pronounced deceased by the police."

Police photographed the fifty-nine-year-old's body and other items of interest, before transporting him to the Maricopa County Medical Examiner's Office for autopsy. They also found his passport, driver's license, and wallet by an open jar of spaghetti and dirty dishes in the sink.

Several medications were in the bathroom, including antidepressants and high blood pressure pills.

The apartment was bare of furniture, and the only pictures on the walls were of his beloved daughter, Tylee.

The case was put on hold until the medical examiner could establish the cause of death. As no one claimed Ryan's body, the local funeral home posted an ad seeking any information about his family, and his body was eventually cremated without a proper funeral.

Ten days after his death, Phoenix police discovered that Lori Vallow was listed as his next of kin. She was informed of his death by Officer Jason Smith.

"Lori told me that she had not heard from Joseph in about two years," Smith later reported. "They did have a child in common. The child's name was Tylee and she was 15 years old. Lori asked what had happened and I explained the situation. Lori stated she would let her daughter know of the death of her father."

Soon afterward Lori took Tylee to Ryan's apartment and removed all his photo albums, files, and other personal papers. She now stood to cash in on her ex-husband's six-figure life insurance policy, as stipulated in their divorce agreement.

A week later, Lori was driving her sister-in-law Kay to the airport when Lori casually asked if Kay had heard about Tylee's father. Kay said she hadn't and asked what had happened. Lori then seemed to light up, saying that God had taken him because he was too evil to be on this earth.

"Now we don't have to worry about him anymore," she said. "And Tylee doesn't have to deal with him."

Kay asked how Joe had died.

"She said, 'Well, he was dead for three weeks,'" Kay recalled, "and nobody even missed him because he was that evil and people didn't want to be around him but they smelled the smell."

Lori then gleefully told her there was a life insurance policy and she expected to receive $150,000 as well as Tylee's monthly Social Security checks from her dad.

"So it's all good," Lori assured Kay. "He was evil and he needed to die."

The Maricopa County medical examiner later determined that Joe Ryan had died of a heart attack, caused by arteriosclerosis, a hardening and narrowing of the arteries.

When Annie Cushing learned of her brother's death from another source, she immediately texted Lori. After getting no response, she followed up with an email, saying she needed to talk to her urgently about Joe.

"When I finally got hold of her," said Cushing, "she already knew and acted like it was no big deal."

Lori also lied, claiming that she didn't know about Joe's death until April 18, although a Phoenix police report shows she was actually called five days earlier.

"Why wouldn't she inform me that Joe had passed?" asked Cushing. "Was she just riding out the clock in hopes that Joe would be cremated before any family had been notified that he had passed?"

Lori invited Annie to come to Phoenix and comfort Tylee, whom Annie hadn't seen since she was a baby. Annie flew in from New York and was met by Lori, who appeared happy that her ex-husband was dead.

"She would actually say," recalled Annie, "'The world is a better place without Joe Ryan.'"

When Lori showed her Joe Ryan's driver's license, issued in September 2017, Annie was shocked. Her once handsome, muscular brother, whom she hadn't seen since 2003, was almost unrecognizable.

"I just stared at it in disbelief," she said. "His face was bloated and he looked like a shell of the man I once knew."

During Annie's stay, Lori proudly showed her all Joe Ryan's treasured photo albums, which she had taken from his apartment. Annie noticed the albums still had a "strong smell of death," but Lori seemed totally oblivious of it, as she cheerfully talked about Joe's decomposed body with a kind of "manic" enthusiasm.

"She went into pretty graphic detail about the state of his mattress," recalled Annie. "Really inappropriate detail. It was grotesque. I had to ask her to stop."

Annie sensed tension between Lori and Tylee. Annie asked her niece when she had last seen her father, and Tylee replied that it had been more than a year.

"There was definitely friction between [Lori] and Tylee," said Annie. "She was very soft and gentle with J.J., but Tylee was much more of a stronger personality—like Lori almost kowtowed to Tylee."

Throughout the visit Lori seemed fixated on the end-times. She repeatedly talked about it, each time with a mounting sense of urgency. Annie was alarmed, as it went far beyond the mainstream Mormon doctrine Lori had once embraced.

"I did notice a tectonic shift," Cushing explained. "Like her focus seemed to have kind of a dark cloud."

Lori said that the end-times would be so scary that she often thought it would be better to put her kids in a car and drive off the side of a cliff.

"And that was definitely very, very shocking," said Annie. "She saw that on my face and immediately walked it back. 'Oh, I'm just kidding. No, I would never do anything to my kids.'"

Lori now avidly listened to podcasts by author and visionary Julie Rowe, who had published five books with Chad Daybell's publishing company, Spring Creek, about her own near-death experiences. She was convinced that wars, earthquakes, and other natural disasters were coming and started to prepare. Charles was so busy working that he was oblivious of the radical changes Lori was going through.

"Lori was infatuated with when Christ was coming back to earth," said her brother Adam Cox. "What's going to happen towards the end of the world. 'We need to prepare the people.'"

On June 26, 2018, Lori celebrated her forty-fifth birthday, and Tylee celebrated by posting a photograph on Facebook of her and J.J. in a swimming pool.

"I won the lottery with this one as my mom," she wrote.

On July 4, Lori brought Tylee to Kauai to visit April Raymond. Lori arrived with $10,000 in cash, explaining that it was from the sale of Juice

Island. It had been fourteen months since Lori and April had last seen each other, and April noticed her friend's dramatic transformation:

"That was my first taste of some of her crazy beliefs. She told me that she had seen Jesus Christ face-to-face and also Angel Moroni. It kind of got shut out pretty quick because it wasn't something I wanted to explore."

Lori was also reading a book by Mormon author Denver C. Snuffer, Jr., called *The Second Comforter: Conversing with the Lord Through the Veil*. She mentioned really connecting with Chad Daybell's two dozen books about the end-times.

"She would talk about this author [Chad Daybell] that she was really interested in," said April. "I would call her a superfan."

ELEVEN

"I WAS GOING TO MURDER HIM"

In October 2018, Lori Vallow attended a church class in Mesa, Arizona, to prepare for the end-times. It was run by a devout Mormon writer and life coach named Melanie Gibb. After the class, Lori sought out Melanie in a hallway to discuss some of Lori's personal spiritual experiences.

"And we just hit it off," said forty-seven-year-old Melanie, who was married to a Gilbert chiropractor and had three young children. "She had a lot of the same energy that I did. We talked a lot about the Second Coming . . . and how excited we are for the things that we'd been studying and learning."

Lori was particularly interested to learn that Melanie knew Chad Daybell, who was about to publish her first book, *Feel the Fire*.

Finally Lori had discovered a direct link to her hero Chad Daybell and a way to meet him. She felt there had been a divine significance to her meeting Melanie, and everything Lori had done up to now had prepared her for what was about to happen.

So Lori began to cultivate Melanie. Lori invited her over to her house to meet her family and get to know each other better. Melanie arrived to find Charles cooking on the barbecue and Tylee and J.J. swimming in the pool.

"J.J. was a lot of work for her," said Melanie, who also has an autistic child. "He was running around and she was trying to make him happy. Then Tylee would every once in a while appear out of the bedroom. She did not have a good relationship with her mom [and] did not talk nicely to her."

Charles was friendly and spoke enthusiastically about his conversion to Mormonism, but Melanie could sense he had underlying tension with Lori, who seemed to disapprove of him.

"There [was] some arguing," recalled Melanie. "She seemed often frustrated with him [and] there seemed to be a lot of contention between the two of them."

On October 19, Melanie Gibb officially invited Lori to a small Preparing a People (PaP) meeting at her house in Gilbert. The religious multimedia organization had many devoted followers nationwide and focused on "helping to prepare the people of this earth for the Second Coming of Jesus Christ."

Melanie, a regular speaker on the PaP circuit, had invited her new friend to tell the group about herself. For a half hour, Lori recounted her long and often torturous spiritual journey.

"I'm a personal witness of the resurrected Jesus Christ," she began. "It was a hard road to get to know him. I sat down with him and we discussed what I would do to get to this point."

Lori explained that she had then embarked on "a very important mission," for which she had been chosen in a "pre-mortal" life. She claimed that she no longer needed to sleep, as angels woke her up to instruct her on doing God's work.

"When people hear my story, they're like, 'I can't believe that you lived through that. I can't believe you're still here.'" She told the group about her "awful" marriage to a man named Joe Ryan, who had "raped" her children.

"After we were divorced, he told everybody that I was this lying, crazy Mormon and got up in court and said all these horrible things about me. He was constantly trying to get custody of my three-year-old daughter, just to rub it in my face.

"I was going to murder him. I was going to kill him like the Scriptures say. Like Nephi killed. Just to stop the pain and to stop him coming after me and to stop him coming after my children."

Lori had scoured the Scriptures to rationalize the act of murder, discovering that the Book of Mormon states that if someone comes against you three times, you can kill them.

"I was like, 'There it is, there's my answer.' I don't want to do anything that's wrong. I did not have a murderous heart. I just wanted to stop the bleeding and stop the pain."

Then, Lori told her avid audience, she had had a vision to go to the temple for guidance. "So I went and met my bishop, and I was like, 'I'm either going to turn my life to the temple or I'm going to commit murder. So do you want to give me a temple recommend?'" (A temple recommend is a ID card that allows LDS members to enter a temple.)

"And I was perfectly honest because at that point I had nothing to lose. You get to the bottom rung. And he gave me a temple recommend."

After that she began going to the temple every week and soon every day. The Lord "was just so patient and kind, and I would be in there just sobbing. I just spent so much time in dark courtrooms, where evil powers overpower these rooms, and [the Lord] washed all of that away from me. And then he sent me on a mission."

Lori then emotionally spoke of her epiphany in the temple sealing room, going beyond the veil to see some of her long-deceased family members.

"I saw a spirit sister. It was one of my husband's aunts . . . and she kissed me on the cheek before she disappeared through the wall."

Lori explained that dead spirits know everything that's going on in the world and are actively involved in our lives.

"The time is now. The Lord is gathering his people. He is calling people to the 144,000 [and] they are already being on their missions. He is preparing us and we promised we would do it."

Lori said it would be a glorious, magnificent mission, as everyone that dies and goes to the other side does so as part of their mission.

Her next statement would be eerily prescient.

"Your kids are adults in eternity. They're your friends. They're loaned to you for this short time. They're adults and they have their own missions and their own eternity to live. We do not need to worry about the souls of . . . our children. We *do not* have to worry."

Lori finished by modestly expressing surprise that God had singled her out for his mission, as she was "totally sweet and innocent."

She explained, "And he gave me a pre-mortal memory of me. And I got to see myself as a warrior fighting for the savior in the pre-mortal world. And I went to other worlds and I fought. And I was one of his strongest warriors. And I saw it. I was not sweet and I was not innocent. I am old. I have fought in this war for millennia. And that's who I am. And I came down here to be a warrior and fight. And I only thought that I was sweet and innocent."

"You should have incredible hope to hear that," gushed Melanie as the audience applauded its brand-new PaP member.

The following week, Lori and Melanie drove 415 miles from Phoenix to St. George, Utah, to attend a Preparing a People conference. Chad Daybell would be the guest speaker, and Lori would finally meet her psychic mentor, whom she had dreamed about for so long.

PART TWO

CHAD DAYBELL

TWELVE

LEAPING INTO ETERNITY

Chad Daybell proudly traces his family back to the 1840s, when his ancestor Finity Daybell and his wife, Mary, joined the LDS Church in England. According to Chad, his ancestor actually came to the rescue of Joseph Fielding Smith—the nephew of the founder of the Church of Jesus Christ of Latter-day Saints—when he visited England on a mission.

The future LDS president was preaching in a town square when several people in the crowd began throwing eggs at him, one hitting his stovepipe hat. Seeing Smith under attack, Finity Daybell leaped into action.

"Finity ran toward the men that were throwing the eggs," wrote Chad in his autobiography, *Living on the Edge of Heaven*. "He grabbed the egg basket from the ringleader and swung it forcefully at the man's head."

The crowd quickly scattered as Finity kept swinging the basket, and a grateful Elder Smith personally thanked him for his courage.

In May 1864, Finity had saved enough to move his family to Utah, finally reaching Salt Lake City. He established a farm in Charleston in the Heber Valley, and his sons became prominent citizens and leading Mormon Church members.

Chad's grandfather Keith Daybell, whom Chad believes to be his main spirit guide from beyond the veil, grew up in Provo, Utah, during the Great Depression. In 1937, he married a pretty young girl named Rosalie Bjarnson, whom he met at the nearby Springville High School junior prom.

The newly married Keith opened a Texaco gas station in Springville and soon had two sons, Ray and Lanny. In early 1944, Keith was drafted into the infantry. After basic training in Southern California, he was shipped off to Europe where he fought on the Western Front.

On December 3, 1944, Keith's platoon came under heavy attack. He was taken prisoner by the Germans and imprisoned in Stalag II outside Frankfurt. The US Army officially listed him as missing in action, and Rosalie and their sons did not know whether he was dead or alive.

Three months later Rosalie received a letter from Keith, saying he was well. The story made the front page of *The Springville Herald* with the headline "Local Woman's Husband in German Prison."

On Sunday, May 20, 1945, Keith was liberated by the Russians, who sent him in the direction of American troops.

"He said he had a pretty long walk," reported *The Springville Herald*, "but had Red Cross food which made it okay."

On his release Keith weighed just ninety-five-pounds, with a long beard and hair past his shoulders. He was later awarded two Purple Hearts for his acts of heroism.

After the war, Keith joined his brothers Theo and LaVar in their new business, the Daybell Lumber Company. Keith's son Jack, Chad's father, was born in 1947, and a daughter, Judy, followed four years later.

On August 9, 1951, Keith Daybell was tragically killed at the age of thirty-two. He had been hoisting a diesel engine onto a lumber truck using a large industrial tripod when the driveshaft broke and the brakes gave way, sending the truck careening down a steep logging road. Keith was thrown into the path of a passing car and died instantly.

He was buried at the Springville Cemetery, where Chad would later work as a gravedigger and sexton.

Five months later, Rosalie took their four children to the Salt Lake Temple, where she and Keith were sealed for eternity.

"Then the children were sealed to their parents," wrote Chad, "preparing for that day when the family would once again be reunited."

(LDS faithful believe that civil marriages finish at death, but a couple that has been sealed in a temple remains married for eternity.)

Chad's father, Jack Daybell, went to Springville High School, where he dated Sheila Chesnut, who was a year below him. After attending Brigham

Young University (BYU) he was drafted into the US Naval Reserve. In September 1967, he and Sheila married, and she joined him at the US Naval Base in San Diego.

On August 11, 1968, Sheila gave birth to a baby boy named Chad Guy Daybell. Jack had scheduled his two-week shore leave so Sheila could have the baby in Utah. After he was born, they brought Chad back to Southern California, settling down in a small apartment in National City, just outside San Diego.

After completing his naval service Jack Daybell moved the family back to Springville, finding work as an electrician at Geneva Steel, one of Utah's biggest employers. He and Rosalie had two more sons and a daughter.

At the age of one, a smiling Chad Daybell made his first appearance in *The Springville Herald,* dressed up in football clothes and grasping a ball. Four years later in 1973, five-year-old Chad started at Grant Elementary School in Springville.

In third grade, according to his memoir, he had his "first encounter with death," when his classmate Randy Perkins was killed in a cave collapse.

"They said Randy was now in heaven," Chad later wrote, "but I didn't really understand what that meant. Death became a very scary topic to me."

As a young child Chad devoted himself to tee-ball and was coached by his father in Springville's Mustang League. His team, the Dodgers, were Springville Tee-Ball Champions several years running.

In June 1979, ten-year-old Cub Scout Chad Daybell won the Arrow of Light Award and was featured in *The Springville Herald,* along with a photo of him in his uniform.

"The award is Cub Scouting's highest honor," read the article. "[Chad] was recognized for [his] hard work and good example to the pack."

He was also a voracious reader, devouring Alfred Hitchcock short stories and the Hardy Boys books. Little Chad was especially fascinated by death, and in fourth grade he wrote his first book, "The Murder of Dr. Jay and His Assistant." The gory handwritten short novel was then bound by a teacher's aide with a cover depicting an evil-looking owl.

From then on Chad would be obsessed by owls, believing that they had secret powers from beyond the veil.

One fine spring day, thirteen-year-old Chad was walking home from school through Memorial Park when he saw a honeybee pollinating flowers. What the meek, timid boy did next revealed a deep underlying violence that would remain hidden for years.

"I peered at it for a moment," Chad would later remember, "then smashed it with my shoe. I spotted another one, then another one. I got a strange fascination from it."

For the next thirty minutes he kept careful count as he savagely killed 120 bees. He was about to stomp on yet another when he heard a loud voice, ordering him to stop killing those beautiful bees.

Startled, Chad stood up and looked around the park, but nobody was there.

"Finally," he wrote, "I realized that maybe an angel was fed up with me killing God's innocent creatures."

In ninth grade, Chad had a spiritual awakening after reading the Book of Mormon. He was seeking confirmation that it was true when the Spirit rushed into his room and he started crying with joy. Soon afterward he received his patriarchal blessing, pointing out what he would be capable of achieving. It gave him great hope for the future.

"The blessing made it clear I had a long, wonderful life ahead of me," he wrote. "It spoke [of] marrying a wonderful woman and raising a strong family. It also mentioned spiritual gifts that would be made known to me later in life that I would cultivate to bless the lives of others."

Growing up, Chad made quite a name for himself in Springville, with his sporting exploits being well documented in *The Springville Herald*. He excelled at basketball and regularly made Springville Junior High School's honor roll and Citizen of the Month. There are numerous photos of the gawky teenager with his long, straight fringe and smug grin.

In January 1983, the fourteen-year-old was profiled in the *Herald*, listing his love of sports, reading, collecting baseball cards, fly-fishing, and hunting pheasant.

"Chad has been on the honor roll every term," the article read, "and is seminary class president and homeroom representative. He plans to go on a mission and attend college."

When he moved up to Springville High School, Chad played on the football team alongside future NFL Miami Dolphin quarterback Scott Mitchell. The two were close friends throughout high school, and years later Chad would publish Scott's autobiography.

Before his senior year, Chad found a summer job as a gravedigger with the Springville City Parks Department. The job fascinated him, and he would return to it again and again over the next three decades.

That August, Chad had his first near-death experience, which would change him forever. He was on a day trip to the Flaming Gorge Reservoir in northern Utah with other LDS Church members. Everyone was leaping off cliffs into the water below when someone dared Chad to jump off one that was sixty feet high. In his autobiography he remembered standing at the edge and staring down at the blue waters before jumping.

It seemed like a lifetime until he finally hit the water, which felt like concrete. Then he saw a blinding flash of white light and felt a sharp shock reverberate through his body. He heard an "audible pop" at the base of his skull and thought he must have broken his neck.

"I quickly realized something even worse was happening," Chad remembered. "My spirit was partly out of my body!"

Chad likened his out-of-body experience to his physical body going far deeper into the water than his spirit had.

"This caused my spirit to pop out through my head," he wrote, "but then it felt like my spirit's knees got stuck in my skull and I didn't make it all the way out."

During his first trip to the other side of the veil, he saw an endless white plain in all directions. He heard a "deep, rich melody" like a synthesizer, as all his pain disappeared. A "soothing warmth" surrounded him, and "energy particles of knowledge" came at him from all directions.

Then his body floated toward the surface and his spirit returned through his head to its proper place, as one of his friends jumped into the water and brought him safely back to the shore.

"I was spiritually changed," wrote Chad. "I had glimpsed another dimension, and it had felt like home."

In retrospect, Chad believes that when his body hit the water his spirit left his body, ripping open his "personal veil," which has never closed.

"To fulfill my mission in life," he explained, "I needed a good shot to the head to tear my veil a little, and the angels fully orchestrated it!"

In May 1986, Chad Daybell graduated from Springville High School with high honors, winning a two-year scholarship to Brigham Young University. The slim, tall seventeen-year-old was now ready to make a mark on the Mormon world.

In his freshman year he commuted to the BYU campus in Provo from his parents' home in Springville. He attended classes and studied in the library, occasionally socializing with old high school friends.

He briefly dated a girl from Florida who was in his communications class, but she dumped him for being too parochial. He felt insulted, having gone to Disneyland three times with his family.

The next summer he worked as a gravedigger again before leaving for Morristown, New Jersey, to serve as a missionary. He arrived at the missionary training center and was immediately sent to some of the neediest New Jersey towns, such as Newark and Union City, to spread the Mormon word.

In this proselytizing mission Chad knocked on doors in tough Spanish-speaking communities, inviting people to learn more about the Mormon religion. He often got the door slammed in his face, but his modest charm sometimes paid off.

While doing the rounds of hundreds of dilapidated apartment buildings lining the Hudson River, he sensed many disembodied spirits lying in limbo. According to his autobiography, he discovered that his torn veil allowed him to differentiate between good and bad spirits.

"I would sense both angels and disembodied spirits in the room," he explained, "and I thought, 'Hey, if these spirits want to listen in, what can it hurt?' I sometimes saw the angels talking to them afterwards."

Chad soon found a tight group of friends in his missionary group to read the Bible and socialize with. Ben Hyde, who grew up in Provo, was immediately struck by how calm and low-key Chad was:

"This is *the* most humble, unassuming guy that I've ever met. He was a very successful missionary. . . . He would just humbly present the message, and people were drawn to him."

Hector Hernandez, who also served with Chad in New Jersey, remembers everybody looking up to him: "Chad was really loved and really respected, and we thought he was really the best of us."

Fellow missionary Trent Price fondly remembers Chad as a "gentle giant," much admired in their missionary community. Price was especially touched by Chad's endearing habit of handwriting thank-you notes.

"We were a pretty solid group, but he was amazing," said Price. "I had a great mission, [but] I just felt like his was extraordinary."

One night Chad, now a zone leader, was walking back to the training center when he sensed the spirit of his grandfather Keith Daybell, who had died seventeen years before Chad was born. It would be his first meeting with the man who would become his main spirit guide.

"I knew instantly who he was," Chad later wrote. "It was as if time stopped for me, because I could sense the spirit of my deceased Grandpa . . . walking along with us on my right side. No actual words passed between us, but I was given the knowledge of how proud he was of my efforts, and that he'll be there for me . . . during my mission."

THIRTEEN

A CEMETERY COURTSHIP

In summer 1989, after completing two years of missionary training, Chad returned to Utah to continue his studies at BYU. He began writing for BYU's *Daily Universe* newspaper, eventually working his way up to city editor.

One day he was idly thumbing through his brother Paul's 1988 high school yearbook when he saw a half page devoted to a blond senior named Tammy Douglas.

"When I saw her face," he later wrote, "I felt the most electrifying shock of my life."

When Chad asked who she was, Paul informed him that Tammy was Springville's cemetery secretary. Chad was instantly smitten, and at the next LDS Springville singles ward event he asked Tammy out on a date. The nineteen-year-old immediately accepted, and they were soon going steady.

Tammy also attended BYU, majoring in advertising as well as working for the Springville Parks Department, where she did all the cemetery's billing. She helped Chad get a part-time job as a gravedigger there.

"Our cemetery courtship allowed us to get better acquainted," explained Chad. "Within a month we took the bold step of actually sitting next to each other during the Singles Ward sacrament meeting—the universal sign to other ward members we were now a couple and pretty much off limits to anyone else."

According to Chad's autobiography, he then prayed to the "Heavenly Father," asking if he should marry Tammy, and received a resounding yes.

At Thanksgiving, Chad proposed to Tammy on bended knee and placed a diamond engagement ring on her finger. They posed for engagement photographs at Springville Cemetery.

On Friday, March 9, 1990, Chad and Tammy were married at the Manti LDS Temple, followed by a wedding reception at the Springville Museum of Art. Tammy's parents and siblings were delighted for Chad to join their family, thinking he was the perfect match for Tammy.

"They really loved each other," said Tammy's sister, Samantha, "and at their wedding you could see how happy they were."

In his final year at BYU, Chad started writing freelance articles for *The Springville Herald*. He covered a variety of subjects, including the Springville City Council, police reports, and profiles of local artists. In April 1992, he graduated with a bachelor's degree in communications.

Garth Douglas Daybell was born a month later, and Tammy gave up her job at the Springville Parks Department to become a full-time mother. That summer, Chad moved his family eighty-five miles north to Ogden to take up his new job on the busy copydesk of Utah's third-largest newspaper, the *Ogden Standard-Examiner*.

"He was just out of school and had spent his summers digging graves," said *Ogden Standard-Examiner* copy chief Peggy Barney, who hired him. "He seemed to be a very mainstream LDS guy with the wife and kid."

He soon earned the nickname Chadderbox as he was so quiet and withdrawn on the otherwise noisy copydesk.

"He was so shy," said Barney, "but he was really dependable and good at his job."

Sports editor Randy Hollis remembers Chad as a mild-mannered, soft-spoken young man who was easily embarrassed.

"I have a kind of potty mouth," explained Hollis, "and sometimes I would say something inappropriate and he would blush. He pretty much only spoke when spoken to."

Chad worked eight-hour shifts five days a week and never socialized with the other copy editors. While they went out drinking at night, Chad went home to Tammy and their baby son.

"I thought the world of him," said Hollis. "This is a fine young man who's a clean liver and goes and does his job. Although we did not socialize outside the building, we had a good friendship."

Soon after they moved, Tammy started working for a local school as a librarian in the computer room. She found an aptitude for the new technology and loved playing computer games.

In May 1993, Chad and Tammy went on a Daybell family vacation to San Diego, where he was reunited with his parents and siblings. One day they went swimming at La Jolla Cove, but Tammy, who was pregnant again, stayed at the hotel with baby Garth.

Everyone else remained on the beach, but Chad, as he later recounted in his autobiography, ventured out into the water to some rocks to look for seashells. Suddenly the sky darkened, the wind squalled, and he heard a loud voice commanding him to cling to the rocks. Then a fifteen-foot wave crashed down on him and he was sucked into another world.

"I found myself in the proverbial tunnel of light," he wrote. "It wasn't a bright white light but more like a yellow heat lamp."

A warm feeling of happiness enveloped him and he looked up to see Finity Daybell and his grandfather Keith hovering ten feet above.

"I was completely out of my body," he wrote, "standing in front of them."

Then, according to Chad, his long-deceased grandfather began telling him about the children he and Tammy would have and their glorious future together. Finity didn't speak but watched intently, as Keith instructed his grandson on all the tasks he had to accomplish to fulfill his spiritual mission.

"Finally, Keith asked if I would be willing to fulfill the assignments he had outlined," wrote Chad. "And I agreed to do so."

Then his grandfather waved his hand and Chad's spirit was reunited with his body, as his concerned father and brothers ran up to see if he was okay. He suffered extensive cuts and bruises to his back, which required hospital treatment.

Chad wrote that his second near-death experience had ripped open his personal veil even wider than before. This time it would remain open, giving him waking visions and experiences of déjà vu.

"I could remember Keith speaking with me," explained Chad, "but the actual conversation about my future tasks was removed from my mind. I just knew it had to do with future earthly missions of my children—four of whom hadn't been born yet."

In March 1994, Tammy gave birth to a baby girl they named Emma Michelle, followed eighteen months later by another son, Seth. Soon afterward Chad invited his boss, Peggy Barney, over to his house to meet Tammy and his small children.

"She was so cute and sweet," Peggy remembered.

At Halloween, the *Ogden Standard-Examiner* organized a costume contest for all the staff. Chad surprised everyone by dressing up as a nun. Although Chad didn't win the contest, which Tammy and Garth attended, he did gamely pose in a line with all the other entrants.

"He was very well received," said Hollis, "because it was so out of character for this quiet, soft-spoken guy on the copydesk to be dressed in drag."

After several years working on the copydesk, Chad quit, making no secret of how much he disliked the job and wanted to move back to Springville. He hated getting up so early with only Sundays and Mondays off, and he wanted to write instead of editing someone else's copy.

"He didn't like copyediting," said Barney. "I don't know if it was the crappy hours or he was sick of the commute."

When Chad heard that Springville's cemetery sexton was retiring, he immediately applied for the job and got it.

"So I went from writing headlines to digging graves," he explained, "but it paid better and allowed us to move back to Springville."

The first week of December 1995, Chad and Tammy moved their three children back to Springville. Unable to afford a house, Chad bought an old double-wide. Tammy dutifully went along with it, but could not have been happy raising three small children in a cramped trailer.

Springville's city administrative manager, Rod Oldroyd, was delighted with his new hire, who now took charge of the city's two cemeteries—the Historic City Cemetery and the Evergreen. Oldroyd had previously employed Tammy as cemetery secretary and now rehired her as a receptionist.

"They were a perfect couple," remembered Oldroyd. "Good mom, good dad, good kids."

Dating back to 1851, the Historic City Cemetery is one of the oldest working cemeteries in Utah. Chad led a team of three, who dug graves, cleaned gravestones, and weeded. One of his first jobs as sexton was to supervise the construction of a new brick fence on the Historic City Cemetery and expand the Evergreen Cemetery with an extra six thousand burial plots.

"I enjoy being a cemetery sexton," he told *The Springville Herald*, "and my only desire is to keep the cemetery looking its best. I am eager to serve you."

FOURTEEN

SPRING CREEK PUBLISHING

Over the next several years, Chad Daybell's sexton job did keep him busy, but hardly resembled his more grandiose dreams of fulfilling his preordained spiritual mission, as dictated by his grandfather. He was frustrated with being a big fish in a small pond and wanted to make his mark on the world. So he decided to become an author—with a nudge from Keith Daybell's spirit.

In the winter of 1997, Springville got hit by a huge snowstorm, paralyzing both cemeteries. For some afternoon-scheduled funerals, Chad and his staff began digging out paths to the grave sites.

Suddenly Chad heard his grandfather's voice telling him it was time to start writing his books.

"I leaned on the shovel," he remembered, "and said aloud, 'That's great, but I have no idea what to write about.'"

Then, as he stood in the snow, the complete plot of his first novel, *Errand for Emma,* suddenly came to him. It centered around his three-year-old daughter, Emma, now a teenager, going back in time to 1868 to solve the mystery of her LDS family history.

On his lunch break he sketched out the outline, and over the next few weeks he began writing at night. He submitted the completed manuscript to the Springville-based LDS publisher Cedar Fort Publishing, which immediately offered him a book contract.

Tammy was now pregnant with the couple's fourth child, and their double-wide was bursting at the seams. Chad realized he needed a real home for his family, so he took out a heavy mortgage on a house in the Imperial Heights section of Springville.

In late April 1998, Chad received an urgent call at the cemetery that Tammy had been rushed to the hospital and gone into labor, a month prematurely. He arrived to find her lying in bed waiting to be seen by a doctor.

"As we talked, she suddenly started bleeding heavily," wrote Chad, "and it turned into a frantic situation. I gave her a quick priesthood blessing, then the nurses rushed her into the operating room."

He watched the doctors perform an emergency cesarean section, fearing Tammy wouldn't survive.

"I was scared," he remembered, "but also felt it wasn't Tammy's time to die."

Leah Tamara Daybell was born small, and doctors told Tammy she would never have another baby. However, she would become pregnant once more, and in March 2000 she gave birth to their fifth and last child, Mark.

After *Errand for Emma* was published Chad Daybell immediately started on book two of what he now saw as a trilogy, *Doug's Dilemma*. That was quickly followed by *Escape to Zion,* in which Emma is launched into the future just before the Second Coming and travels to New Jerusalem.

Chad's novels received positive reviews from local newspapers, and although they didn't make him much money, he enjoyed all the book-signing events he arranged at the area's bookstores.

"*Emma* is a fun story," wrote reviewer Ellen in *The Springville Herald*'s Library Corner column, "easy to read and shows much promise for future books from Mr. Daybell. (And I knew him when he was just a kid!)"

"Unearthing a Passion—LDS Fiction Writer Finds Inspiration Among Generations Past" was the headline of Provo's *Daily Herald* review.

"There aren't many people to interview in a cemetery," it began, "but the stories found there are full of life. Chad Daybell has gone from newspaper reporter to cemetery sexton. He digs the cemetery beat, unearthing an even deeper passion for writing."

Chad told reporter Tawny Archibald that he enjoyed working with the dead in the cemetery, where he found inspiration.

"Working here helps me keep my priorities in line," he explained, "dealing with death every day."

In late 2001, Chad and Tammy embarked on a small promotional tour. At one stop he spoke to the Palmyra Chapter of the Sons of the Utah Pioneers, discussing the work of a sexton, and quoting from the 1892 *Springville City Book:*

"'He had to build coffins, transport the dead, dig graves by hand and they could bury no murderers in the cemetery.'"

His next book, *One Foot in the Grave,* focused on his time working in the cemetery. It laid out in graphic detail every aspect of burying bodies, using Chad's firsthand experience. Later, murder investigators would comb through it to see if he had utilized his unusual expertise.

"Sad times are always when you have to bury babies," he told the *Deseret News.* "That's always a poignant moment."

In 1999, Chad Daybell, now thirty-one, quit his sexton job to become regional sales manager for Access Computer Products. The Colorado-based company, which recycled electronic products, was looking to expand and needed someone to run their new Provo office. For Chad it would mean a big increase in salary from this growing company.

"I didn't want to spend the rest of my life in a cemetery," he would later explain.

For the next two years, Chad worked nine to five selling laser printer cartridges to schools as well as recycling old ones.

"We carved out a niche in the market that had been untapped," he said, "and the company grew rapidly."

In early 2001, Chad's publisher, Cedar Fort, offered him the job of production manager, paying $10,000 a year less than he was making for the computer recycling company. According to Chad, his decision to take a hefty cut in salary was all part of his grandfather's spiritual mission for him.

"I had a wife and five kids at home," he explained, "and taking a pay cut like that would really tighten our budget, almost to the breaking point."

Tammy suggested he call his boss in Colorado, who promptly offered him a $20,000 increase. But just as Chad was about to call his wife with the good news, he heard his grandfather's voice coming from the heavens.

"This is not part of your life plan," it told him. "This isn't the right path."

Suddenly, Chad saw two distinct paths for him to choose from. If he remained with the computer products company and rose through the ranks, it would mean big money and extensive travel. But it would also be spiritually crippling for his family, as he would be away so much.

The other path in publishing would mean "financial challenges" and "stressful situations," but it would strengthen and unify his family.

So, without consulting Tammy, he accepted the job with Cedar Fort, despite the huge drop in salary. His loyal wife would never factor into any of their major life-changing decisions, which he then presented to her as a spiritual fait accompli.

"It was the hardest call I have ever made," he later wrote. "She is a woman of great faith, though, and she felt calm about the decision . . . despite the hardships it might bring."

For Chad Daybell, public acclaim was everything, and in the small LDS literary world he was becoming something of a celebrity. In July 2001, he was one of three authors spotlighted in a *Springville Herald* article for making a strong showing on the LDS classic literature list.

"Springville, known throughout the world as 'The Art City,' has produced many renowned artists and sculptors," the report began. "In recent years, the city has also become a home to many talented writers."

The article singled out Daybell for his Emma Trilogy. The second book, *Doug's Dilemma*, featured a thinly veiled Chad as the heroic Doug Dalton.

"*Doug's Dilemma* begins as a missionary novel," the article continued, "but it quickly turns into an intense race against time as Doug Dalton finds himself in 1944, where he must save his grandfather during World War II."

In September 2001, Chad won a Cedar Fort Publishers' House Award for his Emma Trilogy, despite the conflict of interest as they had published it and just hired him.

For the next three years Chad Daybell worked at Cedar Ford, signing up new LDS authors and writing several new books himself. They were all centered around the end days and the Second Coming of Jesus Christ. He and Tammy also collaborated on a book aimed at LDS children called *Tiny Talks*.

"Authors Tammy and Chad Daybell," read an advertisement, "have written dozens of interesting temple-related stories tied to the 2002 Primary theme. *Tiny Talks* [is] a valuable resource for Family Home Evening as well."

Chad and Tammy spent their Saturdays touring local bookstores for book signings and even went to Las Vegas for a special LDS book fair.

One of the first authors Chad signed at Cedar Ford was Shirley Bahlmann, for a collection of real-life pioneer stories called *Against All Odds*. She would go on to do several more books with him over the next ten years.

"Chad was very friendly," remembered Bahlmann. "He was always willing to listen to my ideas."

Chad and Tammy's *Tiny Talks* was a big hit in the LDS world and spawned a series of six. They filled a void in the children's LDS literary market to provide the basics of Mormonism.

The Daybells presented the perfect picture of young, devout Mormon parents as they traveled around Utah promoting their books.

"We have five children under the age of ten," Tammy told *The Springville Herald,* "so we'll be using the *Talks* ourselves for a long time."

In March 2003, Chad's book *Chasing Paradise* was banned by Deseret Book, the leading LDS bookstore chain in the western United States, for being offensive. It was a serious blow to Chad's future career as an author, and he came out swinging.

"As the managing editor of Cedar Fort Publishing," he told the *Deseret News,* "it's part of my job to watch for offensive material. I certainly didn't think my own novel would fall into that category."

In his promotional copy, Chad described his new novel as "an exciting, uplifting adventure that takes place on both sides of the veil." The controversial passage was on page 99, when a warrior angel named Ruby "swoops in, plucks up a naughty spirit by the nape of the neck and drop-kicks her through the wall."

Chad accused Deseret Book, which is owned by the LDS Church, of censorship, pointing out that it sells many racy *New York Times* bestsellers.

"Is this the new standard?" he asked. "No swearing, no sex and, now, no conflict. LDS novelists might as well put away their word processors because potentially anything can come under fire."

A spokesman for Deseret Book said the real reason for not carrying Chad Daybell's new novel was weak sales of his previous books.

"My understanding is there are a number of problems with the sales potential of this book," he explained.

A year later, Chad decided to start his own publishing company, specializing in LDS literature. Initially Tammy was "not happy" about the idea, but after praying for guidance she agreed to come aboard as accountant and design director. Chad's mother-in-law, Phyllis Douglas, was appointed sales director.

In May 2004, Chad opened the Spring Creek Book Company, operating out of a large warehouse in Provo. He announced ambitious plans to publish up to forty books a year, inviting local LDS authors to submit book proposals.

"The LDS marketplace is growing," Tammy told *The Springville Herald,* "and our goal is to provide quality products for the entire family."

Shirley Bahlmann, who had worked with Chad at Cedar Fort, was one of Spring Creek's first signings. She suggested Chad meet her friend Suzanne Freeman, who had had a recent near-death experience. This led to Chad publishing Freeman's first book, *Led by the Hand of Christ,* followed by several more.

"He was interesting," remembered Freeman. "He was very humble."

After her book was published, Freeman started speaking at various LDS events about her near-death experiences. It would be years before Chad told her about his own, which puzzled her.

"He never mentioned he had a near-death experience," she told the *East Idaho News.* "We had a lot of conversations, and I would think that might come up."

She occasionally visited the Spring Creek warehouse and saw Tammy working away in a back office. She soon realized that Tammy was the driving force of the publishing operation, and that Chad would never have succeeded without her slavish devotion.

"I think she was the heart of the business," said Freeman. "She was just really good at it and very kind and genuine."

Chad would fondly describe Tammy as his soul mate, saying they'd been together in several past lives.

"I was really impressed by that," Freeman said. "I thought, 'Wow, they have a really sweet relationship and that's really tender.'"

In December 2005, the Spring Creek Book Company was named the Outstanding Small Wholesaler of the Year by the LDS Booksellers Association (LDSBA). The award was the result of a ballot of LDS retailers all over the world and a big achievement for the young company that had already published more than fifty books by twenty-six authors, including Chad Daybell.

"We are honored to even be nominated, much less win the award," said Tammy, as she and Chad proudly accepted it at the annual LDSBA convention in Salt Lake City. "This is our first full year in business, and we appreciate the stores taking notice of our efforts to produce quality products."

Over the next three years, Chad and Tammy worked hard establishing the Spring Creek Book Company. They soon moved into bigger premises, and Chad branched out into other areas, such as sports and self-help books.

He published a ghostwritten biography of University of Utah college football star Alex Smith, an autobiography of the 2003 *American Idol* finalist Carmen Rasmusen, and a book about the 2007 Miss Utah, Jill Stevens, who went on to compete in the Miss America Pageant.

In June 2008, Chad's novel *The Celestial City* topped the LDS fiction bestseller charts. It was the second volume in his eventual five-part series, Standing in Holy Places. The first, *The Great Gathering,* had been in the top five since the previous year. He had also enlisted his son Seth to narrate all his audiobooks.

One of the characters in the Standing in Holy Places series was based on Chad's old New Jersey missionary friend Ben Hyde, whom Chad was still in touch with. They occasionally saw each other in church, and Hyde visited Chad and Tammy at their house a few times.

"The [series] was a 'fictionalized' version of the Second Coming of Jesus," said Hyde, "and what it would physically look like in the Utah area where we both lived. He never said, 'Ben, these are visions that I had,' but we both knew that was exactly what he was drawing on for it."

In late 2008, the Spring Creek Book Company abruptly went out of business. Chad Daybell turned over his remaining inventory to an outside distributor, and he and Tammy declared bankruptcy. Their filing revealed that the couple owed more than $200,000 to sixty creditors and that Spring Creek had been far from the success story Chad had presented.

Their bankruptcy filing showed that the Spring Creek Book Company had only generated an annual income of $2,000, and that was decreasing every year. The couple made a joint income of less than $48,000 a year to feed and clothe their five children.

Chad blamed it all on the Great Recession.

"Our sales hit a brick wall," he explained. "It was a nightmare. Tammy and I saw the writing on the wall. We needed to find another way to support our family."

So in January 2009, with his tail between his legs, Chad returned to the cemetery business, finding a job with neighboring Spanish Fork City as their new sexton. To supplement their income Tammy took a part-time job at Art City Elementary School in the computer lab.

After the filing for bankruptcy, Tammy fell into a deep depression and was put on medication. After the Daybells' initial success in the publishing world, they now seemed to be back to square one. And Tammy was starting to get more and more disenchanted with her self-proclaimed visionary husband and their continual financial struggles.

"[Tammy] suffered a mental breakdown," Chad wrote. "It was definitely the most challenging phase of our marriage."

In his autobiography, Chad gamely attempted to transform their growing earthly problems into a wondrous miracle. He wrote of seeing a vision of Tammy in the pre-mortal world, wearing a white dress and addressing a large group of spirits.

"I knew that she was one of Heavenly Father's most valiant children," he wrote. "We had been put through a very tough test, but I assured her we would make it through and be stronger for it."

Chad devoted himself to his sexton job, moonlighting as a writer with his latest series of books, Times of Turmoil. Meanwhile, Tammy spent hours a day on her computer playing *FrontierVille*, a highly addictive game where players' avatars become pioneers of the Old West, using in-game currency to build imaginary towns.

Chad felt threatened by Tammy's new pursuit and tried to get her to quit.

"I went to the temple," he wrote, "and received a strong prompting to tell Tammy she needed to stop playing *FrontierVille* 'cold turkey.'"

When he told Tammy what the spirits had said, she remained unconvinced.

"Tammy knew the game had become an addiction," he explained, "but she didn't fully stop."

Eventually, according to Chad, the angry spirit of Tammy's grandmother came to the rescue, ordering her to stop wasting time on silly computer games. "My descendants are letting Satan lull them to sleep with technology" was her thunderous message, delivered via Chad. "Have Tammy quit her d*** computer game cold turkey!"

In spring 2012, Chad told his author Suzanne Freeman that he was getting out of the book business because the "call out" was coming. In the call out, which is not mainstream Mormon doctrine, the prophets summon the faithful to gather in the (LDS Church–owned) girls' camps, before the end-times.

Chad told her that in July all the righteous would gather for the Second Coming, with large stores of food to survive. Freeman was unconvinced and warned Chad about his increasingly extreme and dangerous beliefs, which he was now incorporating into his books.

"It wasn't good," she explained. "And he kept saying, 'Oh, Suzie, just read them and you'll get it.' But I read some of it and I just couldn't."

In July, when the end-times failed to materialized, Freeman wrote him a letter:

"I do not agree with what you are publishing. I know without a shadow of a doubt what you are preaching will not lead to happiness. It will lead to death and sorrow."

FIFTEEN

A FORK IN THE ROAD

In May 2013, Chad quit his cemetery job in Spanish Fork City to rejoin the Springville City Parks Department as its sexton. He had recently re-launched Spring Creek Books as a part-time venture to publish his latest four-book fictionalized series on the end-times: Days of Turmoil.

After the call out didn't happen, Chad was eager to make a publishing comeback and started looking for new LDS authors to sign up. Each day he would read the Another Voice of Warning (AVOW) website, and in February 2014 something caught his eye in the website's "Dreams and Visions" section.

Arizona mother of three Julie Rowe had had a near-death experience in 2004 and posted an account of it under the avatar Fellow Dreamer. Chad sent her a private message, offering to publish her book. He told her they were fated to meet and that she was the "tall, dark-haired woman" he had seen in visions.

After exchanging several emails and phone calls, Chad signed a contract with Julie to publish her first book, *A Greater Tomorrow: My Journey Beyond the Veil.*

"I gave him the first draft in three weeks," remembered Julie, "and then he edited for a week."

Spring Creek Books published her book on May 14, 2014, and Chad immediately wanted a sequel. He sent her some of his own books to read as inspiration.

"His books were so cheesy," Julie said. "His style of writing really irritated me, and I had a hard time reading them. I mean a lot of people like that, but I didn't."

In mid-July, Julie drove to Provo with her children to meet Chad and Tammy at the Monte L. Bean Museum on the BYU campus.

"He was nice but socially awkward," Julie remembered. "We walked around the museum for an hour or two. He brought the contract for the second book and I signed it that day."

Julie immediately liked Tammy, who kept in the background.

"She's very introverted and also kind of nerdy," Julie said. "I thought she was one of the nicest people I've ever met."

Chad published Julie's second book, *The Time Is Now,* that November. It focused on the latter days and the Second Coming of Jesus Christ. It would far outsell any of Chad's books, and she would write another three books for Spring Creek over the next few years.

Chad's high school friend Scott Mitchell had enjoyed a glorious career with the NFL after graduating from Springville High. He played twelve seasons for leading teams, including the Miami Dolphins, Detroit Lions, and Baltimore Ravens, before he retired.

In 2008, Mitchell returned to Springville to coach his old high school football team and reconnected with Chad. They discussed Spring Creek publishing his autobiography, but nothing came of it at that time.

The six-foot-six-inch quarterback had ballooned to 366 pounds and went on to compete on the 2014 season of NBC's *The Biggest Loser.* He was eventually eliminated on week sixteen after losing more than 120 pounds.

Chad avidly followed Scott's progress on the show and sent him a Facebook message, offering to publish his book on overcoming obesity.

After fielding offers from several other publishers, Mitchell finally signed a contract with Spring Creek Books, and Chad and Tammy got to work.

"He spent about four and a half months in my house writing the book," said Mitchell. "He's the nicest [person] I've ever met in my life. So unassuming."

*   *   *

In August 2014, Chad rented a cabin in Island Park, Idaho, for a family vacation. As he later told it, when they stopped at a gas station on the way there, he suddenly heard his grandfather's ghostly voice ordering him to move to Idaho.

During the vacation he fell in love with the "calm, laid-back" pace of life and decided to move his family there. Back home, he went to the Provo Temple for spiritual guidance, and the spirit told him that he needed to live in Idaho to fulfill his destiny.

In October, Chad resigned as Springville's sexton, and four months later, just a month away from his and Tammy's twenty-fifth anniversary, he received what he would describe as a "fork in the road" vision.

"I saw in the distance a glorious city with a temple on a hill," he wrote. "A voice said, 'Moving to Rexburg will be a tremendous blessing to your children and your grandchildren.'"

Then and there he decided to move the family to Rexburg, Idaho, convinced that it was one of the sacred places where the righteous 144,000 would gather to ride out war, earthquakes, and famine heralding the end-times. But he did not bother to tell Tammy.

A couple of weeks later, during a family dinner, Chad suddenly blurted out that they were soon moving to Idaho. Astonished, Tammy asked what he was talking about, and Chad told her about his visions.

A furious Tammy complained to her sister, Samantha, about Chad's unilateral decision to move three hundred miles north to Rexburg without consulting her first. Tammy, now forty-five, had lived in Springville since she was thirteen, when her family moved there from California.

"She wasn't happy about it," said Samantha. "She prayed about it and tried to decide what it was that she was supposed to do."

Finally, after much prayer, Tammy reluctantly agreed to the move and went online to start looking at real estate listings.

In late March, Chad took the family to Idaho to look at potential homes. He and Tammy had narrowed it down to two possibilities, and they met a realtor to view them. The first disappointed, but the second was a large rambling property with four acres, a large lawn with apple trees, and a pond. They immediately fell in love with the spacious 1,644-square-foot ranch-style home with six bedrooms and one and a half bathrooms in Salem, just four miles away from Rexburg. It was close to the Snake River, the Sand Hills, mountain lakes, and the Teton Mountain Range. The asking price was $181,900, and Chad immediately put in a bid and applied for a mortgage.

On April 23, 2015, Spring Creek Books published Scott Mitchell's autobiography, *Alive Again: The* Biggest Loser *Contestant and Former NFL Quarterback Shares His Intriguing Story.*

Randy Hollis, who had worked with Chad at the *Ogden Standard-Examiner* and was now at the *Deseret News,* interviewed Mitchell and then called his publisher about his publicity plans. It was the first time Hollis and Chad had spoken in almost twenty years.

"Chad seemed like the same quiet, soft-spoken, reserved young man that I'd known years earlier," said Hollis. "He and Scott were going to a couple of local bookstores in Salt Lake City to promote the book and sell it."

In the resulting article, Chad was quoted extensively.

"To me, it's a true hero's journey," said Chad, "where you have a hero who takes a tumble in life and fights his way back to where he wants to be."

Then, in the midst of the publicity tour, Chad suddenly informed Mitchell on the way to a Costco's book signing that he was moving to Idaho. He apologized that he would be unable to help promote Mitchell's book anymore and said that Mitchell was on his own.

"I was furious," said Mitchell. "He goes, 'I just had a vision [and] I've got to move to Idaho.' I was in the middle of promoting this book."

SIXTEEN

REXBURG

On June 8, 2015, Chad and Tammy closed on their new house at 202 N. 1900 E. and moved in. Almost the entire Rexburg population of twenty-eight thousand is Mormon, and the city—whose motto is America's Family Community—is dominated by its historic white tabernacle with a golden figure of the Angel Moroni, holding a horn to his lips to symbolize the Second Coming.

Chad began working on a new novel at the BYU-Idaho campus library in Rexburg. Tammy was hired as an assistant librarian at Madison Middle School, and daughter Emma enrolled in BYU-Idaho.

"Rexburg has always been a strong faith-built community," said the Daybells' new neighbor Matt Price. "The Church of Jesus Christ of Latter-day Saints is very large in this area."

The Daybells were readily accepted by the Rexburg community, and Chad took a sales executive job with the Falls Printing Company, which would now be printing Spring Creek books.

Already an established author, Chad now began promoting himself in Idaho. He started giving talks about his books and his increasingly extreme views of the end-times, now way outside traditional Mormon doctrine. He held book signings and targeted like-minded people who shared his views that the Second Coming was imminent and they needed to prepare.

Cult expert Rick Ross said that Chad had broken away from the mainstream LDS religion and was deliberately targeting Church members to join what would soon become a cult.

"He goes after people that are LDS," said Ross, "and he tries to entice them, recruit them and sell them his books."

Soon after moving to Idaho, Chad participated in a large conference about near-death and other psychic-healing experiences with his best-selling author Julie Rowe, now very much in demand on the Mormon speaking circuit.

Rexburg resident Eric Smith attended the event with his wife, as they were interested in near-death experiences.

"That was when I first got word of Chad," said Smith. "Julie was the primary speaker, and she gave Chad ten minutes to tell his story and introduced him to an audience of about two thousand people."

The doughy-looking evangelist for the end-times soon won over his audience with his self-deprecating delivery about preparing for the Second Coming. What he lacked in charisma he made up for with a "goofy" charm and a wide grin.

"I found his personality to be genuine," said Smith. "He was kind of nerdy but humble and warm. Right away I liked him."

Over the next few months, Chad Daybell developed a staunch following in the Rexburg area, including many prominent local citizens. He would talk about multiple probations and the idea of reincarnation, which was outlawed by the Mormon Church. His followers were mesmerized as he spoke about his thirty-one previous lives on different planets.

"He really had a big fan base," said his former author Suzanne Freeman. "People really followed him and were interested in hearing what he had to say."

Chad Daybell found himself at the right place at the right time. The intriguing subject of the end-times and the Second Coming was fast gaining traction among a section of the LDS Church, although it was officially frowned upon.

His books filled a void in the Church's literary market, and he began to develop his public speaking skills to sell more books and spread his message as far as possible.

On May 22, 2017, the Spring Creek Book Company published Chad Daybell's autobiography, *Living on the Edge of Heaven*. It was dedicated to his devoted wife of twenty-seven years: "To Tammy, my one and only. She doesn't like the limelight but deserves all the credit."

His thin 188-page autobiography was reprinted almost verbatim from his website blog, written over a five-week period on his arrival in Rexburg in 2015.

Chad eagerly promoted it with book signings and small gatherings in people's houses, assiduously building his following in southern Idaho. Eric Smith saw firsthand just how effective the self-effacing author could be at small, intimate events, especially with his growing number of female fans.

"Chad had this charismatic, convincing ability in speaking with people," explained Smith, "and could get followers and glean support."

He also noticed how Chad would target attractive women and then hypnotize them with his doomsday message of survival.

"I've seen him use those skills," said Smith. "There [was] always a little group of women, and he would be drawn to them. They would get that kind of googly-eyed look as they asked him questions, and he would answer in a very personal way."

During their friendship, Smith realized that Chad was far more comfortable with women than men, whom he seemed uneasy with. Smith was an exception.

"He would just talk about the ideas in his books," said Smith, "and what he saw in visions. They were enjoyable to listen to and I felt they were genuine."

Chad was invited to a private home in Rexburg by a group of women who were interested in the controversial subject of polygamy.

"He was kind of clinging around them," recalled Smith. "He liked them. I kind of sensed in some of those conversations they were discussing some yucky stuff. Chad had conversations about those . . . really fringe things that are pretty inappropriate and divisive for families."

Chad happily bathed in all this female attention while Tammy stayed home. Although they were just scraping by on Chad's sales job and Tammy's meager pay as a librarian, he was quite happy to eke out a career selling his doomsday visions to the impressionable.

"I think that business fed his ego," said cult expert Rick Ross, "and made him feel important and powerful. Having adoring fans was something very appealing to him."

In summer 2017, a new company called Preparing a People (PaP) was formed to organize conferences and podcasts focused on surviving the end-times. It grew out of a Springville-based marketing company called Color My Media, which offered an array of marketing services, including Web design and videography.

The entrepreneurial owners, Michael and Nancy James, had known Chad Daybell back in Springville and moved their operations to Rexburg, Idaho, soon after he arrived.

"Chad's one of my favorite people," explained Michael James.

On July 15, 2017, Preparing a People held its first conference at the Rexburg Tabernacle, with Chad Daybell as a key speaker. The venue held eighteen hundred people and was fully catered by BYU-Idaho. Tickets to the all-day event were $50.

Two days before the conference, Michael and Nancy James released their debut PaP podcast, entitled "Rexburg, Idaho: The Promised Land?" It would be the first of fifty-three podcasts released over the next eighteen months, with Chad cohosting many of them. He would enthusiastically discuss subjects as diverse as microchip implants and how he had once heard Van Halen music on the other side of the veil, as well as eagerly promote his autobiography.

The conference with Chad and six other speakers, including Julie Rowe, was a great success. A second in Orem, Utah, was immediately announced, entitled "Come unto Me, and I Will Heal You."

On Saturday, September 9, Chad took the stage to riotous applause at Utah Valley University in Orem. Sporting a crew cut, overweight, and wearing a loose-fitting white shirt and red tie, he radiated confidence as he told his enraptured audience about his two near-death experiences, which had transformed his life and given him visionary powers, before turning to his pet subject of the end-times.

"I've been waiting for twenty years for something to happen," he announced. "I write all these novels and people are like, 'When's it going to start?'"

Chad pressed a button on his laptop and his PowerPoint presentation began. A photograph of Kim Jong Un surrounded by nuclear warheads appeared on the screen behind him.

"North Korea"—Chad gesticulated with his hands—"they're going a little nuts right now. Kim Jong Un seems intent on causing havoc in the world. No question about it with him. Even as we speak Hurricane Irma is on its way to Florida. The earthquake in Mexico. The fires in California and Montana. It just feels like [end-]times are starting to begin."

Then a photo of a frenzied-looking Woody Harrelson as fringe science conspiracy theorist Charlie Frost, in the 2009 movie *2012* came on-screen. The science fiction epic was about a global cataclysm that brings about the end of the world.

"Here's one of my favorite characters, because this is how people think . . . I've acted in the last five years. But *he* was right," declared Chad, as he pumped his fist at the audience.

Chad said his real message was how to prepare to survive all the oncoming trials and tribulations with a smile on our faces. The audience was here, he said, because the spirit had guided them in the role each was destined to play. It might start with baby steps, but, he promised them, they would get there in the end.

"And so old Bill Murray," Chad said, chuckling, as a poster of the iconic star pointing a finger directly at the audience appeared, "just think of him in the movie *Baby Steps* [which was actually *What About Bob?*], as he took it a step at a time. And that's how a lot of us have to do it. You just start small and the Lord will guide you."

Mother of three Angela Stone moved to Rexburg with her husband in July 2015, finding a job with a local accountancy firm. She worked out of her boss's house, and he slowly opened up about his spiritual gifts. He told her he had erected a spiritual shield of protection around his house, to protect his office computers from malfunctioning. He also helped people cast out their bad spirits to cure alcohol, drug, and pornography addictions.

One day he announced that Chad Daybell and Julie Rowe were speaking at a conference in Rexburg, offering to get Angela tickets. She willingly accepted.

"He was so excited," she remembered. "He had read all of her books [and] Chad Daybell was the publisher."

When Angela first heard Chad speak at the July 2017 conference, she sat in awe as he recounted his visions of the end-times and how the faithful would survive.

"It was like [Rexburg] was going to be a city of light and a city of refuge," she said. "A place for the saints and the faithful to gather and be protected from the calamities that come as things fall apart."

A couple of days later, Chad turned up at her boss's house, and Angela met him for the first time.

"He was idolized," she said. "He was just this remarkably well-spoken, kind man who was . . . helping bring people together to prepare for the return of Christ."

Chad often came by to see her boss, and Angela got to know Chad and meet some of his followers. The end-times always dominated the conversation, and Angela learned about multiple probations, and what it meant to be a translated being—an immortal—as Chad claimed to be.

"[It's] essentially an eternal being," explained Angela, "who can pass through portals and travel through the world in a different way, teleporting."

Angela and her husband became deeply involved in Chad's cult, spending around $20,000 to prepare for doomsday. They bought two large canvas tents, sleeping bags designed to withstand below-freezing temperatures, a stove, and a year's supply of gluten-free food with enough charcoal to cook it.

"We believed there would be a time when we would be called out," she explained. "These items would be needed."

SEVENTEEN

THE OWL NECKLACE

Soon after the first Preparing a People conference, Julie Rowe visited Chad and Tammy at their house in Salem before they all dined at Dairy Queen. Tammy took Julie around the house and the large garden outside, where Tammy kept her ducks and chickens. She proudly showed off their pet cemetery, which Chad had recently constructed using his expertise as a gravedigger.

During dinner, Julie sensed that Chad and Tammy seemed uneasy with each other and were having difficulties in their marriage. She later asked him about it. Chad sadly explained that Tammy had stopped taking her prescribed antidepressants, and they were no longer intimate.

Chad also confided that he was having an "emotional affair" with an Arizona woman named Natalie, a fan of his books whom he had met online. During a series of intense phone conversations, Chad had informed Natalie that they had been married to each other in a previous life. Rowe warned Chad that he was being unfaithful to Tammy.

"They had never met in person, but I disagreed with it," said Rowe, "because she was married and he was married. Then he got angry with me."

Soon afterward, Chad told Julie about a vision that he'd had of Tammy dying in a car accident. He saw her driving their black pickup truck in a heavy snowstorm and skidding on ice into a telephone pole. It was the first of three visions of Tammy dying that he would tell Rowe about.

"He said that the Lord had told him that Tammy was going to pass away," said Rowe. "And he was actually quite emotional about it."

* * *

Around that time, Chad Daybell found an old tarnished gold owl necklace on a pew in the tabernacle. He believed it was a gift from God. Since the age of ten, after writing "The Murder of Dr. Jay and His Assistant," with its unsettling owl cover, Chad had been obsessed with the birds of prey, which he considered to have special powers.

He now began using the owl necklace to determine whether people were light or dark spirits. He would also ask it questions to see who various celebrities such as Donald Trump or the Beatles had been in their previous lives.

Initially it was a kind of spiritual parlor game to entertain friends.

"He'd hold it up and let it swing," said Eric Smith, who often witnessed Chad working his magic. "If it swung right to left, it would [mean] yes. If it was a circle, it was a no. It was interesting and fascinating and I was touched by it."

Chad would bring out the necklace during his small gatherings with followers to ingratiate himself with them. But first, according to Smith, he would go online and research certain historical figures to pair them with during his readings.

A particular favorite were the *Mayflower* Pilgrims. He would first look up their names and backgrounds before using his necklace to mesmerize people, like a cheap conjuring trick.

"Chad would personally . . . learn about people's pasts," said Smith, "set up an appointment, and go and visit them in their home and unfold their history to them. Maybe give them a little bit of insight about their future. And in this process he developed quite a following."

He also began making detailed lists of which celebrities were light or dark, finding Oprah Winfrey had the darkest spirit of all.

"I saw a lot of those lists," said Julie Rowe. "I would tell him, 'You're not getting true answers and this isn't coming from God. You shouldn't use that stupid owl necklace.' And the more I did that, the more he distanced himself from me."

In the fall of 2017, Chad met Melanie Gibb at a preparedness camp in Ogden, Utah, where he was one of the speakers. Families came to learn survival skills for the end-times, such as how to cook without an oven and filter pure water. In seminars, people also discussed their spiritual experiences and visions.

Chad found a rapport with the attractive blonde, as they shared similar views of the end-times and the Second Coming. Melanie invited Chad to speak in Mesa, Arizona, where she lived, and they agreed to stay in touch.

A few months later, Chad introduced Melanie to the Preparing a People team, who appointed her as their new Arizona representative. She made her official PaP podcast debut on February 11, 2018, on an episode entitled "Backyard Reflections of Lil' Miss Sunshine: Melanie Gibb."

"We are excited to present to you our New Arizona Branch Representative, Melanie Gibb," PaP proudly announced. "She has been such a force for good as a hub friend to everyone who knows her."

In June 2018, Melanie helped organize PaP's first conference in Arizona, arranging a venue in Mesa and handling logistics. She enlisted her friend and local LDS author Jason Mow to speak alongside Chad Daybell. Mow, a former Phoenix narcotics detective and army paratrooper, would become a PaP rising star, speaking at many future conferences alongside Melanie.

Chad, recently fired from his sales job at the Falls Printing Company because of his increasingly radical ideology, flew into Phoenix for the July 18 event, and Melanie picked him up from his hotel.

"We had an enjoyable early dinner together," he remembered, "where she told me more about the amazing journey she has been on throughout her life."

Chad then brought out his owl necklace and asked it various things about Melanie.

"He created a portal and would ask questions," she explained. "[It] was a gold-colored, pointy pendulum with a string attached."

After the Mesa event, Chad invited Melanie to write a book about her spiritual experiences, with the title *Feel the Fire*.

Five weeks later, they were reunited at the next Preparing a People conference in St. George, Utah, where she brought along her new friend, Lori Vallow.

PART THREE

GASOLINE AND FIRE

EIGHTEEN

"IF CHAD IS SATAN, HE SURE IS A GOOD ONE"

Lori Vallow and Melanie Gibb drove 415 miles north to St. George, Utah, for the Preparing a People conference, entitled "Bringing to Life Hidden Things Through Personal Revelation." The two-day event was held over the last weekend of October 2018, at St. George Academy high school. It featured "fifteen amazing speakers," including NDE and end-times author and publisher Chad Daybell, who had conveniently left his wife, Tammy, and five children back in Rexburg.

After Chad delivered a fiery Friday-night speech from the stage, he retired to a side table to meet his fans and sign books. Lori immediately approached and said she had read all his books. Chad looked up at the beautiful blond apparition standing before him and was instantly smitten.

Then, as Melanie watched, they began exchanging spiritual experiences, beliefs, and visions, blissfully staring into each other's eyes. It was as if a lightning bolt hit both of them. They would never again be the same.

Chad immediately told Lori that his spiritual gifts had revealed that she was a translated being, and they had been married seven times before in previous lives, while she hung on his every word. He told her she was one of the chosen ones and together they would change the world.

"She talked to him a lot about his books," Gibb later told the *East Idaho News.* "She asked a lot of questions and she was very interested in what he thought, and he was interested in what she knew. And they started developing that connection right there."

For the rest of the conference Lori and Chad were inseparable, as he revealed to her the secret spiritual powers she possessed that he alone could unleash. With his marriage to Tammy fading, the stunningly beautiful blonde was his dream come true; the kind of woman who had once been unattainable now idealized him as his biggest fan. He immediately saw the possibilities of a glamorous new life without Tammy holding him back.

As for Lori, her whole life suddenly came into focus. Her messy history of failed marriages, bitter custody battles, and verbal abuse all evaporated into thin air. She felt an otherworldly connection with this soft-spoken, attentive man, whom she had admired for so long. She finally felt validated, as Chad softly assured her that God had brought them together again, entrusting them with a sacred mission they alone could accomplish.

Lori asked Chad to gauge who in her life were light or dark spirits. She told him all about her previous husbands, her children, and other extended-family members, as he took careful notes.

At the end of the conference Chad and Lori exchanged phone numbers, agreeing to meet up again in a couple of weeks when he was due to speak in Mesa, Arizona.

On the long drive back to Phoenix, Lori couldn't stop talking about Chad, although she knew he was married with five children. She told Melanie how attracted she was to him on a spiritual level and was particularly "intrigued" by their having been married so many times before on this and other planets.

Back in Rexburg, Chad Daybell immediately began work on a detailed light and dark spirit analysis of Lori's entire family, including ex-husbands and dead relatives, using his owl necklace. He judged sixteen-year-old Tylee a dark spirit and J.J. a light one.

Chad also helpfully provided a rubric for Lori to interpret his readings. This practice did not remotely have anything to do with LDS Church doctrine and would be considered utter heresy.

Family History Information

Barry Cox—3L (1500s France)

Janice Cox—3L (1600s England)

Stacey—Was 3L on earth, has graduated to 4.1L

Alex Cox—2L

Adam Cox—3L

Laura—Was 3L on earth, has graduated to 4.1L

Lori—4.3L

Summer Cox Shiflet—3L Husband is 2L, but borderline 2D

First husband—2L

Second husband: William Lagioia—2D

Son: Colby Ryan—3L Kelsee Ryan—3D

Third husband: Joseph Ryan—4.3D Is now sealed away

Daughter: Tylee Ryan—4.1D

Fourth husband: Charles Vallow—3L (1700s London)

First wife: 2D

Cole Vallow—3D

Zach Vallow—3L

Joshua Vallow—4.2L

Niece Melani Boudreaux—3L

Husband: Brandon—3D

4 kids—Both boys are 3L, Older girl—3L, Younger girl—4.1L

On October 30—just four days after they first met—Chad emailed his findings to Lori's email address: lori4style@hotmail.com.

Over the next two weeks, Lori and Chad were in constant touch, emailing and talking on their new burner cell phones, which they had bought for secrecy. Lori also began shooting sexy videos of her nightly dancing sessions and sending them to Chad.

They both counted the days until they would see each other again.

* * *

Cult expert Rick Ross has studied Chad Daybell's light/dark spirit document and believes he used it to brainwash Lori. Ross labeled it a classic example of "thought reform," which many cult leaders, including Adolf Hitler, have been using on their followers for centuries.

By the time Chad met the beautiful, adoring woman of his dreams, he had tired of Tammy. After almost thirty years of marriage she no longer wanted him physically and was pressuring him to get a real job. Now he saw a way out of his stagnant life—but first he had to get rid of Charles Vallow, Tylee, J.J., and Tammy, who would all be obstacles to his blissful future with Lori.

"Chad Daybell was relegating people to a category of subhuman," said Ross. "So that if someone came to him and said, 'I'm going to kill them [because] they're zombies and possessed by dark spirits,' Lori would say, 'That is the only way that they can be free.'"

On Thursday, November 15 an excited Chad Daybell drove more than nine hundred miles to Mesa, Arizona, for the next PaP conference. He arrived a day early to see Lori, who had invited him to stay at her house in Chandler. Charles and the children would conveniently be out of town.

That night Lori hosted a small group of women, including Melanie Gibb and Lisa Clarke (not her real name), an old friend from Utah who had once organized Chad's Utah book-signing events.

When Lisa came into the kitchen, she found Lori and Chad discussing sleeping arrangements. Chad seemed nervous, making a point of telling Lisa that he would be sleeping in J.J.'s room. She later realized that Lori and Chad planned to be intimate that night, but didn't want anybody else to know.

"And I thought, 'Well, so what?'" Lisa later told *Inside Edition*. "But now I see why he was concerned. If you look back, you go, 'Oh, that's why. Because they were having an affair.'"

On Friday, Chad was the key speaker on the first night of the two-day PaP conference. Afterward, Chad, Melanie Gibb, and about thirty other out-of-towners went to Lori's house. They split into small groups, with Melanie finding herself in the same one as Chad and Lori.

"[Chad] was telling us some of the deeper mysteries of God that we weren't familiar with," Melanie recalled. "He seemed to know things that most people had never heard of before . . . and he was convinced that [Lori] was a very powerful woman."

Chad then brought out his owl necklace, telling the small crowd around him which Old Testament prophets or other biblical characters they had been in past lives. Chad claimed he'd had thirty-one previous lives, where he'd been, among others, Martin Luther and Methuselah. Lori had had twenty-one lives and had been married to the prophet Moroni. Chad told Melanie that all three of them had known one another in several past lives.

That evening, Lori's teenage nephew Zac Cox, who was living at the house, came back to find around thirty cars parked in the driveway and down the street. The front door was open and he heard loud voices coming from the living room. He walked in to find it full of strangers.

"Everybody in that room all turned around and stared at me," Zac remembered. "They stopped talking and my heart dropped. It was the scariest thing . . . and I felt like it was a horror movie."

On Saturday morning, Lori took Chad out to a nearby park, where they went for a long walk together holding hands. Chad told her more about their past lives together, as well as the secret meanings of his books. She luxuriated in his lavish praise and compliments.

Then he informed her that the two of them had been chosen by God to lead a select group of 144,000 souls who would usher in the end-times and the Second Coming of Jesus Christ.

To Lori it was as if one of Chad's end-times novels had magically come to life, and she was the heroine who would help him fulfill this divine calling. She had long thought that she was one of the 144,000, but now, according to Chad, they would lead them all as king and queen.

After that weekend, Lori's whole attitude toward Charles Vallow abruptly changed. She became cold and critical of everything he did. He had no idea what was going on.

"She seemed to be upset a lot," said Melanie Gibb, now a frequent visitor to their house. "He was frustrated."

Charles called his sister Kay in Louisiana to complain that Lori had changed, but he didn't know why. He said she was no longer the same person that he had married and he hardly recognized her.

"Charles started confiding to me that they were having problems [and] she's just not acting right," said Kay. "But my brother was in love with her and she could do no wrong."

Suspicious, Charles checked Lori's computer and discovered she was emailing videos of herself dancing to a man named Chad. Charles called his sister for advice.

"I said, 'Charles, if she hasn't had an affair, she is about to. She is with this man and that's what all this is about.'"

Lori breathlessly confided to Melanie that Chad had constructed a spiritual portal in her closet so he could come and visit her. They could now commune ethereally whenever they wanted and begin fulfilling their mission.

"He created this portal for her," said Melanie. "It's not like he could come through it physically, but it was a way for them to interact spiritually."

Lori informed Melanie that a vital part of their mission was to rid the world of evil spirits, or "zombies," as Chad now referred to them. First, they would say a special prayer for a particular state and then check in the portal to see how many zombies had died.

"And the number would come up," explained Melanie. "Ten thousand died [in Texas] or whatever."

Although Melanie thought it all "pretty extreme," she kept an open mind to all these new spiritual revelations she was learning from Chad via Lori. Her spiritual sister appeared to believe everything he said, but Melanie sensed a slight doubt.

"Two or three times she said to me," remembered Melanie, "'If Chad is Satan, he sure is a good one.'"

On November 26, Lori Vallow made her podcast debut in a new series entitled "Time to Warrior Up." The PaP website announced the first episode, "Find Your Closet," which would star "our warrior trio, Melanie, Lori and Jason."

At the beginning of the podcast, former Phoenix narcotics detective turned author Jason Mow officially introduced Melanie and Lori as the "gatherers."

"Lori is so cool," he began. "Lori and I met in a very, very unique situation."

Then Lori, describing herself as a spiritual "cheerleader," explained how she had been sent to the temple on a certain day to receive a message from someone she didn't know. In walked Jason Mow.

"I instantly knew you were one of us," said Mow. "You're a gatherer. You get it. You understand that there's something bigger going on here than just church on Sunday."

Mow said he had then put Lori in touch with Melanie, and that's how they first met.

Lori declared that she loved both of them and was so grateful to them for helping her develop spiritually.

"I feel like I work for the Lord," she explained. "I have turned my life to him from circumstances that have happened to me."

Later in the one-hour podcast, Lori touched upon her sacred new mission with Chad to begin gathering the 144,000 souls for the end-times.

"We're gathering as saints," she announced, "preparing for the Second Coming of Christ. We're mothers with lots of children. We're sisters. We're aunts. We're daughters. We're friends, so it applies to everybody."

At the end of the podcast Lori told listeners that she loved a challenge and had a special message for all the young people out there:

"You're dying for direction. Our society does not instill that. And I just say this is the time to warrior up. Here we are. We're getting started."

Lori started sending emergency thirty-day supplies of food to various family members, to tide them through the end-times. Her older brother Adam and his wife, Nicole, received several large food packages, which they did not want.

"We all started receiving buckets of food," said Nicole, "in preparation for the end of the world. And I'm thinking, 'If it's the end of the world, I don't want to live. I want to go with everybody else, so stop sending me food.'"

Lori had become so "madly infatuated" with Chad Daybell that Melanie suggested the two should divorce their respective spouses so they could be together. Lori said that was forbidden.

"They felt it was okay to have this infatuated love," explained Gibb, "because Jesus knew it was their mission to be the head of the 144,000."

But Lori did confide that she and Chad had secretly snuck into the temple and sealed themselves together for eternity, which was absolutely blasphemous in the Mormon Church.

But in the real world Lori was still married to Charles Vallow and Chad to Tammy. When Melanie brought up that dilemma, Lori had an answer ready.

"She said that it was okay," remembered Melanie, "because they had been married so many times before that their spouses would understand someday."

In mid-December, Julie Rowe met Chad for a business breakfast in Idaho Falls to discuss her book rights. During the meal she warned Chad about Lori Vallow, whom she had heard that Chad was growing close to.

"Lori was like a groupie," said Rowe. "She really looked up to him. I think Lori was falling in love with Chad from a distance."

When Chad said that he and Lori had been married before in previous lives, Julie reminded him that he had said the same thing to her.

After breakfast, they went to a private energy-healing session at a house in Rexburg. She would later accuse Chad of sexually assaulting her that day.

"He came on to me," said Julie. "I had no idea what he was going to do [and] I felt very betrayed. It was very unprofessional."

After the assault Chad burst into tears, questioning why he had done it. She later told Eric Smith and a member of her security team what had happened, and they both back up her account.

"She was not specific with me, but she made it clear that he made an advance on her and she was pretty upset," said Smith.

That was the last time Julie Rowe ever saw Chad, although he would later apologize for his behavior in several emotional texts.

NINETEEN

NICK SCHNEIDER

All through the holidays, Chad and Lori spoke daily on their disposable pay-as-you-go phones, exchanging texts, photos, and videos. Chad had begun poisoning Lori's mind against Charles Vallow, whom Chad viewed as his biggest obstacle. She told close friends that Charles was "blocking" her spiritual gifts.

Lori had a revelation that Charles would die before the end of the year in a car accident, traveling from Arizona to Texas. When it didn't happen, Lori was crestfallen and asked Chad why. He explained that it was because of "people's choices."

"She was greatly disappointed when he didn't [die]," said Melanie, whom Lori had confided in about her vision.

On January 1, 2019, Charles and Lori moved into a new rental house at 2267 E. Tomahawk Drive in Gilbert. Days later, Chad called to inform Lori that Charles Vallow's body had been taken over by an unclean spirit named Nick Schneider. An old acquaintance of Charles's, Schneider had recently died and been "roaming around" in limbo as a demon and had now managed to take over Charles's body.

"Charles is no longer Charles," Chad told Lori. "He's Nick Schneider."

Melanie Gibb was over at Lori's house when she got the news.

"Lori seemed a little overwhelmed by this idea, but wanted to believe Chad," Melanie remembered. "She was trying to absorb it. It was new for her."

*   *   *

In mid-January 2019, Chad Daybell came to Arizona to be the special guest on a two-part episode of Lori and Melanie Gibbs's new podcast, "Time to Warrior Up."

"Our Arizona Team invited Chad to the Mesa area," read an online PaP advance blurb, "to speak and do this podcast about his life, having died twice when he was younger. Melanie and Lori dig deeper into many of Chad's understandings of what is coming to America and the World, based upon his spiritual gifts, visions, dreams and understandings."

Chad was now regularly instructing Lori in his beliefs. She would pass them on to Melanie, saying, "I have been told." He claimed to be receiving divine revelations from the "Book of Life," which only he could receive.

"He said the veil [between heaven and earth] was open all the time," said Melanie, "and he had a way of seeing things that Lori could not. . . . She would tell me, 'He's so much better at getting revelation than me. I used to get [them], but I rely upon him a lot more now.'"

On his return to Rexburg, Chad emailed Lori a list of the seven missions that they had to accomplish together to prepare for the end-times:

> *Translating ancient records*
> *Write a book together*
> *Identify locations in northeast Arizona for "white camps"* (where survivors of the end-times would live in tents)
> *Establish the presidency of the Church of Firstborn*
> *Organize food distribution as the tribulations start*
> *Ordain individuals to translation as the camps begin*
> *Provide supplies to righteous members of families*

Chad also introduced the word *zombie* into Lori's vocabulary, meaning an unfortunate person whose spirit has left the person's body to be replaced by a dark spirit. They both told Melanie that they were on a sacred mission to rid the world of zombies before the tribulations came.

Initially, Chad and Lori would say special prayers to exorcise dark spirits from human bodies that were possessed, but that would soon change.

On January 22, 2019, Chad sent Lori an email with the subject "Demon with a name, Nick Schneider." It also included a breakdown of some of Lori's, J.J.'s, and Melanie's past lives that Chad's owl bracelet had revealed.

He categorized Lori as a light 4.3 spirit, the highest possible under his own perfect rating. He found that she was descended from Methuselah's daughter Lania and married to the Prophet Moroni and Robert Smith, Jr., as well as to Chad, in her many previous lives.

J.J. was a 4.2 light spirit who in 400 BC had been a member of the Lost Tribe of Manasseh. In a previous incarnation J.J. had been the eighteenth-century theologian Jonathan Elliot Edwards, famous for defending orthodox evangelical doctrine and a linguistics pioneer.

Chad also analyzed Melanie Gibb, whom he made a 4.2 light, divining that in her many previous lives she had been Mormon founder Joseph Smith's granddaughter Phoebe Smith and Alabama prison reformer and educator Julia S. Tutwiler.

Although Tylee wasn't specifically mentioned, Chad told Lori that her daughter was a dark spirit, as she was Joe Ryan's daughter.

After receiving this email, Lori appears to have stopped filling J.J.'s prescription for risperidone, a strong antipsychotic medication he took for his autism. And for the next eight months, J.J.'s condition worsened.

Lori was now actively recruiting family and close friends into her and Chad's growing cult. It was already understood that Melanie Gibb was part of the 144,000, but Lori now enlisted her brother Alex and niece Melani, now married to Brandon Boudreaux and mother to four young children. The several other members of their inner circle included an older woman named Zulema Pastenes, a self-described Emotional Code practitioner. Zulema believed that she had been told by God to protect Lori against Charles, whom she called Hiplos. She informed Lori that she had had a vision that she could create storms and fire and now had the "eye of the Lord."

They were all honored to have been chosen as part of this sacred mission, believing they had known each other in past lives.

"I met Alex for the first time at Lori's house," said Gibb. "He often came over to visit [and] Melani, too. We'd just talk about all kinds of . . . spiritual stuff."

Alex had read every single one of Chad's books and was a firm believer in his teachings.

"Al actually gave me one of [Chad's] books one time," said his nephew Zac Cox, "and he said, 'If you read this, I'll give you one hundred dollars.' He really believed it was a true story."

The teenager, who was living at the Vallow house to look after J.J., had always been wary of Alex and saw how easily Lori converted him into believing her increasingly radical ideology. As a long-distance truck driver, Alex spent many hours on the road listening to Preparing a People podcast hosts expound on their radical beliefs.

"The thing about Alex," said Zac, "is mentally he was always off. He was a weird guy and definitely easy to manipulate, and Lori was very manipulative."

Lori also tried to recruit Zac's father, Adam, but he had no interest. She told Adam that she was becoming "an immortal being" and no longer needed to eat or go to the bathroom, that even if she was shot, the bullet would just pass through her body without harming her.

Zac said Lori's increasingly strange behavior started freaking him out: "We could be in the kitchen, and she would mention seeing spirits walking around the house. She told me one time she had an encounter with the devil, and they screamed at each other."

TWENTY

"I LOVE HER TO DEATH"

On Tuesday, January 29, 2019, a month away from their thirteenth anniversary, Lori coolly executed a plan to rid herself of Charles Vallow. It had Chad Daybell's fingerprints all over it, prosecutors would later allege.

Lori's sixty-two-year-old husband left home at 5:00 A.M. for an overnight business trip, catching an early-morning flight to Houston. As soon as he left, Lori transferred $35,000 from his business account into a new one she'd recently set up in her name. Only $7 remained in his business account, so he wouldn't be able to make his upcoming payroll for his finance business.

As soon as Charles landed in Houston, Lori called to tell him what she had done. But he was far more stunned when she coldly informed him that she was now a god, busy gathering the 144,000 for the Second Coming of Jesus Christ, which would happen in July 2020. She warned that if he dared to interfere with her mission, she would murder him. Then she hung up.

Charles could not believe what he was hearing and immediately called her back. When Lori finally answered, she referred to him as Nick Schneider, saying she knew he had taken over her husband's body. Puzzled, Vallow asked who Nick Schneider was, and Lori replied that he was the evil spirit who had killed the real Charles and now inhabited his body.

"You're not Charles," she told him. "You're Nick Schneider. I don't know who you are or what you did with Charles, but I can murder you now with my powers."

* * *

Lori stopped taking Charles's increasingly frantic calls and summoned Melanie Gibb over to help her. They first went to Phoenix Sky Harbor Airport and used a spare key to drive Charles's Ford truck from the long-term parking lot to another friend's house. Lori then canceled Charles's plane ticket home the next day and had a locksmith come over and change all the locks.

She ordered Zac to pack up his things and go stay with his grandparents Janis and Barry. Tylee was told to go and collect J.J. from school and take him to a movie for the rest of the afternoon.

Then Lori and Melanie packed up all Charles's clothes and belongings in boxes and removed all his computers and business files from his office. They hid everything behind the massive amounts of food stored in a closet, thinking he would never find it there.

Lori then checked into a Hyatt hotel with Tylee, J.J., and his service dog, Bailey.

On Wednesday morning Charles desperately called his friend and ward bishop, Gabe Bonilla, saying Lori had lost her mind and had threatened to kill him. Charles put his friend on hold and called Lori, so Bonilla could listen in on a conference call.

"I thought it was a recording at first," said Bonilla, "and then it dawned on me after a minute or so that this wasn't."

During the brief call, Lori threatened to "destroy" Charles and told him not to bother coming home, as all his stuff was gone. When he asked about J.J., Lori said Charles could have him as she didn't want him anymore.

"That actually concerned me," said Bonilla. "[It] was a bit strange for a mom to say. She seemed coherent but her statements were strangely irrational."

When Charles arrived at the Houston airport that afternoon, he found his return ticket had been canceled. He scraped together $600 for a standby, though Lori had cleaned out his business bank account.

While waiting for his flight home, he called the Gilbert Police for help. They sent him the necessary paperwork to file an emergency mental health petition for his wife to undergo a mandatory psychiatric evaluation at Community Bridges Inc. (CBI) health care.

* * *

After the two-and-a-half-hour flight back to Phoenix, Charles went to the long-term parking lot to find his Ford truck missing. He frantically called Lori's cell phone, but she didn't pick up.

Instead, he took a taxi to the Community Bridges in Mesa, where he filed the emergency health petition for a voluntary seventy-two-hour hold and evaluation. A pickup order for Lori Vallow was then sent to the Gilbert Police.

Minister Bonilla met Charles in Mesa and drove him back to his house on Tomahawk Drive. On their way there, Lori called to say she and the children had checked into a hotel for the night. She said that she would drop J.J. off at school in the morning and that Charles was welcome to collect him in the afternoon.

Before hanging up, Lori declared that she wanted nothing further to do with Charles or the kids, as she had "a more important mission to carry out."

When Charles Vallow arrived home, he discovered that Lori had changed the locks and he couldn't get in. So he called Gilbert Police to carry out a welfare check for Tylee and J.J., as he feared for their safety.

Just before midnight, Officer Chris Dorenbush arrived at the Tomahawk Drive house to find an exasperated Charles waiting outside.

"So what's going on tonight?" asked the officer.

Charles approached wearing a gray T-shirt and a red baseball cap, while Bonilla waited in his car. "I can't get in touch with my kids," Charles replied.

"How old are your kids?" asked Dorenbush.

"Six and a half and sixteen."

"How long have you been trying?"

"Two days," Charles answered emotionally. "But she's lost her mind. I don't know how to say it. . . . We're LDS. She thinks she's a resurrected being and a god and a member of the 144,000. She thinks Jesus is coming next year."

Charles explained how Lori had taken all the money out of his business bank account, canceled his flight home, and stolen his truck.

"Okay, so what makes her a danger to herself or others?" asked Officer Dorenbush.

"She threatened to murder me, kill me. . . ."

"She threatened to murder you?" asked Dorenbush, aghast.

"Yes. She said, 'I will have you destroyed.'"

When Officer Dorenbush pointed out that wasn't a direct threat to kill him, Vallow replied that Lori had told him that he wasn't Charles and she could murder him with her powers.

"She's not here," he told the officer, wiping his brow. "She's lost her reality."

"Is this just recent?"

"It's been going on for about four or five years. It's gotten really, really bad lately. She goes to temple every day and speaks with Moroni and Jesus Christ, and they tell her what to do."

Charles said he was most concerned about his son J.J., who suffered from autism and needed his medication.

"So how does she pose a threat to your children?" asked Officer Dorenbush.

"I don't know what she's going to do with them. I don't know if she's going to flee with them [or] she's going to hurt them. I just want to see if my boy's okay."

Dorenbush asked if Lori was on any medications or seeing a doctor.

"She won't go to the doctor," replied Vallow, "because she's a translated being and they would find out. She cannot be killed. She cannot die. I love her to death. This is killing me, Officer. Our thirteenth anniversary's next week. We had a great marriage. All of a sudden last month it just blew up. She just lost connection."

Charles noted that although Lori seemed disconnected from reality, she still had the wherewithal to take $35,000 out of his business account. "She knows what she's doing. I can't make payroll Friday for my company. She changed our bank account numbers. I've got seven bucks to my name."

Dorenbush's supervisor, Sergeant John Gillis, arrived and was briefed on the situation. They all walked toward the house to try to get in. Charles said Lori had a rifle in the house, although he was unsure if she knew how to use it.

Charles finally managed to open the garage door, and they walked in to find it empty. Then they went back outside and walked around to the back door, which was locked.

"You don't have a hidden key?" asked Dorenbush.

"No. "It's in the house. J.J. can open it so we have to keep these locks really closed. He's a runner."

"So the dog has gone, too?"

"Yeah, obviously he'd be barking. He's a service dog. Very well trained, but he'd be barking. He's part of the family. I'm going to go and try the back door. I may break a window."

They walked back into the garage, and the officers advised breaking the inner door to the house. Using all his strength, Charles tried to kick the door open eight times without success.

"She's taken my son," sighed Charles. "If he's not at school tomorrow, I'll have to report that. I have no choice. He's special needs. I don't know what she's done."

Charles tried to kick down the door one final time and pulled a muscle, recoiling in pain. Sergeant Gillis offered to give it a try, and on his sixth mule kick, the door burst open.

"Gilbert Police!" he shouted. "Anybody in the house?"

When there was no answer, Charles led them into the house with a flashlight. It was completely bare, every closet empty. The officers went upstairs into each of the bedrooms to find all Charles's clothes were gone.

"Oh my God!" cried Charles in exasperation. "I went in my office. She took my computer and I need it tomorrow."

Outside, the officers questioned Gabe Bonilla, who had walked over to see what was happening. Officer Dorenbush asked if Bonilla had heard Lori threaten to kill Charles during the conversation he was patched into earlier.

"No," Bonilla replied. "She used the word *destroy,* which again is subject[ive]. She could have meant a number of things. There was a level of disconnect from reality that was a bit disturbing."

The officers advised Charles to report his truck stolen to Phoenix Police, who covered the airport, but as far as the officers were concerned, no crime had been committed.

"We understand that you're in a tough situation," sympathized Officer Dorenbush, "and it's kind of alarming to you. But what we're providing is what we can do on our end."

At 8:00 A.M. Thursday morning, Charles Vallow was outside the L.I.F.E. school when Lori drew up in her black Infiniti QX80, with its handicapped plates, to drop off J.J. While she was inside the school, Charles took her purse and her iPhone out of the car, where she had left Bailey. He drove off in his rental car, going through her purse and finding her credit cards, ID, and a hotel key to the Hyatt. Then he called the Gilbert Police Department, asking for an officer to meet him outside the hotel.

An hour later, Charles Vallow met Officers Marianne Robb and Thomas Wiederhold outside the Hyatt in downtown Gilbert. Charles had changed clothes since the night before and looked refreshed.

"What's going on?" asked Sergeant Robb.

"It's a long story," Charles replied sadly. "She's kind of had a break from reality."

He asked Sergeant Robb if she was LDS and she said that she was.

"[My wife] thinks she's married to Moroni in the past." Charles explained that he was referring to the gold statue atop most Mormon temples. "Her religious stuff has gone way off the deep end."

On the verge of tears, Charles told the astonished officers how his wife wanted to kill him, claiming he had been possessed by an evil spirit called Nick Schneider. "I just never thought she'd do anything like this, but she's just lost touch with reality. I'm not me, she yells. She's unhinged. It just scared the crap out of me."

Charles stepped away to the Hyatt reception desk to see if Lori was registered as a guest and if he could gain access to her room. While he was gone, the two officers discussed the bizarre situation with more than a hint of sarcasm.

"Now the biggest thing is she wants to marry Moroni," observed Sergeant Robb, "which is great, fantastic, fine and dandy. That's not as bad as the UFO thing."

After several minutes Vallow exited the hotel, reporting that Lori was not there and had probably checked out. He knew that she would be picking J.J. up at 3:45 P.M., suggesting they all reconvene there later.

Sergeant Scott Gallas of the Special Victims Unit had arrived and was briefed on the situation. He informed Charles that it was a tricky situation for law enforcement: "It's not real black-and-white, like somebody commits a crime and we just arrest them. So we're getting the story second- and thirdhand. We need to be real careful."

"I called the police," said Charles defensively. "I'm not irrational or stupid or anything like that."

"I don't get that impression at all," said Sergeant Gallas.

"I want her to get help," Charles said desperately. "She's not right. I love her to death but something's wrong. And if she wants me gone . . . goodbye . . . that's fine. I just don't want her to hurt J.J."

TWENTY-ONE

"I DON'T SEE YOU BEING A DANGER"

After leaving the Hyatt, Charles went to his bank to stop Lori's cashier's check, so he could meet his upcoming $8,000 payroll for his staff. He also called an attorney to get a restraining order against her.

Next, using Lori's iPhone, he texted her family and friends to try to locate her. When Melanie Gibb received the urgent text asking to meet at the Tomahawk Drive house, she thought it was coming from Lori.

At around 11:00 A.M., she arrived to find an agitated Charles waiting outside. Several locksmiths were busy changing the front-door locks. She confronted Charles about using Lori's phone and he apologized, explaining he needed to find out why Lori was acting this way.

"He was asking, 'What's got into her? Where is she?'" Gibb later told the police. "Of course I didn't say where she was [because] I didn't know."

She asked Charles to give her Lori's purse and phone, but he refused, saying he would return them after Lori underwent a psychiatric evaluation.

Leaving Charles at the house, Gibb drove off and went straight to her fellow "Feel the Fire" podcaster Jason Mow. She told the former narcotics detective how Charles had taken Lori's purse and phone without permission, and he said Lori must report it to police immediately as harassment.

At 12:36 P.M., Lori, Tylee, and Melanie Gibb arrived at the Gilbert Police Department, where they met Officers Thomas Edgerton and John Riportella in the lobby. They all went into an interview room, with Lori and Tylee sitting across a table from the two officers and Melanie sitting off to the side.

"My friend [Jason], who's a police officer, told me to file a report," announced Lori as she sat down. "If I could just get to have it on record."

"Yeah, I have a little bit of info from dispatch," said Officer Edgerton. "He stole your phone and your purse."

He asked Lori to explain what happened.

"So yesterday I got into an argument with my husband on the phone," she began, gesticulating wildly with her hands. "He was in Texas working and I found some stuff that he'd been doing, so he was really defensive. And so I took the kids. We spent the night in a hotel because I knew he was coming home."

She told the officers how she had taken J.J. to school that morning, and Charles had been waiting and stole her iPhone and purse, containing all her money and credit cards. She said her autistic son had thrown a fit because they'd spent the night in a hotel and he was out of his element.

Lori said her husband had then texted her friends and family pretending to be her and "lured" Melanie to their house.

"He told her how crazy I was and stuff like that," said Lori manically.

Tylee looked on, tense, and folded her arms.

"He just basically wanted me to take his side, I think," added Gibb.

Officer Edgerton asked if Charles had behaved this way before.

"Yeah, unfortunately," replied Lori. "We've had to leave and go to hotels until he calms down."

"What is it that motivates him doing this kind of stuff?" asked Edgerton sympathetically.

"He just goes nuts sometimes," said Tylee.

"But this time I caught him cheating," her mother snapped, "and I had evidence and I told him about it. I told him not to come home and that all his stuff would be *gone* and that his car would be *gone*. And I was thinking, 'He's alone now.'"

"She's just trying to protect herself," Melanie added supportively.

"But I just left with the kids because I didn't want them in all the drama."

Edgerton asked if she would be willing to meet with Charles if he brought her stuff back to Community Bridges.

"I don't really want to talk to him today if I don't have to," Lori replied. "He's very sneaky, so what he'll do is meet me in the parking lot and mess around with me. Like he's not going to just let me walk into therapy."

The officer offered to call Charles and ask him to come to the police station with her purse and iPhone. Lori said that would be fine, and Tylee brought out her phone so her mother could read out some of the texts Charles had been sending.

"He was acting like my son was in danger," said Lori. "'I've been worried about J.J.'s safety.' He sent me a strange link to a website about our church."

"Preparing a People," explained Gibb.

Tylee said her stepfather had texted her just before midnight, saying he had no choice other than what he had done.

"But he didn't file a police report or anything as far as we know," said Tylee. "I'm just assuming he was trying to get a response . . . and then 'I love you.'"

"A police report about what?" asked Edgerton.

"I don't know," replied Tylee, "but he was acting like he did something."

"And those text messages . . . do you have it entered as 'Mom's phone'?"

"No," said Tylee. "And he was sending word for word the same text to my cousin [Zac]."

Lori said that her friend Jason Mow had told her to file a police report and restraining order against her husband. But she emphasized that she did not want to press charges. "I don't want to do all of that stuff. If you can get the purse back, that would be lovely, because all my stuff's in there. Really *mad* about the lip gloss."

Officer Edgerton laughed at that, apparently swayed by her charm, before asking about her credit cards.

"He has all the cards," snapped Lori angrily, "so I took the money out of our account. It's a joint account so he wants me to give him money."

"Okay, that's all a civil issue," noted the officer. "There's no reason why he's walking around with your purse, your ID. . . . He doesn't have a right to, married or not."

At 1:12 P.M., Charles Vallow anxiously called the emergency dispatcher at the Gilbert Police Department, saying he now had the necessary order required for Lori to undergo a psychiatric examination. He knew Lori was with police, accusing him of stealing her purse, and wanted to make sure they didn't let her go before he could bring over the order.

"I'm going to go over there," he said. "The officer said he won't hold her because he doesn't have an active order. Could you get that to him immediately?"

The operator asked Charles to stay on the line while she made inquiries.

"She's supposed to be retained for Bridges," said Vallow. "I got an order last night. She's lost her marbles."

The dispatcher took his number, saying that an officer would call him back.

A few minutes later, an exasperated Vallow called again, repeating that he had all the necessary paperwork to hold Lori for a mental evaluation. "They said someone would call me back in a minute, and I just want to make sure that's going to happen. She needs serious help."

Once again, he was told that somebody would call him back, before the same operator hung up again.

Lori was informed that her husband was "all upset" and on his way over with an order to have her psychiatrically evaluated. Officer Edgerton explained that after the order was verified by his sergeant, she'd be taken to the CBI health center, where she could be committed for up to forty-eight hours.

"It's just based on what your husband says," Edgerton explained. "Doctors play it safe."

"I just think it's funny because he's trying to tell everybody . . . I'm really the one that did something wrong." Lori laughed.

Tylee grabbed her arm to calm her down. "Hey, just let him explain," Tylee told her mother.

"I don't know and I'm not going to take sides," continued Edgerton. "Just talking to you I don't see you being a danger to yourself or anybody else. You get your kids to school."

He warned that if she was still there when the evaluation order was approved, he'd have no choice but to take her to CBI, by force if necessary. But, he pointed out, she was free to leave while the order was still being processed.

"Will they be looking for me?" asked Lori. "That's the whole thing."

"We don't bust down doors to get you, but we will knock. So if you see police officers knocking, talk to them through the door if you really don't want to go."

Then Lori asked if the facility had a gym she could work out in.

"You are going to get a padded room," quipped Melanie Gibb, as everyone laughed.

"So you can just say anything you want about someone and get a mental health order against them?" asked Lori.

"It's a family member," said Edgerton, "and depending on what he told the doctors, they'll usually do it just to be safe."

"But do you know what he said?" asked Lori, sounding concerned.

Officer Edgerton then got a call on his cell phone and stepped out, leaving Officer Riportella alone with the women in the interview room.

Lori started making small talk, saying Tylee had graduated at just sixteen and wanted to go into law enforcement.

"She's going to apply to the academy now she's a high school graduate," said Lori proudly. "Yeah, she got her GEDs so she's moving on with her life."

"So you really want to be a police officer?" asked Riportella.

"Maybe," replied Tylee. "You never know."

"I'm actually pretty new myself," he said. "It's my first month on training after I got out of the academy. This is a more unique call from what I've seen."

Lori replied that her husband "rolls with this kind of stuff" and was "creepy," adding that she'd had a rough morning and was worried that he had changed the locks, so she wouldn't be able to get in the house. "He's trying to lock me out. I'm on the lease as well. I'll kick the door down, too."

Then Melanie said how relieved she had been that the two locksmiths were there earlier, so she wouldn't have to have been alone with "creepy" Charles.

"You were just being a good friend to me," Lori told her. "I'm sorry you're caught up in [this] and he's got to tee up everybody."

Officer Riportella asked if Charles had done this before.

Lori said yes. "He's been ballistic where we had to leave because he was being awful and I don't want him to hurt one of the kids or something."

"Probably three or four times that I can remember," added Tylee in support of her mother. "He's really just a stand-up guy overall."

After the interview, Lori went straight to the CBI health center of her own volition and underwent a psychiatric evaluation, which she passed with flying colors. Tylee and Melanie waited outside during the exam, then drove her back to the police station to collect her purse and cell phone, which Charles had returned earlier.

In his subsequent report, Officer Edgerton wrote that he had found Lori completely normal, except for being "slightly upset" at not having her belongings. "Lori showed no sign of mental distress and appeared to be in a good mood. Talking with Lori's daughter and friend, they did not seem concerned for anything other than Lori getting her property back. This incident is cleared, non-crime resolved."

Four days later, Charles Vallow filed an order of protection against Lori in Maricopa County Court. He claimed that his wife, Lori, was a danger to their son, J.J., requesting that she be ordered to stay away from their home and the L.I.F.E. school.

In the protection order request, Vallow outlined Lori's bizarre claims:

"She told me that she was a GOD and was assigned to carry out the work of the 144,000 at Christ's second coming in July of 2020. She said I was in the way and she would have to murder me if I tried to stop her.

"The next day on a business trip to Houston she called and told me she didn't trust me and would have to kill me when I got home. She would have an angel there to help dispose of my body. She also said she knew my real name was Nick Schneider and said I'd have to go."

Lori was now staying with her brother Alex, thirty miles away in San Tan Valley. The process servers did go to Alex's house and saw Lori's car in the driveway, but were unable to serve the protection order. Lori had also stopped going to church to avoid being served.

Lori had returned J.J. to his father, but Tylee remained with her. Lori refused to return J.J.'s medication and iPad with its special developmental apps, but had eventually told Charles where he could find his truck.

Charles had tried to contact Lori numerous times to ask her to return J.J.'s medication and iPad, but received no response. Then he discovered the "Family History Information" that Chad Daybell had sent Lori three months earlier.

"He just flipped," said Lori's niece Melani Boudreaux. "He came over to our house and said, 'Lori is crazy.' He showed us these documents . . . that said something about Tylee being dark and J.J. being light. Charles just went ballistic."

He also desperately reached out to his own family for help and reassurance. Even after everything that had happened, he still loved Lori, but his main priority was to protect J.J. from her.

"Some nights he'd call me just crying like a baby," said Charles's brother-in-law Larry Woodcock, "and it hurt my soul."

Kay said her brother had secretly recorded Lori expounding on her new religious beliefs that she was an immortal god with a divine mission to fulfill.

"As he's telling me these things," said Kay, "I'm thinking, 'Where's that coming from?' It was so outrageous."

On February 8, 2019, Charles Vallow filed for divorce and custody of J.J., stating that his marriage was now irreparably broken. Days earlier, he had discovered that Lori had transferred two thousand Enterprise Rent-A-Car points out of their joint reward account and called the L.I.F.E.

school to check if J.J. was in class. Charles feared she would try to flee with their son.

He hired Mesa divorce attorney Taylor Larson, scraping together enough money to pay the $349 divorce filing charge and legal fees.

"My impression right off the bat was 'this is a broken man,'" Larson told *Dateline NBC* in March 2020. "He had been crying. Everything he knew was gone."

But the young attorney was totally unprepared for Charles's reasons for wanting a divorce. "It's not every day that we have someone come in and say that their wife has threatened their life and that she's got angels ready to dispose of his body."

The ten-page divorce motion Larson filed in the Maricopa County division of Arizona Superior Court read like a bizarre sci-fi novel.

During their first meeting, Vallow had warned the attorney that if anything happened to him, Lori and her brother Alex would be behind it. The "instigator" would be Lori, he said, but it would be done through Alex's hands.

After hearing this, Larson advised Charles to immediately remove Lori from his $1 million life insurance policy, as it provided motive to kill him. Charles agreed to make his sister Kay his sole beneficiary.

But when he tried to access his life insurance policy, he discovered that Lori had changed the password. He emailed the Banner Life Insurance Company demanding an investigation into how this had happened. He wrote that he suspected his "soon to be ex-wife" Lori, who had recently threatened his life, was behind it.

The company made Vallow fill out a notarized beneficiary-change form to make the necessary changes. After putting the change through, he sent a final email to Banner, writing, "I want nothing to go to Lori or any member of her family."

The last week of January, Julie Rowe called Chad Daybell. He told her that he and Tammy were struggling financially and that their marriage was in trouble. He spoke of new visions he'd received of Tammy dying soon.

"He was doing his best to keep his marriage together," said Rowe, "but he really felt like she was going to pass away."

Rowe then accused her former publisher of exploiting her and using her psychic gifts to his own advantage. "And when I confronted him on his abuse of me, he sent me a text back and said, 'Wow, you really know how to burn bridges. You don't know me at all.'"

TWENTY-TWO

HIDING OUT IN KAUAI

On Sunday, February 10, Lori flew to Kauai with Tylee, swearing everyone to secrecy about where she had gone.

As soon as she landed, she called her old friend April Raymond, telling her that she and Charles were getting a divorce and asking if she and Tylee could stay with her. April already knew from a mutual friend that Charles was desperately searching for his wife.

April told them to come straight over and stay as long as they wanted, giving them the master bedroom for privacy.

"[Lori] seemed very disorganized and a little manic," April remembered. "She started out telling me Charles had had an affair, and that didn't make sense to me. Then she talked about him being a zombie, with a demon living inside of him named Nick Schneider."

Lori gleefully bragged about cleaning out Charles's business account, canceling his return flight, and taking his truck from the airport. "She was laughing about it. I felt like she was almost baiting him, so he would become enraged and she could have proof to say, 'Look how irate and out of control this guy is.' It made me sick to my stomach."

April was even more alarmed when Lori casually announced that she was expecting a call soon that Charles was dead. But April gave her old friend the benefit of the doubt, hoping Lori was simply having a midlife crisis after becoming a grandmother, as her son Colby and his wife had just had a baby girl.

Lori arrived in Hawaii with $10,000 in cash, as well as bundles of papers and notebooks crammed with strange religious doctrine. She also had half a dozen pay-as-you-go phones, which she'd fumble through when one went off. Tylee joked that the phones made her look like a drug dealer.

It was the first time April had seen Lori since the previous July. She was shocked by Lori's new extreme religious beliefs, which veered off the mainstream Mormon chart.

Over the next couple of days, Lori constantly spoke about the amazing new podcast group she was involved in. Although the name Chad Daybell was mentioned several times, nothing she said about him stood out more than remarks about the rest of the podcast group she was so enamored with.

Lori also talked about her many past lives on different planets, and how she was a god with supernatural powers to eliminate evil.

"It was very much like a self-deification," said April, "elevating herself above everybody else. And it was just all so crazy and such a departure from the Lori that I had known. I couldn't make sense of it."

Eventually, Lori told April the real reason for her visit: "I'm here to gather you because you're one of the 144,000."

Lori informed April that she would have to leave her two young sons behind and come to Rexburg to fulfill her sacred mission. As a practicing Mormon, April was well aware of the 144,000 from the book of Revelation and didn't want anything to do with it. She politely declined the invitation.

Lori showed April the huge stack of Chad Daybell's papers she had brought with her, with pages and pages of people's names, alongside their light and dark ratings. April noticed that her own name had been handwritten over someone else's that had been crossed out. When she asked why, Lori explained it was because that person had gone dark.

"They had a whole rubric system," explained April. "She did say that Tylee was a dark spirit because she was like her father, who was also a dark spirit."

Tylee spent most of her time in the bedroom, sleeping or chatting with friends on her tablet. When she heard her mother preaching her religious fanaticism, Tylee seemed unfazed, as if she'd heard it all before.

"Tylee just seemed along for the ride," said April. "She was just present, I guess."

*   *   *

Soon after she arrived, Lori announced she wanted to start a new life in Kauai with Tylee when her divorce came through. Lori told April she was done with J.J., and he would now be his grandparents' responsibility.

She also opened a bank account on the island and asked April to help her and Tylee find jobs at the St. Regis Princeville Resort, where April worked. She got them application forms and helped them fill them out. Then Lori discovered she had lost her Social Security card, so she had to apply for a new one.

Over dinner one night, Lori boasted about receiving $80,000 from Joe Ryan's life insurance policy, saying he had finally done something worthwhile in his life.

"She was also using a debit card attached to money that Tylee had received from her father's passing," said April. "She would use it for dinner and say, 'Thanks, Joe.'"

A day after Lori and Tylee flew to Kauai, Charles Vallow turned up at the L.I.F.E. school. He told the principal that Lori had "gone crazy" and J.J. was in danger, so Charles was pulling his son out of the school and taking him out of state until he was safe.

Charles was beside himself after Lori disappeared. He just couldn't believe that she would just abandon J.J. and disappear into thin air. He turned to his close friend and Realtor Joe Pongratz for help. Pongratz had rented Charles and Lori their first home in Chandler and had even stayed with them in Kauai.

"He came to my house and cried," Pongratz recalled. "He can't believe she just abandoned J.J."

Charles filed for sole custody of J.J. Using the pseudonyms "Mother" and "Father," the custody motion outlined in painful detail Lori Vallow's recent strange behavior, claiming that she was no longer "mentally stable enough" to make decisions for herself and J.J.

"Father is extremely worried that Mother would abandon J.J.," read the filing. "Mother's recent decision-making has caused emotional harm to J.J., who has special needs and is unable to understand the circumstances or situation happening."

*   *   *

After staying with April Raymond, Lori and Tylee checked into the luxurious Kauai Beach Resort in Kapaa. Since arriving with $10,000 in cash from Charles's business account, Lori had been spending freely, but it wouldn't last forever.

"Kauai is one of the most expensive places in the world," said April. "But Lori never seemed to worry about money. It was easy come, easy go."

A few days later, Lori announced she had to go back to the mainland, as Tylee had gotten a job. She promised April she would soon be back.

On Saturday, February 16, 2019, Chad Daybell and Melanie Gibb were both featured speakers at a Preparing a People event in Boise, Idaho. It was entitled "Near Death Experiences, Dreams of Future Events, Overcoming Disappointments." That same week Chad was publishing Melanie's first book, *Feel the Fire*.

Charles Vallow believed that Lori would attend the conference. His attorney had process servers stationed at Boise Airport to serve divorce papers, but she never showed.

Charles was now certain that Lori was having an affair with Chad Daybell, telling Kay that he had found evidence. He asked his sister to take over his finances, which Lori had been handling up until then.

"Charles supported her entire family," said Kay. "He wasn't a money guy, so I was helping him with that and with J.J."

Kay was shocked to see that Charles had been paying for Lori's parents' and brother Alex's telephone and cable accounts. She told him it had to stop.

"It was crazy," said Kay. "I said, 'Charles, are you out of your mind?' [His response was,] 'Well, they're family.'"

On March 1, for some inexplicable reason, Charles Vallow told his attorney to drop the divorce. Four days later, Maricopa County Superior Court judge Rodrick Coffey officially dismissed it.

For the next six weeks, Lori bounced between Kauai and the mainland. On Mother's Day, Tylee posted a photo of Lori tenderly kissing her on the cheek in a Hawaiian park, alongside the caption "Who needs words when parks and rec has you covered."

In mid-March, Lori checked into the Kauai Beach Resort with Melanie Gibb. Lori invited April Raymond to lunch to meet Melanie, who struck April as almost subservient to Lori.

"Melanie just seemed like a passenger on Lori's bus," explained April. "Lori was definitely running the show, and Melanie was pretty quiet. There would be times when Lori was going on and on about her doctrine, and Melanie would just be staring at the wall."

A couple of days later, they were all dining out at a restaurant when Lori suddenly became paranoid that a woman at a nearby table was filming her with a cell phone. April said it was probably nothing, but Lori was convinced that Charles had sent the stranger to spy on her.

"And I was like, 'I thought you said Charles didn't know where you were,'" said April. "So now I'm really confused."

Every day since Lori had disappeared, Charles had texted her a photo of J.J., never receiving one reply.

On Saturday, March 9, he emailed Lori begging her to come home for the sake of J.J., who was missing her desperately.

"Lori," he wrote. "The purpose of this email is, again, try and establish a family connection with you and our son. It's been 38 days since you've made any contact with us."

He had just seen Alex, who had accused him of snatching J.J. and trying to put his sister in jail.

"What Alex said was confusing," he wrote. "I was really further confused that the entire family had refused contact, not just with me, but also J.J."

It was only after speaking to Alex, he told her, that he had realized she was telling everyone in her family that he had been unfaithful.

"You and I BOTH know it is ridiculous," he wrote. "You are my one and only for 14 years. Period."

Eleven days later, Charles fired off another email, giving Lori one last chance to return before he and J.J. moved to Texas.

"I'm hoping and praying with JJ that you may reconsider," he told her. "Therefore I will keep the house until the end of April, in hopes that you'll come see your son. He's doing well. He's actually taking his own tubby, washing his own hair and getting on his jammies."

Charles wrote that J.J. did scriptures every night before he goes to sleep and was now being homeschooled.

"I make no judgement Lori," he told her. "I only want what is best for JJ and having you in his life in crucial to his well being and development. PLEASE see your son or at least call him. He does miss you terribly and simply cannot understand where you went."

After receiving no answer, Charles sent J.J. off to visit his grandparents in Lake Charles, Louisiana, while he packed up and prepared to move to Houston. He was a broken man as he tried to make sense of what had happened to his once happy family.

"Things have changed so dramatically in the last six months," Charles wrote in an email to a friend. "Something snapped. It is so unbelievable and scary. I'm thankful she doesn't see J.J. . . . . She wants him and for me to disappear. Seriously . . . it's the most freakiest thing I've ever experienced."

He told his friend how Lori was involved with a group called Preparing a People, who had warped her mind. His friend said he couldn't believe it.

"Believe it," wrote Charles. "The beautiful sweet Lori you and I knew is gone. She actually believes I'm not Charles. She says an evil spirit named Nick Schneider murdered me and is using me to 'violate' her and her family. Not kidding. Gotta get out of here."

"Who the fake is Nick Shhneider [sic]?" asked the friend. "The last time I saw Lori she couldn't say enough wonderful things about [you]."

"I truly feel there is no good ending for her," replied Charles. "Emotionally J.J. is about 4. He will remember bits and pieces. But thankfully not the pain she's put a lot of people thru for her 'Mission from God.'"

At the end of March, Lori Vallow suddenly reappeared in Arizona as if nothing had happened, wanting a reconciliation. Charles and Kay were packing up the E. Tomahawk Drive house for his move to Houston when Lori suddenly waltzed in. She had her phone out and recording as if expecting a huge drama. But Charles only burst into tears.

As Kay watched aghast, Lori demanded to know why he was keeping J.J. away from her. Charles explained that she was the one who had disappeared and her family was ignoring him, so he was moving to Houston to be near his.

"And she said, 'What family?'" said Kay. "And he said, 'My family in Louisiana.'"

Lori and Charles went into the bedroom to talk. Eventually Lori came out and apologized to Kay for everything that had happened. Lori suddenly burst into tears, saying how much she had missed her.

"She never even cried when Charles was talking to her," said Kay. "The whole thing was weird."

Charles offered to fly Lori to Lake Charles to be reunited with J.J. after two months apart. Lori said she had a previous commitment that took precedence over her son.

Later that day, a delighted Charles Vallow texted his friend, "We have our Lori back. J.J. is over the moon."

The friend asked if Lori could be trusted after everything that had happened.

"Yes, without any doubt," Charles replied. "Like I said a lot of misunderstanding."

"Seriously!" his friend texted back. "What a turnaround . . . your [sic] happy about it."

A joyful Charles also informed his attorney, Taylor Larson, that he was back with Lori in an email with the subject line "Love Wins."

"And I said, 'Charles, I'm happy for you,'" Larson remembered. "Privately I thought maybe this wasn't the best idea."

The first week of April, Lori and Tylee moved into Charles Vallow's new rental house at Harbour Sands Drive in Houston. When Melanie Gibb learned that Lori was back with Charles, she was surprised. Lori explained to her friend that she had been told by the Lord to get Charles's finances in order.

Lori was now completely under Chad Daybell's spell. Behind the scenes he was secretly pulling her strings as if she were a marionette, assuring her things were moving fast toward the end of the world in July 2020.

Charles's $1 million life insurance policy would help finance their preparations.

Less than a week after moving to Houston, Charles had a $9,000 insurance-commission check deposited into his bank account. Within a day Lori had transferred $6,000 of it into one of her accounts that he couldn't access. Soon afterward she moved out the remaining $3,000.

"The money flew out of that account so quickly," said Kay, who was now overseeing his finances. "[He gave] Lori the keys to the kingdom."

Lori spent less than two months in Houston with Charles before leaving him again. In mid-June he called Joe Pongratz, asking him to find a rental property for Lori, Tylee, and J.J. in Chandler, Arizona.

Charles ended up renting a condo on South Four Peaks Place for them, while he remained in Houston. Although he still wanted to save the marriage, Lori was adamant it was over. But she refused to give Charles a divorce, explaining she did not want a fourth one to her name.

Chad and Lori were now actively gathering couples to join their growing cult. For some of Lori's closest friends and family, it would mean divorcing their present spouses to remarry others more sympathetic to the cause.

On May 21, 2019, Clifford Gibb started divorce proceedings against his wife, Melanie, the mother of his three children. She would soon embark on a relationship with one of Preparing a People's leading podcasters and speakers, David Warwick, eventually leading to marriage.

In early July, Brandon Boudreaux filed for divorce from Lori's niece Melani, initiating a bitter custody battle for their four children. Just a few months later, Alex Cox, who had never had a steady girlfriend, would marry podcaster and self-proclaimed spiritual teacher Zulema Pastenes, who was close to Lori and Melanie Gibb and shared some of their extreme beliefs.

Soon they would all move to Rexburg, Idaho, where Chad Daybell lived, to ride out the end-times together.

TWENTY-THREE

A DEATH WARRANT

After moving back to suburban Phoenix, Lori enrolled J.J. in a summer program at the L.I.F.E. school and found him a live-in nanny. She then went traveling to meet people and groups affiliated to Preparing a People, seeing her lover, Chad Daybell, whenever she could.

That spring she visited Utah and Idaho and went as far east as Connecticut. She remained in close touch with April, apparently still trying to recruit her into Chad's cult.

"She was bouncing around to a lot of different places on the mainland," said April. "She was staying with different members of this group, and she would call me and say, 'Hey, this is where I'm at this weekend, let me fly you out. Let's have some girl time.'"

One day Lori called April asking for a favor. Out of the blue she explained that Alex had been excommunicated from the Mormon Church and needed support to help him through it. She asked if Alex could call April to discuss spiritual things.

"Alex and I maybe had two or three conversations," said April, "and he was just too strange for me to even tolerate. I ended up blocking his number."

Lori was also instructing Alex in Chad Daybell's teachings. She explained the concept of light and dark spirits, telling him how Chad had designated Charles a zombie called Nick Schneider or Hiplos. She explained that when someone became a zombie, the person's true spirit was trapped in limbo and could not progress any further. Therefore the only way the spirit could ascend to paradise was for the person's physical body to die. Killing the person, she said, would be a kindness.

Lori and her fellow cult members were now using their perceived spiritual powers against Charles Vallow, and things were coming to a head. They were regularly meeting at the temple to pray and summon up forces to defeat him.

"Just got home and got J.J. to sleep," Lori texted one of them on June 3. "Let's go spiritually tonight and work on him. We give the timing to the Lord but we don't need to relent. This is war."

Two weeks later, another cult member texted Lori, "Can you meet me at the temple in the morning? I have time tomorrow and we can work on Hiplos."

On June 21, Lori went online to find out how many Social Security disability payments she would be entitled to in the event of her husband's untimely death, in addition to his $1 million in life insurance. She filled in an application form for a free benefits evaluation and discovered she would receive around $4,000 a month.

On June 29, Charles told Adam Cox that his sister was having an affair with Chad Daybell, and that he was going to tell Chad's wife, Tammy. The previous day, Charles, who knew how to access Lori's computer, had discovered a new email account set up in his name. There he found an email, purportedly from himself to Chad Daybell, inviting him to come to Arizona to discuss a book project. When Charles had confronted her, Lori denied knowing anything about it.

> Hello Chad,
> I hope you are doing well. This is Charles Vallow from Arizona. We really enjoyed having you stay with us in November when you came to the Preparing A People Conference. I appreciated you taking time to talk to me about the book I've been working on. Well, more than six months later I still haven't made much progress on it, but I feel an urgency to get it done.

So I will cut to the chase. I'm willing to pay you well to help me get this book into shape as my ghostwriter. I really liked your autobiography and the tone you took in sharing experiences without preaching. Is there any way you could come here for a couple of days and help me get the book underway? I feel talking in person would be much more valuable than a phone call or video chat, mainly because I would like you to read through some of my journals and explain to me how the publishing industry works.

I'm out of town until Saturday, but would gladly fly you down here early next week before the holiday and cover your expenses. You could stay in our guest room like before, or in a hotel if you prefer. I hate to take you away from your family, but I know this book is vital to my speaking success. I understand if you don't want to take part in the project, but I would definitely make it worth your time.
With Admiration,
Charles

Charles told Adam he was certain that Lori had written it with an ulterior motive. He realized that Lori had written it especially for Chad to show Tammy, as a ruse to allow him to spend a few days in Arizona with Lori. Charles pleaded with Lori to come clean about her affair with Chad Daybell within twenty-four hours, or Charles would inform Tammy about what was going on.

Charles then forwarded the email to Adam with the subject line "Chad Letter From Lori."

Adam
Open this letter and see what she did. I'm not sure [of] the relationship with her and Chad Daybell but they are up to something. She created an email alias for me as I've never set this one up. She sent this yesterday and I guess she forgot all her emails are on the computer at my house. I asked her to explain it and she started blaming you, Brandon and me for perpetuating a scheme against her. Just more of her paranoia. She will not explain it. I am going to send it to Chad Daybell's wife. Her name is Tammy and I found her email

address on their website. I've got her cell number too. Sounds very suspicious to me. What do you think? Whenever she gets caught doing this kind of stuff she starts blaming everybody else. Mostly me, you and Brandon. Brandon and I are victims of her craziness. I wish you luck trying to help her. I was the only one brave enough to try to get her help in January and look what happened to me. The whole family put a scarlet letter on me. Maybe now they can see what they're up against.

Thanks.

Then Charles asked Adam to fly to Phoenix and help Charles stage an intervention on July 10 to bring Lori to her senses. He also wanted Adam to record some of Lori's heretical religious statements, so Charles could take them to a Mormon bishop and have her excommunicated.

"Charles thought if he could get her excommunicated from the Church," said Adam's son Zac, who was in on the plan, "that she wouldn't be able to go to the temple anymore . . . and she'd snap out of it."

After confronting Lori about an affair with Chad Daybell and threatening to tell Tammy, Charles signed his own death warrant. The lovers knew that if Tammy discovered their affair, it would jeopardize everything. And as Lori had warned Charles six months earlier, he would now have to die. He was interfering with their mission.

On Wednesday, July 10, Charles was flying in from Houston to see J.J. and stage the intervention. Lori found out about it from her mother and invited Alex to stay the night at her new home in Chandler, Arizona, which she had just moved into with Tylee and J.J.

She told Alex that it was now time to do the Lord's work, as Charles and Adam were planning "some kind of intervention."

"It's coming to a head!" she texted Alex. "This week will change everything. I will be like nephi I am told! And so will you."

Alex arrived in Chandler with a Springfield XD-M .45-caliber handgun, for which he had a concealed-weapons permit. Then, it is believed, Lori and Alex carefully planned Charles's murder to make it look like self-defense.

* * *

At 7:35 A.M. on Thursday, Charles Vallow drew up outside 5531 South Four Peaks Place in a crimson rental SUV. He had just come from the gym and was dressed in a sleeveless shirt, athletic shorts, and tennis shoes. When he realized Alex was inside the house he texted Adam saying he was concerned. Adam texted him straight back warning him to be careful as he thought his siblings were up to something. There was no reply.

Exactly what happened next only Lori knows, but within an hour her fourth husband lay dead on the bare living room floor in a pool of blood, after two .45 bullets had ripped through his chest.

After Charles's murder Lori left with Tylee to take J.J. to school, taking Charles's rental car and cell phone. She casually stopped off at Burger King for breakfast before going to Walgreens to buy flip-flops for her and Tylee.

Back at the house, Alex hit himself on the back of his head with a metal baseball bat, making sure to draw a little blood. He called Lori several times for updates. Then approximately forty-three minutes after killing Charles, he finally called 911.

"Nine one one, where is your emergency?" said the operator.

"It's at 5531 South Four Peaks Lane," replied Alex casually, without a hint of emotion.

"What's the emergency there?"

"I got in a fight with my brother-in-law, and I shot him in self-defense."

"Okay. Let me get medics on the phone. Is he hurt? Is he alive?"

"Yeah, there's blood. He's not moving."

A fire department medic came on the line, asking what happened.

"I shot my brother-in-law," said Alex matter-of-factly.

The medic walked Alex through CPR procedure, and for the next few minutes he feigned doing chest compressions.

"What happened there?" asked the medic.

"He came at me with a bat. I've never seen him that enraged before."

Alex was instructed to go outside with his hands up, where Chandler police officer Irwin Wierzbicki was waiting.

"Come out this way, man." He beckoned Alex over. "You have no weapons?"

"No weapons." Alex had both hands raised, his cell phone pressed against his right ear. Officer Wierzbicki told him to sit on the curb outside.

Then he went into Lori's house with his gun drawn.

"Chandler Police Department!" shouted Officer Wierzbicki. He walked into the empty living room and saw Charles Vallow's body on the floor lying in a pool of blood, with two .45-caliber shell casings to the right of his body. Officer Wierzbicki checked for a pulse but found none.

"We've got one subject down," he said into his walkie-talkie. "Apparent gunshot wound to the chest."

Then he walked through the condo, which was bare of furniture. In a front bedroom was a mattress and Alex's yellow duffel bag, containing a gun case with .45-caliber magazines and ammunition. Next to it on the floor was a handgun, still smelling of gunshot residue.

Outside, Officer Robert Krautheim questioned Alex about how his brother-in-law had died. Alex seemed strangely unemotional after killing Charles Vallow. He would occasionally dab the back of his head with a tissue and look at the blood, which was minimal.

"Let me see your head," said Officer Krautheim. "You've got a little laceration, do you want me to call paramedics?"

"No. I'd really like some water, though."

Officer Krautheim asked what had happened.

"I don't know. He was enraged."

"What's going on? What happened?"

"Well, he was talking about my sister earlier. . . ."

"What happened today though?" said Krautheim impatiently. "Just in the last twenty minutes."

"He came at me with a bat, hit me on the head." Alex pointed to the back of his head. He explained that Charles had come by to pick up his seven-year-old son, who had been taken to school by Alex's sister.

"Okay, so it was just you at the house?"

"Yes. I think they were talking earlier, then she left and then he got in it with me."

"What do you mean?"

"I don't know." Alex shook his head. "He was accusing me."

Alex said that after he had broken up "a tussle" with his sister in the living room, Charles became angry.

"He told me not to interfere anymore with them or I'd pay." Alex gesticulated with his hands. "And he came at me with a bat."

Pressed for more details, Alex claimed that his niece Tylee had grabbed the baseball bat to defend her mother, and Charles had taken it away from her. Alex had then stepped in and told them to separate, before Lori left with his niece and nephew.

"And then he came at me. He hit me on the back of the head with the bat, so I went to my room and got my gun that I always carry. I told him to put the bat down and he wouldn't. And he came at me again."

Officer Krautheim questioned why Alex hadn't just gone to his bedroom and closed the door. Alex replied that hadn't occurred to him. Instead he'd returned to the living room with the gun drawn, asking Charles what his problem was.

"And I said, 'I want you to put that bat down,' And he wouldn't do it . . . and he came at me with that bat again, after he'd already hit me in the head. So I shot him to stop him."

At this point Lori and Tylee pulled up in Charles's rental vehicle. They parked across the street, which was now lined with several red fire trucks and police vehicles. Officer Krautheim told them to wait there while he finishing talking to Alex.

"Are you and your sister pretty close?" Officer Krautheim asked.

"Yeah, we're planning to go and do something fun today."

Homicide detective Nathan Moffat had arrived to lead the investigation. Asked his brother-in-law's name, Alex erroneously spelled it V-A-L-L-O, even though Lori had been married to him for thirteen years.

Then Officer Krautheim went across the road to interview Lori, and Tylee, who looked apprehensive, her arms tightly folded.

He did not tell them that Charles was dead. "Does your husband live here?"

"No, he lives in Houston," a smiling Lori replied. "We're separated."

She handed the officer her driver's license, saying her middle initial stood for "Norene."

"How long have you lived here?"

"Like three weeks." She giggled. "That's why the neighbors don't know us very well. I'm like, 'Hi, neighbors . . . sorry.'"

The officer then turned to Tylee, who wore a blue Kauai T-shirt and looked pensive.

"Hello, young lady. Let me get your information. How old are you?"

"Sixteen."

Asked if she had a driver's license, Tylee said it was inside the house.

"Nice," said Officer Krautheim. "So you're a new driver?"

"Yeah, well, almost seventeen."

"Almost up . . . so you're old hat then?"

"Yeah, I drove here from Texas by myself," said Tylee proudly, "so I'm used to it by now."

Asked her height and weight, Tylee said she was five foot one and weighed 160 pounds.

"I'm going to list you as a blonde," joked Krautheim. "And then blue eyes? You have very blue eyes, that's not under debate."

Krautheim walked back to the house to brief Detectives Nathan Moffat and Cassandra Ynclan.

"What's the wife's name?" asked Moffat.

"Her name is Lori. She's unaware of anything."

"Yeah," said Moffat, "we're going to go and take her to victim's assistance."

TWENTY-FOUR

SOMETHING'S WRONG

During the short drive to the Chandler police station, Alex Cox made casual small talk with Officer Krautheim. They soon found a rapport and were on first-name terms. Alex described the kind of heavy trucks he drove hazardous waste in around the Midwest.

When they arrived at the station, Officer Krautheim brought Alex into an interview room. While they were waiting for a detective, Alex complained of feeling nauseous.

"Do you want me to call paramedics to check you out?"

"No. It's more adrenaline than anything."

"Do you have any medical issues that might be underlying? High blood pressure, do you take medication?"

"Yeah, I'm slightly overweight. It was a little high at my last physical, but nothing major. No medication or anything like that."

Then Detective Moffat arrived to interview Alex. The session was video recorded. Alex repeated his version of how Charles Vallow had died, saying he was in his bedroom when he heard arguing. He came out to find Charles aggressively yelling at his sister and tried to push him away. Tylee then emerged with her metal baseball bat and came toward her stepfather.

"Alex said Tylee was tiny and wanted to defend her mom," Detective Moffat later wrote in his incident report. "Alex said there was some shoving between him and Charles, and he got spun around and hit."

Then Alex went into the bedroom to get his gun. He returned to the living room with the gun in both hands, telling Charles to put the bat down. Charles said, "Fuck you," and came toward him with the bat, and Alex shot him.

"I asked [Alex] how many times he had fired the gun," wrote Moffat, "and he said it was a couple."

After shooting Charles, Alex walked into the kitchen to wash the blood off his hands. He then put the gun back in his bedroom and called 911.

Alex said that since Lori had separated from Charles in January, he had been acting "insane" and "erratic," and that he had once shown up at Alex's house looking for Lori "and threatened him."

After Detective Cassandra Ynclan informed Lori and Tylee that Charles Vallow was dead, the detective drove them to the Chandler police station, where they were formally interviewed in separate rooms.

At 9:43 A.M., Detective Ynclan switched on the video recorder and asked Lori about her separation from Charles. Lori said that Charles would often get angry with her and cared far more about J.J. than her daughter, Tylee, whom he was horrible to. She explained that they had both adopted J.J., who was actually Charles's great-nephew, referring to him as "a drug baby."

Since Lori's move to Chandler three weeks ago, Charles had made "all these threats" and was constantly mad at her. Lori said she wanted a divorce, so she wouldn't have to deal with him anymore.

Lori then gave her version of what had happened after Charles had made her get a mental evaluation at the end of January. She described it as "a nightmare," blaming Charles for ripping J.J. out of school and moving him to Houston.

"Lori said she just didn't talk to him for thirty days and let him take care of their son," wrote Ynclan in her subsequent report, "to let her husband see what she has been doing for the last 7 years. She knew he would be begging her to pick him up, which she stated he did."

Then Detective Ynclan asked about the events leading up to her husband's shooting. Lori said Charles had announced he was arriving from Houston and would pick up J.J. on Thursday morning to take him to school. Lori said she told him that was fine, but he couldn't stay at the house because of Tylee, and so she would book him a hotel room for the night.

"Lori stated that Tylee is a minor and she lives there," wrote Ynclan, "and that he gets in huge fights with Tylee and Tylee hates him."

Lori had then asked Alex to come over and spend the night, as she didn't want to be alone with Charles when he arrived.

"Lori said she trusts her brother," wrote Ynclan. "She had to go live at her brother's when her husband took J.J."

She told the detective that Charles often "went nuts" and she'd left him five times during their marriage to stay in hotels with the kids. Tylee was "mad" at her for always going back to him, she said.

"I asked what she means when she says he goes nuts?" wrote Ynclan. "Lori said yelling and screaming and I asked about physical violence. Lori confirmed grabbing and pushing them but never punching them."

Lori claimed that Charles had got in a physical fight with Colby when he was sixteen and had twice gone after Tylee in Hawaii and would have hit her if Lori hadn't gotten between them.

The detective asked what Charles did for a living. Lori said he had the "freedom" of constantly traveling on business trips and didn't have to stay home to care for a special needs kid as she did.

Lori said she had been expecting "an ambush" when Charles arrived in Chandler because that was his "macho kind of attitude."

According to Lori, Charles had arrived at around 8:40 A.M. and started banging on her front door. J.J. came out to meet his dad, and she started getting his stuff ready for school.

"Lori said her husband was just being real 'smirky' and real 'jerky,' to her," wrote Ynclan. "So Lori was ignoring [him]."

After packing J.J.'s backpack, Lori had kissed him goodbye, and the little boy had got in the car with his father. Suddenly, Charles realized he'd left his cell phone in the house and returned to retrieve it, leaving J.J. in the car.

Lori said that when Charles came back in the house she was holding his phone, which had been on the counter. He demanded she give it back, but she asked to see his texts

"Lori said he's been acting really 'weird,'" wrote Detective Ynclan, "like he's been 'plotting something.'"

Lori had asked Charles about his recent texts to Adam, and if that was the real reason he was there. She wanted to know why Charles had suddenly started texting her brother. Lori must have read Charles's email to Adam, as she told Ynclan that Charles blamed her for not only breaking up their marriage but someone else's, calling her "a destroyer of marriages."

When Lori refused to return Charles's phone, he started screaming at her. She had walked around the house with his phone, as Charles trailed behind, yelling for her to give it back. Lori told the detective that something was on the phone he didn't want her to see, and she feared he would turn violent.

"Lori said Tylee came out of her room upset and she had a bat," Ynclan wrote, "and Tylee told him to 'leave her mother alone.' Her brother Alex heard the commotion and came into the main room. Lori said her husband is screaming and is super upset. Lori doesn't know if Tylee swung at him or what, but he grabbed the bat from Tylee and went to hit Tylee with the bat."

Lori said Alex had grabbed Charles from behind, to stop him hitting Tylee with the baseball bat. Charles then started hitting Alex with the baseball bat and they had gone to the ground grappling.

Detective Ynclan asked if Charles hit Alex with the baseball bat while they were on the floor, and Lori said Charles was just swinging it back and forth. She said he was "freaking out" and began swinging her right arm downward to demonstrate.

Then Charles got up and came toward her with the bat, and she stepped back to avoid being hit. She ordered Tylee to go to the car with J.J., as she didn't want him coming in and seeing whatever "this fight was going to be."

Lori had gone into the kitchen to get away from Charles, when suddenly she heard a gunshot.

"Lori said she didn't see the shot," wrote the detective. "She heard it and she came back around and she saw him on the ground. [I] asked where her brother was and . . . if she saw him. Lori stated [her brother] was right in front of [Charles] and it all happened very quickly. I asked if her brother said anything to her and Lori said no, that they were both in shock."

She claimed she had then gone outside to the car and was "freaking out." Not knowing what else to do, she took J.J. to school, stopping off at Burger King for breakfast on the way.

Lori's version of the events leading to Charles's death was very different from Alex's, who had claimed that she was not in the house when it happened.

After the thirty-minute interview with Lori, Detective Ynclan went next door where Tylee was waiting. The recorded interview began at 10:14 A.M., and the detective was struck by how flat and unemotional the sixteen-year-old appeared to be after the violent death of her stepfather.

Tylee said she had been woken up at around 7:50 A.M. by yelling outside her door and had picked up her baseball bat for protection. She came out to find Charles screaming at her mother and uncle in the hallway.

She had followed them into the living room, and Charles warned that if she hit him with the baseball bat, she was going to jail. He had grabbed it from her and she had fallen onto the floor. Her uncle Alex had then grappled Charles to the floor, and her mom told her to go to the car and look after J.J.

Tylee ran out of the house and stayed with J.J., who was trying to get out of his child's car seat. Eventually Lori came out and they left.

Detective Ynclan asked if her mom had told her what had happened.

"Tylee said she heard a noise," wrote Ynclan, "and that she knows what it was now, but she thought it was someone taking the bat and hitting it really hard against the floor."

The detective asked what Charles's demeanor had been when he had taken the bat away from her. Tylee replied that he looked like "a crazy person, screaming and his face was beet red."

Ynclan wrote, "He looked like pure rage. Tylee said that was the craziest she had ever seen him. Tylee stated her uncle was kind of calm . . . and just standing there in the doorway being protective of her mom."

After the interviews, Detectives Moffat and Ynclan met to compare notes and arranged for Lori to meet with a victims services advocate for counseling.

Both detectives were uneasy and felt something was wrong. In Alex's account he had been alone in the house when Charles was shot, while Lori said she had been in another room when she heard the shot and gone into the living room and seen the body. The detectives secured a search warrant for the residence.

"We essentially had Charles deceased on the floor," explained Detective Moffat. "The blood on the ground. A couple of shell casings. So at least initially there was not a whole lot to examine or to look at there."

The two detectives then drove Lori, Alex, and Tylee back to South Four Peaks Place. None of the three seemed to be the slightest bit upset about Charles Vallow's violent death, and his new widow actually appeared in a celebratory mood.

"The van ride was straight-up bizarre for me," recalled Detective Moffat. "The odd part about it was just the complete lack of emotion. Lori had a big smile on her face."

Lori gleefully spoke about her daughter passing her GED and soon going to BYU-Hawaii. There was not one mention of Charles Vallow during the trip, which struck the detectives as odd. By the time they dropped the three back at the house, the detectives were sure something was very wrong.

"Just the behavior and the interaction was just so far out of what I was expecting," said Moffat. "I started getting concerned there might be something more."

Detective Ynclan, who has a young daughter, observed how Tylee seemed to idolize her mother and wanted to impress her. The teenager obviously cared a lot about what her mother thought of her. It was as if Tylee had been coached how to describe the day's events and had performed well.

"She wants her mother's approval," said Ynclan. "And you could see that in just how they interact with each other."

When the detectives arrived back at the house, crime scene investigators were still busy taking measurements and photographs. The detectives decided to stage a crime scene walk-through with Alex Cox, who was totally cooperative.

"The claim had been made that the shooting was in self-defense," wrote Detective Daniel Coons in his report, "and there was a desire to have the shooter be present in the scene to help explain the dynamics and locations of the parties involved. An attempt was made to clean the blood from the floor to help minimize the trauma that could be created from exposing [him] to the gore."

Apparently Alex convinced the detectives he had acted in self-defense and nothing was amiss. The victim's body was then removed to the medical examiner's office for autopsy, and police left the house.

Finally, Lori was able to call Chad Daybell with the good news that Charles Vallow was dead, and the police did not suspect a thing. They had gotten away with murder and were now ready to move on to the next stage of their divine mission, so Lori and Chad could be together.

That same afternoon Lori threw a pool party. There was loud music and swimming, and several neighbors complained to the landlord. Lori left to call her son Colby at work, saying Charles had suffered a fatal heart attack at her house. He was stunned and horrified, thinking his stepfather had died in front of Tylee and J.J.

"I'm just freaking out," he recalled. "I just sat there in shock."

After composing himself, he asked his mother what had happened, but she was evasive. Colby said he would come straight after work to offer support.

At 7:30 P.M., Colby walked through the door and was greeted by Tylee, who hugged him and burst into tears. He still thought Charles had died from a heart attack.

Then Colby walked into the kitchen and saw his uncle Alex with a bandage on the back of his head. Colby asked where his mom was, and Alex pointed to the garden, where Lori was by the pool calmly talking on her cell phone. As soon as she saw her son, she hung up.

Colby asked what was going on, and if they were okay.

"And she kind of hesitated," remembered Colby, "and just tells me about a fight [and] that he was shot. I immediately froze up. I had no words."

Stunned, Colby asked why she had said it was a heart attack. Lori explained that she and Charles had gotten into a huge fight, and it had escalated into Alex shooting Charles.

"A bat was brought into it," Colby said. "Al got hit and then he came out and shot him. I just said, 'I don't understand why [Al] took his life.' If you pull a gun on me, I'm not Superman, and I'm not going to come at you . . . no matter how angry. So it really didn't make sense."

Three days after the killing, Alex Cox flew to Colombia for a five-day vacation until things calmed down.

TWENTY-FIVE

"I HAVE SOME VERY SAD NEWS"

The next morning, all the local Phoenix TV stations and newspapers reported Charles Vallow's strange death. "Chandler Police: Man Shot Dead by In-Law" was the headline in the *Arizona Daily Star*.

Neither Lori nor Alex Cox were named by police, who only said they had been released with no charges filed. The case would now be sent to the Maricopa County Attorney's Office for review.

On Friday afternoon, Lori texted Charles's two sons from his previous marriage, Cole, twenty-four, and Zach, twenty-one, to coldly inform them of their father's death, a day and a half after it happened.

"Hi Boys," she wrote. "I have some very sad news. Your dad passed away yesterday. I'm working on making arrangements and I'll keep you informed with what's going on. Im [sic] still not sure how to handle things. Just want you to know that I love you and so did your dad !!"

Cole immediately texted Lori back, demanding to know more.

"We are still waiting for the ME [medical examiner] report," she replied. "I'll let you know more when I can."

"Where is he and what happened?"

"I'll call you when I can bub. He is here in Arizona."

Alarmed at the stunning news, Cole sent four emails in quick succession, asking, Where in Arizona? When did it happen? How was J.J. doing? And what funeral home was handling the arrangements?

Two hours later, when there was no reply, Cole sent another text to his stepmother: "Lori what the **** happened. You can't just tell us our [*sic*] dad died. You're not too busy to just let us know he died and disappear."

At 8:20 P.M., when there was still no reply, he texted again: "Lori it's been 3 hours. You're not that busy. I don't care what you're doing."

Finally Lori responded: "I'm sorry you are so upset. I'm upset too. I'm trying to get jj [*sic*] ready for bed. I'm waiting to hear back from the Medical examiner to make sense out of all of this myself. Please be patient with me. It's a crushing situation all the way around. I'm still trying to process it too and what it means for JJ."

"When and where is the funeral," Cole immediately texted back. "How did this all happen? I want an explanation."

For the next twenty-four hours, Cole desperately fired off text after text to Lori without getting a response.

When Charles's ex-wife, Cheryl Wheeler, learned of his death and how heartlessly Lori had broken the tragic news to their sons, she was speechless.

"I couldn't believe that she did it in that way," said Wheeler. "I wish she could have called me and said, 'Will you please tell [them],' but to do it so brutal through a text was just horrible."

Kay Woodcock was at a nail salon when she got a frantic call from her nephew Cole with the sad news. "He was extremely upset. And he said that Lori said that Dad's dead . . . and that she's making funeral arrangements."

Kay asked if she could call him back because she needed a couple of minutes to compose herself. "So I hung up, and I was just thinking, 'Okay, wait a minute, this is a joke. Charles is as healthy as a horse.'"

She then called Lori's and Charles's cell phones, but there was no answer. Then she received a call from her husband, Larry, who had just read about the shooting online.

"I said, 'What are you talking about?'" remembered Kay. "He said, 'I googled Charles Vallow, Chandler, Arizona, and they murdered him yesterday morning. They said it was justifiable.' We knew it wasn't true. He told us and other family members, 'If something happens to me, it's Alex and Lori.'"

* * *

On Saturday morning, the Maricopa County medical examiner performed an autopsy on Charles Vallow's body. It was witnessed by Detectives Nathan Moffat and Daniel Coons.

The autopsy revealed that the trajectory of the bullets that killed Charles was inconsistent with Alex Cox's account of what had happened. The first shot passed through his body and ended up in the baseboard; however, the second one entered below Charles's rib cage, exiting through his upper left shoulder. That proved that Charles was already lying on the floor when it was fired.

The medical examiner found that Charles Vallow died from multiple gunshot wounds and the manner of death was homicide. The bullets that had killed him had exited through his chest. The case remained open, pending further investigation, and it would be another two years before any action would be taken against his killers.

Adam Cox and his son Zac were visiting friends in Tucson when they found out about Charles Vallow's death. They were convinced that Lori and Chad were behind it and drove straight to Janis and Barry's home in Phoenix for more details.

"We got there, and Tylee's in the kitchen crying to my grandma," said Zac. "She's hugging her and getting ready to leave."

As soon as Tylee saw her cousin, she stared at him with a helpless look in her eyes, as if she wanted to tell him something but couldn't with the rest of the family present.

"I could just tell that she wanted to say . . . what happened on Thursday [with Charles]," said Zac. "She started walking towards me and my grandma guided her shoulders and moved her out. And that was the last time that I saw Tylee."

Later that day, Lori finally replied to her stepson Cole's flood of texts, demanding more details of their father's death and funeral arrangements.

"I'm still waiting," she wrote, "working on arrangements and sorting things out the best I can. I'll let you know when I know."

"Why aren't you telling me what happened?" Cole responded. "I've asked numerous times. Just tell me."

After hearing nothing further over the weekend, a frustrated Cole texted Lori on Monday afternoon: "Okay Lori, it's been 3 days. You let us know our father passed away over a text message. 3 days and we haven't heard from anyone. The only information we have is that one text from you saying he passed away. You disappeared after that. We need any information you have. What happened, when did it happen, how did it happen. Where is he now. Are there any funeral plans and can Zach and I be a part of it. We talked to him all the time and now he's gone. He was our dad and we loved him very much. We deserve answers. Also why have you been the only one to contact us? We haven't heard from Colby or Tylee. I know they are affected too. I called Colby recently too but he didn't answer. Is JJ safe and what does he know?

"I need to be kept in the loop about this all. This isn't a nonchalant topic you can just throw a text at and be done with it."

Lori responded the following day, still not addressing how Charles had died. She was evasive, leaving far more questions than answers.

"These are your dads [*sic*] wishes. He and I discussed this a lot over the years we have been together. My plan is to have him cremated as he wished and then take all 5 of you kids to Hawaii to spread his ashes. He did not want a funeral. He wants a celebration of his life. I've been overwhelmed but I am going to try to start these arrangements today. Jj [*sic*] is doing good but he does not know his daddy is gone. It's so tough because he doesn't really understand. He says daddy is in California working. I know how much he loves you boys and always has. I have a lot of things to do with the business and contacting people and it's still so difficult. Today I'm trying to put up a memorial page on the funeral home website. I'll send the link to you when I have it. I love you and so does your dad!"

Cole immediately fired back a text, demanding real answers: "I appreciate this information but I will ask these question [*sic*] again because I still haven't been given an answer. What happened? When did it happen? How did it happen? Where is he now? Is there a funeral? When is it? Who have you told about his death? Give me all the information you have. Please. My brother and I deserve to know."

There was no reply from Lori, and by Saturday evening Cole appeared to have given up trying to get answers from her. He then asked if he and his brother could have Charles's valuable collection of watches.

"Of course," Lori replied an hour later. "Send me the address you want me to send you [sic] stuff to. Kay is supposed to clean out the Houston House. I told her to let you and Zach have whatever you want first, then she could . . . have or give away the rest. I know he wanted to you to have all that you want."

Cole later told the *East Idaho News* that Lori did send him some watches, but not the fancy expensive ones his father so treasured. "The package arrived and inside were two cheap Timex watches you'd find at CVS. Anything that was worth money, we didn't get. I'm assuming she sold everything else."

Lori never did give Charles a proper funeral and mailed his ashes to Lake Charles, Louisiana. On August 3, the Vallow family held a memorial service, but Lori never showed up and refused to allow J.J. to go either.

On Monday, July 15, four days after Charles Vallow was killed, Lori called the Banner Life Insurance Company to claim his $1 million in life insurance. When she discovered that Kay had been made the sole beneficiary, Lori was furious that she would not be receiving the fortune she and Chad had been expecting.

Three days later she texted Chad that she had talked to the insurance company and discovered Charles had changed it in March.

"So it was probably Ned before we got rid of him," she told Chad. "It's done [but] I'll still get the 4000 a month from SS."

Lori took a photo of the change-of-beneficiary form and sent it to Kay in a text, writing, "Five kids and no money and his sister gets everything."

That was the last time Kay and Larry ever heard from Lori, and from then on Lori began restricting their FaceTime sessions with J.J.

"That's when I started fearing for J.J.," said Kay. "Will [we] ever get to see him again?"

After messaging Kay, Lori called Melanie Gibb, fuming that her former sister-in-law, whom she called a zombie, would be getting all Charles's life insurance money.

"I did not know about [his death] until four days after it happened," said Melanie. "She called me and she says, 'Hey, did you see the news?' I said, 'I don't watch the news.' And she said, 'Charles was shot.' And I'm like, 'What! Tell me what happened?'"

Lori explained that Nick Schneider, who had taken over Charles's body, had come down from Texas to kill her, and Alex had shot him to protect her.

Adam and Zac Cox now feared for their lives. Lori was telling everyone that they had been conspiring with Charles Vallow against her. She claimed they wanted to kill her for her life insurance, and they had become outcasts in the Cox family.

After a huge fight following Charles Vallow's death, Barry and Janis kicked the two out of the house, and Zac, who had been staying with them, moved to Wichita, Kansas, to be with his father.

"The whole family had blocked us on everything," Zac told Fox 10 reporter Justin Lum. "They all took Lori's side. Everyone split up [and] the family is destroyed."

For the next few months Zac and his father were frightened that Lori would set Alex on them next, as she now considered them dark spirits.

"Every day we were really scared that Al was going to come and kill us," said Zac. "We were really worried that we were going to be next."

TWENTY-SIX

MOVING TO REXBURG

Now that Charles Vallow was dead, his widow prepared to move to Rexburg to ride out the end-times with Chad Daybell. They would soon be joined by her brother Alex and niece Melani, now divorcing her husband, Brandon. Melanie Gibb was also considering moving there with her new boyfriend, David Warwick.

"That is the typical dynamic of a personality-driven destructive cult," explained cult expert Rick Ross. "You move to the leader, and the leader's in Rexburg, a place of safety. And the purpose is so the leader can control your life, can isolate you and more easily manipulate you."

Chad now fully controlled Lori. After Charles Vallow's demise, Chad moved on to the other dark spirits keeping them apart. He started telling her what now needed to be done for the mission to proceed, using her brother Alex as their hit man. Alex was only too willing to kill for Lori and Chad's divine mission and started going to a local gun range to improve his shooting skills.

On July 30, Chad and Lori exchanged text messages regarding "death percentages" for J.J. and Tammy.

"I got the inspiration to go back to my original death percentages," Chad told Lori, "that helped us track Charles, Ned, etcetera. Tammy is very close. Her percentage has fallen steadily since Hiplos left. It is encouraging!"

Chad said his wife was already in limbo, having been possessed by a spirit named Viola.

"Lori Vallow became his number one disciple and romantic interest," said Ross. "The children were an impediment. He indoctrinated Lori Vallow to believe that her children were possessed by evil spirits, and the only way to free them was death."

A couple of weeks after Charles's death, Lori called the L.I.F.E. school to inform them that J.J.'s father had committed suicide. The school's co-founder Margaret Travillion immediately googled Charles Vallow's name and discovered the truth.

"It just didn't make any sense," said Travillion. "Why would you tell us that he committed suicide . . . and he was actually shot by your brother? What is happening?"

In late July, Lori put J.J.'s beloved service dog, Bailey, up for sale for $2,500.

"Bailey has such a sweet spirit [and] has brought so much love to his home," she wrote on AnimalDirect.com, "but his owner recently died and he needs a new home."

When warned it was illegal to sell a specially trained service dog, she called Dog Training Elite asking them to rehome Bailey because her husband had passed away.

Bailey's trainer, Neal Mestas, was shocked; he had spent almost a year at the Vallow house, getting to know Charles. He called Lori to offer his condolences and sympathy.

"I told her Charles was such a great guy and asked her what happened," said Mestas. "And she goes, 'It's too hard to talk about now. I'm sorry I can't get into it with you.'"

He then questioned why she wanted to rehome Bailey, as J.J. would be needing him more than ever. Lori replied that Bailey was more "Charles's thing," and it would be too hard having him around. Mestas agreed to start looking for a new home for Bailey.

The first week of August, recently divorced Melanie Gibb and her new boyfriend, David Warwick, visited Lori's house. Tylee and J.J. were there, and Alex came over and met Warwick for the first time.

"Alex was just kind of a fun guy [with a] sense of humor," Warwick remembered. "He doesn't take anything real serious, so we had a light conversation about nothing in depth."

Lori spoke about the pressure she was facing from Chad to move to Idaho. She told Melanie that she had originally thought he would move to Arizona to be with her, but then he said she needed to be in Rexburg.

Melanie wondered whether Chad's wife, Tammy, and their five children would complicate things.

"Well, that was part of their plan," said Gibb. "Their whole goal was to get together, because they expressed so many times that Tammy would be okay with this. She'd just move on and fulfill her mission, so it didn't seem unusual to either one of them."

Melanie was used to listening to Lori and Chad's talk of zombies and kept an open mind. Once during a phone call, she had heard Lori call Tylee a zombie. "Not me, Mom," Tylee had shouted back.

Although Melanie wasn't fully convinced about everything Lori and Chad were preaching, Melanie never dared disagree for fear she would be designated a zombie. But she did ask Lori why those in her life were turning into zombies.

"Well, it's because Satan really hates me," Lori replied. "Because of . . . the level I'm exalted to, they're coming straight after me."

Chad was now a regular visitor to Chandler, often staying over at Lori's condo. He took a special interest in Alex Cox, who was mesmerized by him and his teachings. Chad flattered Alex by saying he had been a special protector to important figures in past lives, and Alex gullibly lapped up every word.

"Chad encouraged him in his thoughts," said Gibb, who often saw them together. "It made him feel good about who he was."

In his quiet, gentle voice, Chad repeatedly told Alex that he had been put on this earth especially to protect Lori from the zombies who threatened her. Alex now viewed himself as an essential part of their end-times mission and would do anything it took to achieve it.

"He had really convinced Alex," said Gibb, "and he was one hundred percent sure that zombies really were zombies."

*   *   *

On August 5, Lori brought J.J. to L.I.F.E to start the new school year. During the two years he had been at the school, J.J. had blossomed and was loved by all his teachers. He had arrived in 2017 a withdrawn and difficult child, but over time he had come out of his shell to show just how creative and gifted he was. He loved painting and dancing and entertaining his teachers and classmates.

"He was a spitfire, for sure," his teacher Julia Allen told CBS *48 Hours*. "He had a lot of energy. When J.J. was there, you knew he was there."

Five days later, J.J. made his last FaceTime call to Kay and Larry Woodcock. Right away, they sensed something was different. J.J. would usually call them throughout the day on his iPad, just to say hi and chat a little before hanging up.

This call lasted just thirty-five seconds and seemed scripted. They suspected Lori of holding something up for him to read out.

"He's, 'Hey, Maw Maw, hey, Paw Paw,'" said Kay, "and then he looks up and . . . you can see his eyes move and he goes, 'I've gotta go, I've gotta go. Bye.'"

After the FaceTime, Kay and Larry feared something was wrong. That night Kay emailed Lori, thanking her for letting J.J. FaceTime them. Kay offered to fly to Phoenix to spend time with J.J., saying she and Larry would stay in a hotel so Lori would not be inconvenienced.

"We can work out details to suit your schedule," Kay wrote. "Plz let us know. We're not up to anything except to see our beautiful boy. We can take him to zoo, arcade, indoor jumpy park. Larry and I need hugs and kisses."

Lori never responded. On August 25 a desperate Kay sent another email with the subject line "JJ FaceTime & visit request. PLZ."

It read, "Lori, I ask again. Plz let us visit JJ. Please let him FT us. Yes Lori. I'm begging. I'll do anything in order to see him. Thx Kay Woodcock."

There was still no reply.

On August 27—seven weeks after Charles Vallow's shooting—Lori and Alex took out leases on neighboring condos at the 565 Pioneer Road complex in Rexburg, Idaho. Melani Boudreaux would soon rent a third, after telling her husband, Brandon, she wanted a divorce. Just a short walk from the Jesus Christ of Latter-day Saints Church, Lori's new $1,225 a month condo was only a few miles away from Chad's property.

For the next two days, Lori and Tylee packed up for the seven-hundred-mile move to Idaho. A couple of weeks earlier Lori had arranged for Tylee's Social Security benefits to be paid directly into Lori's personal BBVA bank account instead of her daughter's. Tylee was not happy.

On August 30, Lori swung by Colby's workplace. He came out to the parking lot where his mother, Tylee, and J.J. were waiting in the Jeep. Tylee was crying and J.J. jumped out to hug Colby.

Lori announced they were leaving tomorrow and had come to say goodbye. She explained they were moving "somewhere cold" for her new job, but could not tell him where.

"[Tylee] didn't really say anything," Colby later told Fox 10 reporter Justin Lum. "She just looked so emotional [and] sad like she didn't want to go. All her friends are here and it just seemed like she wasn't ready to move again."

Colby didn't press his mother about where they were going, assuming they wanted to start fresh after Charles's death. He was also worn-out from his mother's constant drama and wanted to concentrate on bringing up his new daughter, Riley, who had been born in February.

"And I remember saying, 'Take care of the kids,'" he said, "'and make sure that they're safe. Please give them a base, give them somewhere to settle . . . and just stay there.'"

Later that night, Colby FaceTimed Tylee, who was babysitting J.J. He asked his half sister why she had been crying and if she was sad about the latest move. But J.J. mischievously hung up the phone, and Tylee immediately texted that she was sorry.

The next morning, Lori asked Neal Mestas of Dog Training Elite to collect Bailey immediately. She told him the family were moving to Idaho for her daughter to attend college there.

"She said, 'We're leaving now and I need you to come and get the dog,'"

Mestas remembered. "I literally dropped everything and drove over to her house to pick him up."

He arrived to find Lori loading big boxes into an SUV backed into the garage. J.J. was buckled in the back seat and playing a video game on his tablet. He looked up and acknowledged Bailey's trainer, who felt uncomfortable taking away J.J.'s beloved service dog.

Lori went in to get Bailey's stuff, reappearing with a huge Tupperware container with a dog bed, leashes, toys, and some doggy treats. Then she went back inside to get Bailey. J.J. was too busy on his iPad to notice what was happening.

"Lori brought Bailey out on a leash," said the trainer. "She said, 'Have you found a home for him yet?' And I said, 'No, Lori, I haven't.' She said, 'Tylee's in there packing, and if she comes out and asks, just please tell her that you've already found Bailey a home. She's really upset I'm rehoming him.'"

On Sunday, September 1, Lori, her children, and Alex Cox moved into unit 175 at 565 Pioneer Road in Rexburg. Alex had quit his truck driver's job to be with his sister and would soon move into unit 107 in the same complex.

Lori could now see Chad as often as they wanted. BYU-Idaho was just down the street, so the lovers could meet on campus for long romantic walks together.

When Chad had summoned Lori to Rexburg, her only reservation was Tammy. Chad had promised she would die in a car accident before Lori's arrival, but Tammy was still alive, making Lori uncomfortable. Chad assured her that Tammy would soon die, but in the meantime they were safe meeting up on the BYU campus, as nobody there knew what Tammy looked like.

Chad avoided coming to Lori's new town house because of Tylee. Upset at being uprooted, Tylee now spent most of her time in her room texting and emailing her friends back in Arizona. Chad coming over would prompt too many questions from Lori's judgmental daughter.

Under Chad's supervision, Lori now devoted herself to preparing for the end-times. She began stockpiling food rations, water, and medical supplies to tide them through the Second Coming. Melanie Gibb was also excited when Lori and Alex moved to Rexburg, viewing it as a sign that things were finally starting to happen.

"Chad and Lori gave this impression to all of us," Melanie said, "that . . . when they were able to get together, things were going to start changing in the world."

On September 3, Lori enrolled J.J. at Kennedy Elementary School in Rexburg, and he started the next day. She also emailed the L.I.F.E. school back in Gilbert, saying J.J. wouldn't be coming back.

"Since the circumstances in our lives have changed drastically since my husband passed away last month," she wrote, "I have been offered a job out of state and have had to accept it. We have to move quickly since the job started ASAP. So I'm sad to inform you that Joshua won't be returning this year."

She went on to thank the school for everything it had done for J.J. during his time there.

"We are doing our best to adjust to our new life. Thank you again Life Academy. We really loved our time with you."

For the next few months, Lori would constantly monitor the school's Bloomz app, used for communications between the teachers and parents. It allowed teachers to share photos and classroom updates with parents, and Lori wanted to know what people back in Gilbert were saying about her. When the school administrators eventually realized what she was doing, they removed her access to the system, baffled as to why she still cared so much.

In Rexburg, J.J. soon made friends with another little boy who lived next door, and they often played together outside.

"J.J. seemed really happy," said the boy's mother, Leah Bernard. "He was very energetic and running around all the time."

Although autistic, J.J. was imaginative. He loved to put on his favorite backpack and pretend it was a jetpack and go running around the complex. He also rode his scooter all over the place, setting up jumps to go over.

Later, neighbors would recall how Lori would coldly describe J.J. as her niece's "drug baby."

On Sunday, September 8, one week after the move to Idaho, Alex and Lori took Tylee and J.J. for a day out to Yellowstone National Park in Montana, seventy-five miles north of Rexburg. They drove there in his silver Ford F-150 pickup.

At the entrance to the park Alex posed with the children as Lori took photos on her iPhone. The images show Tylee with a big grin, holding J.J., now sporting a punky new haircut with shaved sides, courtesy of his mother. Behind them was Uncle Alex, looking relaxed and smiling. They look like any other happy, normal family on a sightseeing trip to the dramatically scenic national monument.

They spent the day sightseeing and were clocked leaving through the west entrance at 6:40 P.M. They stopped off at Buckaroo Bill's BBQ Grill in West Yellowstone for a twenty-minute dinner before heading back to Rexburg.

Alex was at Lori's condo at 8:37 P.M. and spent an hour there before going out to the Maverik gas station and convenience store on Main Street for ten minutes. He then came back to Lori's for half an hour, before returning to his own apartment.

TWENTY-SEVEN

"FUN TIMES!"

We may never know what exactly happened to Tylee after she returned to Rexburg from Yellowstone National Park. Using Alex's cell phone pings from nearby towers, FBI experts later stitched together a timeline of his movements during the gruesome killing and disposing of her body in Chad's pet cemetery.

At 2:42 A.M. Monday, Alex was in his sister's town house for almost an hour. Investigators believe that he killed Tylee then, but exactly how, only Alex, who is now dead, will ever know.

He left Lori's place at 3:37 A.M., perhaps carrying Tylee's body out and putting it in his pickup, where he spent the next hour dismembering her body. Then he returned to his own condo, heading out again at 8:59 A.M.

At 9:21 A.M., investigators believe, Alex brought Tylee's remains onto Chad Daybell's property, going behind the home and east of the barn to the pet cemetery. With years of gravedigging experience, Chad likely dug her grave, while Alex burned the body parts at the firepit near the pet cemetery. A day earlier, Chad had visited a weather website for wind direction, to ensure that his neighbors would not smell the foul odor of burning human remains.

First her head was buried a few feet under the surface. Then her burned, tangled mass of human flesh and bones were put into a green bucket, which melted from the heat. It was placed on top of the head and covered with earth, leaving little trace of her grave.

At 10:47 A.M., Alex left the property briefly to go to the city of St. Anthony, just a five-minute drive away. He was back at the pet cemetery ten minutes later, where allegedly he and Chad spent the next forty-two minutes finishing their gruesome work.

Alex finally left at 11:39 A.M. and ate lunch at Del Taco in Rexburg, before spending the rest of the day relaxing in his apartment.

The distinct smell of burning human flesh hung over the pet cemetery for hours. Soon after Alex left, Chad texted Tammy with an explanation, in case she smelled it and got suspicious. It would be worthy of one of his novels:

"Well, I've had an interesting morning! I felt I should burn all of the limb debris by the fire pit before it got too soaked by the coming storms. While I did so, I spotted a big racoon along the fence. I hurried and got my gun, and he was still walking along. I got close enough that one shot did the trick. He is now in our pet cemetery. Fun times!"

A week later, Chad joined Lori and Melanie Gibb for their next "Feel the Fire" podcast, entitled "Chad Daybell Sharing Jesus' Love."

"Emerging from a Spring and Summer break," read the podcast's description on the PaP website, "Chad Daybell joins Lori and Melanie to share things he has been shown about the Savior of the World with insights from 2 Near-Death Experiences and a visionary gift that was opened up to him because of his visits 'Beyond the Veil.' You can see a 10 Episode Series with Chad called 'Beyond the Veil' here."

During the thirty-minute podcast, Chad aggressively pushed Melanie's new book, which came out the following day. Lori then asked him superficial questions, such as how Jesus looked, what his personality was like, and if he had a sense of humor.

"We want people to know that [Jesus] is real," exclaimed Lori toward the end of the episode. "He *is* real."

"Yes, I testify that he is real," agreed Chad. "He does appear to people and . . . he learned from his father what to teach the world, and that is the plan that will help us return to live with our heavenly father and with Jesus. And there is really no other way that is going to help us find true happiness."

"That is awesome," gushed Lori. "Thank you for your testimony."

* * *

After Tylee's death, Lori continued to proudly tell people that Tylee was away studying at BYU-Idaho University. How she explained his big sister's sudden disappearance to J.J. remains a mystery.

On Sunday, September 14, Lori photographed J.J. happily sitting on a ride at Yellowstone Bear World, just outside Rexburg. Two days later, the rambunctious seven-year-old boy was captured on a neighbor's doorbell surveillance camera, playing in his front yard. He looks happy as he runs toward his house with a new friend.

The next day Lori went onto the Care.com website to find a nanny. She messaged Charlotte Pearce (not her real name), saying she was interested in her services for her son Josh, who was autistic. She invited her over to the town house for an interview.

Charlotte was impressed by how clean the home was, noting a picture of a Mormon temple on the wall.

"She was very welcoming and gave me a hug," said Charlotte. "She explained to me, as we watched J.J. play outside with the neighbor kids, some of his tendencies."

Lori said her son often became emotional, frustrated, and distracted. Although he had difficulty communicating, he could follow orders if you looked him straight in the eye. Lori explained they had recently moved to Rexburg from Arizona, after her husband had passed away from a heart attack, but J.J. still didn't understand his father was dead.

Lori told the nanny that her daughter, Tylee, lived in Rexburg and was in college. Tylee didn't like to babysit without being paid, which was why Lori was hiring a nanny.

"Occasionally her daughter would come visit for dinner or to do laundry," said Charlotte, "but she never said she lived there with them."

After showing Charlotte how to work the television and explaining J.J.'s dietary needs, Lori asked if Charlotte could start work the next day, as Lori was going to the airport to pick up her friend Melanie.

"She was kind but seemed stressed-out," said Charlotte, "being a newly widowed mom alone with her autistic son."

Kay and Larry Woodcock were becoming increasingly concerned about J.J. It had been five weeks since their last FaceTime, and Lori was not responding to their texts and emails. They had no idea that she had moved J.J. to Idaho.

"Lori, Plz allow JJ to call/FT us," Kay emailed on September 18. "We need to see that he's ok. When can we get him for weekend?"

Kay repeated her offer to fly to Phoenix for a weekend with her and Larry's beloved grandson, saying they only needed seven days' notice.

I'm begging you to have . . . humanity & let us visit him. PLEASE!!!!
LORI: what are you thinking??? Are you even thinking ???
Kay Woodcock.

Soon after Kay pressed Send, Chad informed Lori that J.J. had now become a zombie. A dark spirit had entered his body, and J.J. had to die for his own good, so he could move on to his next spiritual level.

On Thursday morning, Charlotte arrived at Lori's town house to start her nanny job. Lori told her that her brother Alex was on his way over to take her to the airport, and if she was back late, to give J.J. his medicine just before bed, as it made him tired. Lori even joked about how she looked forward to giving J.J. his medicine when he was "extra tough to handle," so he would give her a break. Then Alex arrived and the two went to pick up Melanie Gibb.

After his mother left, J.J. became upset and went into the garage. He spent most of the day playing hide-and-seek and other games with his new friends.

"He seemed to be in his own little world, kind of talking to himself," said Charlotte. "He had this toy he really loved called Ducky . . . and carried it everywhere with him."

At dinnertime she fed him mac and cheese and then he went back outside to play. After tidying up the house, Charlotte went to fetch J.J., who was arguing with one of his friends about a toy. When the boy said he didn't want to play with him anymore, J.J. threw a tantrum.

"He started crying and screaming," said Charlotte. "He threw the chair from their wooden table down, flipped the ottoman over by their couch, and then ran upstairs."

Charlotte found him hiding under his mother's bed. As soon as he saw her, he crawled out and knocked a mirror off the wall and ran downstairs.

He said that he hated her and his mother wouldn't want her to come over anymore.

Soon afterward, Lori arrived home with Alex and Melanie Gibb, whom Lori introduced to Charlotte, saying they did podcasts together. Lori asked how J.J. had been and Charlotte told her about his outburst.

"I explained the situation," said Charlotte, "and she babied him, as if he could do no wrong. It felt a little overwhelming, the amount of love she was showing him, instead of trying to teach him to calm down."

Lori then handed Charlotte $40 in cash and thanked her, neglecting to set up any future babysitting dates.

Melanie Gibbs's boyfriend, David Warwick, was due to arrive the next day to attend a conference and record a new podcast. The couple were also interested in moving to Rexburg, and Chad had arranged for a realtor to show them some land available to build on.

Lori brought Melanie Gibb up-to-date with the developments since Lori's move, assuring Gibb that the end-times were fast approaching. Lori said Chad had decided that J.J. was a zombie and loved Satan. She cited her son's growing vocabulary and how he would sit still and watch TV as further evidence of his being a dark spirit.

"I was looking at him and thought, 'I don't know. He looks just like J.J. to me,'" said Gibb.

Lori also explained that Tylee was now studying at BYU-Idaho with some of her friends. Gibb knew Tylee had gotten her GED in December, but wondered how the sixteen-year-old could possibly be in college so soon.

Lori said that J.J. was going to live in Louisiana with his grandparents because he was interfering in their spiritual mission. She planned to tell Kay that she had breast cancer and couldn't care for J.J. anymore.

On Friday morning, Chad joined them for a walk around the BYU-Idaho campus running track. He would be a constant presence at Lori's house during Melanie's four-day visit.

Lori and Chad acted like teenagers in love with constant public displays of affection. They held hands, hugged and kissed right in front of Melanie, who was pleased for them.

Chad Daybell believed that his grandfather Keith, who died in a logging accident before he was born, was his main spirit guide from the other side of the veil. *(Courtesy of* The Springville Herald*)*

Lori with her close-knit high school friends. *(Courtesy of Rose Vaughan)*

The Eisenhower High School cheerleading squad flyer, Lori Cox lived for the applause she got at games. *(Courtesy of Rose Vaughan)*

Chad during his LDS mission to New Jersey with some of his fellow missionaries. *(Courtesy of Ben Hyde)*

Vaisia Itaaehau was like a sister to Tylee Ryan. After their move to Kauai, Vaisia often came to visit. *(Courtesy of Echo Itaaehau)*

Lori's brother Alex Cox became close friends with fellow comedian Mary Tracy when they did stand-up together in Phoenix in 2006. *(Courtesy of Mary Tracy)*

Lori Ryan looked very glamorous competing in the 2004 Mrs. Texas Pageant. "I'm a ticking time bomb," she told the judges. *(Courtesy of Tracy Crist)*

Lori had breast implants to give her an edge in the Mrs. Texas Pageant. Unfortunately, she did not make the final five. *(Courtesy of Tracy Crist)*

Publisher and prolific novelist Chad often appeared at promotional events to sell his books.
(Courtesy of Julie Rowe)

Chad was a major draw at the large Preparing a People conferences he spoke at.
(Courtesy of Julie Rowe)

Lori and J.J. playing in Kauai. By all accounts, Lori was then an excellent mother. *(Courtesy of Echo Itaaehau)*

"Hi, neighbors . . . sorry," Lori told Chandler police officer Robert Krautheim a few minutes after Alex shot Charles Vallow dead. *(Courtesy of the Chandler Police Department)*

On September 8, 2019, Lori and Alex took J.J. and Tylee on a day trip to Yellowstone National Park. This is the last known photograph of Tylee before she disappeared. *(Courtesy of the Federal Bureau of Investigation)*

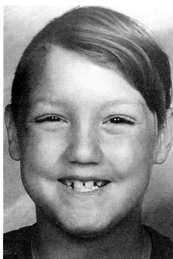

The Rexburg Police Department released these headshots of J.J. and Tylee in December 2019 in a nationwide hunt to find them. *(Courtesy of the Rexburg Police Department)*

Chad delivered the eulogy at Tammy's memorial service in Rexburg. *(Courtesy of Eric Smith)*

During her move to Rexburg to be closer to her Aunt Lori and Uncle Alex, Melani Boudreaux dumped all her children's clothes and toys on the sidewalk with a sign saying they were free. *(Courtesy of Rich Robertson)*

A smiling Lori at her first court appearance in Rexburg on March 6, 2020. She was wearing a bulletproof vest and bright red lipstick made by other inmates from Jolly Rancher candy. *(Courtesy of Pool Photo/John Roark–Post Register)*

J.J.'s grandparents Larry and Kay Woodcock attended Lori's court appearance in Rexburg, when Judge Eddins reduced her bail from $5 million to $1 million. *(Courtesy of Pool Photo/John Roark–Post Register)*

Lori and her new attorney, Mark Means, who she reportedly said had been her son in a previous life. *(Courtesy of Pool Photo/John Roark–Post Register)*

The Daybell property, where the missing children were finally found in June 2020. Tylee's dismembered and burnt remains were buried in the pet cemetery on the left and J.J.'s were found adjacent to an empty pond on the right. *(Courtesy of Lisa Smith)*

Chad Daybell's mugshot after his arrest on June 10, 2020, following the desecrated bodies of J.J. and Tylee being found on his property. *(Courtesy of the Rexburg Police Department)*

Chad and his defense attorney, John Prior, at his preliminary hearing. *(Courtesy of Pool Photo/John Roark–Post Register)*

Tenacious special prosecutor Rob Wood has vowed to make sure that J.J. and Tylee get justice. *(Courtesy of Pool Photo/John Roark-Post Register)*

Melanie Gibb giving dramatic testimony against her one-time friend Chad Daybell. *(Courtesy of Pool Photo/ John Roark–Post Register)*

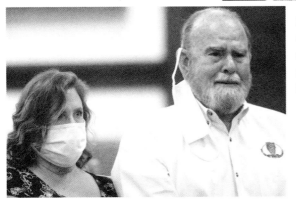

Kay and Larry hear gruesome details from an FBI special agent about how J.J.'s body was recovered. *(Courtesy of Pool Photo/John Roark–Post Register)*

Lori and Tylee photographed in Hawaii in early 2019. *(Courtesy of the Chandler Police Department)*

"They were very much in love," Gibb later testified, "and wanted to be together as soon as possible."

When Melanie expressed surprise at how open they were, Lori explained that Tammy didn't go out much and never on campus.

Lori described her relationship with Chad as "full of love and lust," saying that after the massive earthquake Chad had predicted would hit Utah by the end of the year, no one would care about their personal lives.

That night, Melanie's soft-spoken boyfriend, David Warwick, arrived at Lori's apartment for the weekend. Over dinner they discussed Melanie's new book, as well as her and Warwick's move to Rexburg for the Second Coming.

One recurring topic for Lori the entire weekend was J.J.'s out-of-control behavior and his acting like a zombie. J.J. spent most of the visit playing outside or in the family room next to the kitchen.

"She was obsessed," said Gibb, "to the point where she was saying, 'Look how he's behaving. Look how hyper he is.' She believed he was a zombie."

At noon on Sunday, Lori and her guests went to see an available real estate lot near the Daybell property. Chad wanted David, who was a general contractor, to develop it as part of their end-times survival plan. Alex joined them as Chad arrived with a realtor, spending an hour discussing the land's potential.

That night, Lori recorded a podcast in the kitchen from 9:00 P.M. to midnight with Melanie and David. Lori told them that Alex was babysitting J.J. in his condo, as he was acting up.

"We were interviewing David," said Melanie Gibb, "and he was sharing a lot of his personal spiritual experiences and conversion to our Church."

In the middle of the recording Alex came in with J.J., who appeared to be asleep with his head on his uncle's shoulder. Alex carried J.J. up to Lori's bedroom.

That would be the last time J.J. would ever be seen.

TWENTY-EIGHT

J.J. WAS BEING A ZOMBIE

On Monday morning, Melanie and David packed up their belongings to leave. At around 9:00 A.M., they came downstairs to say goodbye to Lori, who was in the kitchen. There was no sign of J.J., so David asked where he was.

"She said he was being a zombie," David later testified, "and [that he] climbed up on the top of the fridge and smashed her picture of Christ down. He then climbed onto the upper cabinets and got between the top of the cabinet and the ceiling."

David asked to see J.J. and say goodbye, but Lori said he was out of control so she had asked Alex to come over and get him.

After Alex brought J.J. back to Lori's condo, the boy was never again seen alive. Exactly how he murdered the helpless seven-year-old in cold blood, no one will ever know. Later, investigators would attempt to reconstruct how Alex killed his nephew, but their horrific findings have never been revealed, probably for the sake of J.J.'s family.

What Alex did next is beyond comprehension. Always rambunctious, J.J. must have fought for his life, but the little boy was no match for his six-foot-one-inch, 227-pound uncle. To stop J.J. from screaming and trying to escape, Alex wrapped a strip of heavy-duty duct tape tightly over his mouth and looped it several times around his chin to his forehead.

J.J. was probably still alive when Alex began binding his feet and hands. He folded J.J.'s hands over his chest and bound his wrists, before wrapping the duct tape tightly around his arms, over his hands, and all the way over to his right elbow. Alex wrapped the tape around and around his ankles.

Then Uncle Alex put a white plastic trash bag over J.J.'s head and tied it tightly with its red drawstring before putting his small body into a black trash bag.

At 9:55 A.M., Alex Cox brought the trash bag containing his nephew's bound-and-gagged body into Chad Daybell's backyard. He spent the next seventeen minutes at the northern edge of Chad's property near the pond, across from the pet cemetery where they had buried Tylee two weeks earlier.

As experts suggest, it would have been impossible for Alex alone to dig the clandestine grave, bury J.J.'s body, then refill it in such a short time. It would have taken the gravedigging expertise of Chad Daybell, who literally wrote a book on the subject, to accomplish this feat.

After the grave was dug, J.J.'s remains were placed inside. Three thin wooden panels were placed over the black trash bag containing his body, with three heavy white stones put on top to secure it in place. They filled in the hole with earth and smoothed it over.

Chad and Alex then went their separate ways, confident that no one would ever find J.J.'s body.

On Tuesday morning, which would have been Tylee's seventeenth birthday, Lori called Kennedy Elementary School to inform them that J.J. would be absent for a while. She explained that he would be staying in Louisiana with his grandparents and would not be back until the end of October at the earliest.

A few hours later, Charlotte Pearce texted Lori to see when her babysitting services would again be needed. Lori told her that J.J. was spending a month with his grandmother in Louisiana while she vacationed in Hawaii. She promised that when she returned to Rexburg there would be more work for Charlotte.

"It seemed irresponsible for a mother to dump her kid off to the grandparents," said Charlotte, "while she had a good time in Hawaii."

Later that day, Lori's sister Summer Shiflet texted birthday greetings to her niece Tylee's cell phone, now in her mother's possession, and received a reply:

"Thank you, Sunny. Love you and Happy Birthday to you too."

Four days later, Colby texted his sister's phone to wish her a belated happy birthday and had a brief exchange. But whoever was replying to his texts did not want to speak over the phone.

Colby: Hey Ty!! Happy Birthday. I'm so proud of you! I know you have been through [a lot]. . . . Trust god, it's all going to be okay. . . .

Tylee: Thanks colbs. I love you

Colby: Hey Ty are you okay?

Tylee: I'm good just tired. . . . Call you back later. Love you

Colby: Okay call me tonight please

Tylee: at the movie. I'll call you after

Colby: Ty, please call me after your movie. I'm worried about you!

Tylee: Worried about me? What?

Colby: I just want to hear you talk. . . .

Tylee: Ok this week was just busy. I'll call you soon

Colby: Okay please call me tonight if you can.

After the text exchange, Colby felt something was wrong. Tylee usually used lots of emoji in her texts, but now there were none. She also didn't seem receptive to calling him.

"[It's] not sounding right," he later told Dr. Phil McGraw. "Just the way she spoke didn't fit her personality."

About a week after her stay in Rexburg, Melanie Gibb asked Lori what was happening with J.J. Lori said she had told Kay that she had breast cancer and was too ill to take care of him. Lori claimed to have personally taken J.J. to Louisiana and handed him over to Kay at the airport.

Lori also mentioned that Tammy was suspicious that Chad was being unfaithful, but did not elaborate further.

*   *   *

That fall, Chad Daybell was officially excommunicated from the Church of Jesus Christ of Latter-day Saints for declaring himself a prophet. His public appearances and podcasts had angered Mormon Church leaders, who disliked his self-styled end-times Prepper message.

He was stripped of his Church membership and could no longer partake in the sacrament. He was also banned from preaching in public or entering Mormon temples.

A Mormon Church spokesman refused to comment on Chad's excommunication except to say, "It is a personal matter that is left to him to discuss if he wishes."

TWENTY-NINE

"SOMETHING REALLY WEIRD JUST HAPPENED"

Now that J.J. and Tylee were out of the picture, Lori was eager to move on in her new life with Chad Daybell. Everything was going according to Chad's plan, but several obstacles were still in their way before they could fly off to Hawaii for their romantic beach wedding, already in the planning.

After Lori failed to receive her expected $1 million payout from Charles Vallow's life insurance policy, Chad made "significant increases" on several life insurance policies he had taken out on Tammy, bringing them to the maximum legal payout allowed.

Lori's niece Melani's estranged husband, Brandon Boudreaux, also had a life insurance policy worth more than a million dollars. It is believed that Alex Cox was assigned to kill him next so that Melani, who was about to move to Rexburg to be with the cult, would get the money. The day after J.J. was last seen, Lori visited The Gun Shop in Idaho Falls where she photographed boxes of 5.56 mm rifle ammunition. Investigators believe it was for the firearm Alex planned to use to kill Brandon and Tammy.

On Tuesday, October 1, Lori rented a ten-foot-by-ten-foot storage unit in the name of Lori Ryan. She signed a $53-a-month rental agreement for unit C52 with Self Storage Plus on Airport Road in Rexburg, just 350 yards from the city dump.

Over the next two days, she visited the unit with either Chad or Alex half a dozen times. They brought boxes of family memorabilia, including photo albums of J.J. and Tylee. She also left sports equipment, her children's clothes, and J.J.'s beloved bike and backpack with his initials on it.

Back at his apartment complex, Alex removed the spare tire and rear car seat from the 2018 green Jeep Wrangler still registered to Charles Vallow, which Tylee had driven. Alex left the tire and car seat in Lori's garage for her and Chad to take to the storage locker.

He then took one of his rifles with a silencer and set out on the thirteen-hour drive south to Gilbert, Arizona, to kill Brandon Boudreaux.

A few hours later, Chad called Julie Rowe about book royalties he still owed her. They talked for an hour about a variety of subjects, including his wife, Tammy.

"I said to him, 'Do you still see Tammy dying?'" remembered Rowe. "And he said, 'Yes, I wouldn't be surprised if she died in her sleep.'"

Early Wednesday morning, Alex Cox parked the Jeep directly opposite Brandon Boudreaux's house in Gilbert. He carefully positioned himself where the rear seats and tire had been, giving him a perfect line of fire to the driveway. He then got out his rifle and waited.

Just before 9:00 A.M., Brandon arrived back from the gym. He was about to pull his black Tesla Model X into his driveway when he recognized Tylee's green Jeep Wrangler with Texas license plates parked across from his house. The back window opened and he saw Alex Cox poke a rife and silencer out of it, aimed straight at him.

Brandon heard a muffled gunshot and for a split second thought it was a paintball gun. Then, as if in slow motion, his driver's-side window shattered, as a real bullet whizzed by, missing his head by inches and hitting the doorframe.

Fearing for his life, Brandon hit the accelerator hard and sped off. The Jeep followed for a few blocks before peeling off in a different direction.

Terrified, Brandon called 911 to report the attempt on his life.

"Someone shot my window," he told the operator breathlessly. "I was pulling in my house. I drove away but I can see them driving off."

"Okay," replied the 911 operator, trying to calm him down. "Someone shot at your vehicle?"

"Yes. And it hit my window. It shattered my driver's-side window. Sorry . . . I'm a little out of breath. I saw them drive off."

After getting more details, the operator said officers were on the way, asking if he wanted to wait for them in his house. Brandon said he was too scared to go home and would meet them a few miles down the road, in case his assailant returned to try again.

After giving a statement to Gilbert police, Brandon gathered up his four children and went into hiding at his parents' house in American Fork, Utah, fearful that Alex Cox would strike again.

At 2:30 P.M., Lori and Chad Daybell came by the storage unit to drop off the spare tire and rear car seat. On the way out Chad patted Lori's behind affectionately. Twenty-four hours later, Lori would return with Alex to collect the tire and seat and put it back in the Jeep.

That night, Lori accessed Charles Vallow's Amazon account, which she was now using regularly. She ordered matching size 4 and 11 sterling silver Southwestern-style malachite gemstone wedding rings for a total of $206, which were delivered to her Rexburg address five days later. Malachite, according to Chad, had healing properties.

She also used her late husband's Amazon account to buy Chad an extra large button-down white cotton shirt and Oyamiki linen slacks for their upcoming wedding.

Two days later, with Chad's encouragement, Tammy Daybell drove to Springville, Utah, to see her parents and sister, Samantha. It was the first time Tammy had been back since moving to Idaho four years earlier. Tammy drove the 290 miles alone, as Chad said he was too busy to join her.

After a family dinner at her parents' home, Tammy demonstrated some new steps she had learned in her clogging class. She seemed in excellent health and talked about training for a marathon. She stayed the night with Samantha and left at 9:00 A.M. the next morning for the long drive back to Rexburg. If Tammy had any suspicions about Chad's faithfulness, she never mentioned them to her family.

"It was a really fun visit," remembered Samantha. "She was happy. We stayed up late visiting and talking and she never said anything. So if it had been weighing on her mind, she was keeping it hidden from me."

Five days later, Tammy was in her driveway taking some shopping bags out of the back seat of her car when Alex Cox suddenly appeared wearing a ski mask. He was carrying what she assumed was a paintball gun and shot at her several times, but missed. When she yelled for Chad, Alex ran away.

Shaken, Tammy called the Fremont County Sheriff's Office to report the incident. A deputy came to investigate, but was unable to find anything and put it down to pranksters.

Soon afterward, Tammy went on Facebook to post about the bizarre incident.

Okay Neighbors—
Something really weird just happened and I want you to know so you can watch out.

    I had gotten home and parked in our front driveway. As I was getting stuff out of the back seat, a guy wearing a ski mask was suddenly standing by the back of my car with a paintball gun. He shot at me several times, although I don't think it was loaded. I yelled for Chad and he ran off around the back of my house.

    I have no idea what his motive was, and he never spoke, even after I asked him several times what he thought he was doing. I was about to smack him with my freezer meals from Enrichment tonight when I decided to yell for Chad instead.

Tammy also told her sister, Samantha, about the incident. Although Tammy was shaken, she did not think it was anything more serious than a paintball prankster.

"It seemed kind of ridiculous," said Samantha. "Who'd want to shoot a paintball at you?"

* * *

On October 14, Kay and Larry Woodcock were desperate and fed up with Lori's stonewalling them. Kay sent one last text to Lori, begging to see J.J.:

"Lori, PLZ allow JJ to FT us. We really miss him. No need to cut him out of our lives. PLZ work something out for us visitation?? PLZ tell him we love him. Give him maw maw & paw paw kisses."

THIRTY

"MY BEAUTIFUL, TALENTED WIFE TAMMY PASSED AWAY"

On Saturday, October 19, Tammy Daybell died in her sleep at the age of forty-nine. She was found by Chad, who called 911 to report her death, explaining she had gone to bed with a cough and didn't wake up. Pink foam was coming out of her mouth.

A Fremont County sheriff's deputy soon arrived at the Daybell residence in Salem to investigate the unattended death, but found nothing suspicious. The grieving husband calmly answered all questions, saying Tammy had been ill for some time.

"He was responding like anybody would whose spouse had just passed away," said Sheriff Len Humphries. "They didn't see anything that alarmed them."

The Fremont County coroner Brenda Dye arrived and ruled that Tammy had died of natural causes. Her body was transported directly to the Flamm Funeral Home, as Chad did not want an autopsy.

Meanwhile, Chad called Tammy's sister, Samantha, to tell her Tammy passed away in her sleep.

"He sounded upset and devastated," said Samantha. "I was crying and he was crying and it was a really hard moment."

Chad explained that Tammy had recently been sick and having coughing fits, speculating it had led to her death.

"She hadn't been sick when I saw her," said Samantha, "but I don't know if she'd gotten something in the two weeks after."

When Samantha asked why there was no autopsy, Chad said that the body was already at the funeral home, so there was no need for one.

After hearing the sad news, neighbor Matt Price came over to offer his condolences to Chad, who seemed unaffected by his wife's sudden death.

"I don't know how he was grieving," said Price. "He didn't show a lot of emotion. It was very odd."

Later that morning, Chad announced Tammy's passing on Facebook. His post seemed cold and stoic, especially after a thirty-year marriage that had produced five children. It was also surprising that within hours of her death, he had already arranged her funeral back in Springville, Utah, as well as several memorial services.

"I am saddened to share that my beautiful, talented wife Tammy passed away early this morning in her sleep," the post began. "It is a shock to all of us. She was so beautiful in every way! We are still working out the details, but we plan to hold a viewing Monday evening in Springville, Utah, then hold the funeral and burial there on Tuesday. We will hold memorial services in Rexburg on Wednesday at 11 a.m. at the Henry's Fork Stake Center. We are overwhelmed with the outpouring of love and support. Thank you so much!"

At 1:15 P.M., Chad's eldest daughter, Emma, called Julie Rowe for emotional support.

"She was sobbing," remembered Julie, "and very upset about Tammy dying."

Emma asked if her father had ever talked about Tammy dying. Julie told her that Chad had spoken of her mother dying in various ways several times recently.

"She felt betrayed," said Julie, "because he hadn't said anything to her that he'd had a vision of it."

Toward the end of their forty-minute conversation, Emma said what most scared her was the idea of her father getting remarried. It was as if Chad had been preparing his daughter for the new life he was planning.

"And I asked, 'Why are you afraid of that?'" said Rowe. "And she said, 'Because he taught me about multiple probations and I'm not okay with polygamy. I have problems with it.'"

Emma said she had to get off the phone, as her father needed her.

"And I could see Chad in a vision standing next to her and take the phone," said Julie, "and her energy changed. After that she wouldn't respond to any of my texts or calls and we've had no contact since."

Melanie Gibb learned of Tammy's death on social media and immediately remembered Lori saying that Chad's wife would soon die. When she called to find out what had happened, Lori seemed surprised, claiming not to have not heard the news. This puzzled Melanie, as Chad and Lori had both told her that Tammy would have to die for them to complete their mission.

"Their whole goal was to get together," said Melanie, "because they expressed to me many times that Tammy would be okay with this. She'd just move on and fulfill her mission."

Three days after she died, Tammy Daybell was buried at the Evergreen Cemetery in Springville, Utah. Ironically, it was where she had fallen in love with Chad when he was a gravedigger there. The small service was attended by family and a few close friends.

A memorial service was held back in Rexburg at the Henry's Fork Stake Center. Bishop Ryan Bradshaw officiated, and Chad delivered the eulogy from the pulpit.

"He brought in humor," recalled Eric Smith. "He got people laughing a little bit, although there was some emotion."

The Daybell children took part in the service with the exception of Mark, now serving an LDS mission in South Africa. The closing song was the LDS hymn #300 "Families Can Be Together Forever."

After the memorial service, Chad made a beeline for Smith and his friends. As they offered their condolences, Chad said Tammy's spirit had already visited him to help set his affairs in order and give advice on their children.

"It seemed rehearsed," said Smith. "'Hey, it's okay, she's visited me and things are going fine.' He was unusually at peace, which I thought odd, but, well, he does have these gifts and a visitation from your wife . . . could really help calm you."

Smith and his friends were also struck by how much weight Chad had lost; his baggy suit was now hanging off him. In the last few months, under Lori's supervision, Chad had started working out and had lost more than fifty pounds.

"He had changed his whole physique, his dress and appearance," said Smith. "He looked good. He looked trendy."

Later, Smith was alone in the parking lot when Chad came over to say goodbye. He suddenly began discussing Tammy's life insurance policy and said that he would soon be getting out of the publishing business.

"He was clearly making this point that he would be okay financially," said Smith. "The Lord's taking care of him."

Although Lori did not attend the memorial service, Chad and his children went over to her town house that afternoon for tea and cookies. She later boasted to Melanie Gibb that it had been a big success and that Chad's children adored her.

A couple of days later, Chad and Lori bought tickets to fly to Kauai to get married. Chad had no problem getting his $440,000 life insurance payment, and they now had more than enough money to celebrate in style.

To ensure that no one would question Tylee's sudden absence, Lori was regularly using her daughter's phone to text people.

"tylee I'm just thinking about you," a friend texted her on October 25.

"Hi. Miss you guys too . . . luv ya," came the text back.

Lori frequently texted Colby, as well as sending him several payments through Tylee's Venmo account.

Lori was also busy moving more and more stuff into the storage locker before she left for Hawaii to marry Chad.

On Sunday, October 27, Brandon Boudreaux, who had been in hiding with his four children since the attempt on his life almost a month earlier, hired private investigator Rich Robertson of R3 Investigations. Gilbert Police had told Brandon that they could not launch an investigation until they found Alex Cox and the Jeep. They had advised Brandon to hire a private investigator to find something concrete for them to work with.

"Brandon called me in a panic," said Robertson. "He wanted to meet right away and just started spewing [everything] out about being the target of a shooting. It was just a crazy story."

Brandon said his soon-to-be-ex-wife, Melani, was part of a doomsday cult led by her aunt Lori and Chad Daybell. He told the PI how Alex Cox had tasered Lori's third husband, Joe Ryan, before shooting her fourth, Charles Vallow, dead. Now Brandon was convinced that Alex had tried to kill him and wanted him stopped.

As far as motive, Brandon told Robertson that he had a million-dollar life insurance policy for which Melani was the beneficiary.

The next day, Melani was in Rexburg to sign a lease on a town house right next door to Lori's and a stone's throw away from her uncle Alex's.

All the members of the cult were coming together in Rexburg. As Melani was signing the paperwork, Lori and Chad were preparing to leave for Hawaii to get married.

On Halloween, Chad posted a personal essay about his late wife, Tammy, in an LDS newsletter:

As I See It
BY CHAD DAYBELL

Moving into the Second Half of my Life

My dear wife Tammy passed away in her sleep early Saturday, October 19. When I awoke at around 6 a.m., it was clear she had been gone for several hours. It came as a shock. I couldn't believe I hadn't been awakened somehow, but all indications are that her spirit simply slipped away during the night. Her face looked serene, with her eyes closed and a slight smile. It was devastating to discover her that way, but I'm so grateful that her death was peaceful.

Tammy really was the anchor of our family and our publishing business. We have worked side by side from the moment we were married in the Manti Temple in 1990. It is safe to say I never would have become an author without her faith in me and her constant encouragement. Tammy herself wasn't a visionary woman, but she believed what I told her and trusted my decisions. She often said that she felt like Lehi's wife Sariah in the Book of Mormon, where her faith was often tested by the unexpected twists and turns of our lives.

Stepping into the Future

Tammy conveyed to me several messages . . . and I'm in the process of implementing what she has told me. She has indicated that my life has two parts that were planned even before I came to earth.

At 3:29 P.M. that afternoon, Alex and Melani flew to Phoenix, to pack up Melani's belongings for her move to Rexburg. She had hired a U-Haul moving truck, giving her aunt Lori's storage unit as the drop-off address.

"Alex helped me move on Halloween night," said Melani. "We were going to have a fresh start."

At around 8:30 P.M., Brandon Boudreaux's private investigator, Rich Robertson, pulled up a few doors down from Melani's old rental home in Chandler, Arizona. He had been busy running down leads to locate Melani, Alex, and the Jeep. Several days earlier, after finding Melani's house empty, he had left business cards with neighbors, asking them to call if she returned.

"I got a call from two of the neighbors [that night]," said Robertson. "I was out trick-or-treating with my grandkids and I dropped everything and said, 'I've got to go.'"

He arrived to find Melani and Alex in the garage, loading up a U-Haul truck with furniture, mattresses, and bags of clothing. They also dumped large plastic bags of young children's clothes and toys on the curb, with a sign reading FREE.

"It was creepy," said Robertson.

When they went inside the house, the PI sneaked up and slapped a GPS tracker underneath the U-Haul.

At around midnight they left the house and drove five miles into neighboring Gilbert to spend the night at their friend Zulema Pastenes's house.

Early Friday morning, Robertson showed up to stake out Pastenes's house. Around 8:00 A.M., Melani and Alex came out and drove off, stopping at Los Favoritos Mexican restaurant about a mile away. Robertson followed them in, taking a table nearby.

"My purpose was primarily to get a close enough eyeball look at him to verify it was Alex, and it was," said Robertson. "They were talking very quietly and I couldn't hear anything they were saying."

After leaving the restaurant, Melani and Alex returned to the rental house to finish packing. For the rest of the day they drove the U-Haul around, stopping at various people's houses with Robertson on their tail.

The private investigator was reporting back to Brandon Boudreaux on Melani and Alex's movements. Boudreaux breathed a sigh of relief knowing exactly where they were.

Robertson also sent him a photo of his children's clothes lying on the curb, asking if he wanted any of them. He did, so the PI gathered up the best ones and sent them to his client.

In the early hours of Saturday morning, Melani Boudreaux went on Facebook to post a bizarre, rambling attack on her ex-husband. She offered a $10,000 reward for any information about his and the children's whereabouts.

"Please help!" it began. "My ex-husband **Brandon Boudreaux** and four beautiful children have been missing. He began hiding with our children and he has not taken them to school since Oct 15, so they have now been unenrolled due to truant unexcused absences."

She complained that the police refused to help her, as something "fishy" was going on with their ongoing custody battle.

"My children could be in danger," she wrote. "I feel I should ask for help on here." Melani said that after eleven years of marriage she had discovered that Brandon was a wolf in sheep's clothing. "All I have is my testimony in our Savior Jesus Christ. Everything else has been taken from me."

She appealed for prayers and quoted seven passages from the Book of Mormon Doctrine and Covenants.

The next morning, Alex and Melani set out for Rexburg. Robertson's GPS tracker was monitoring their journey, and he had a colleague in Rexburg watch them unload the U-Haul at Melani's new town house at 565 Pioneer Road.

A few hours earlier, the Gilbert Police Department had asked Rexburg police to seize the green Jeep Wrangler that Alex had been driving during the attempt on Brandon's life. As it was now in Lori's possession, Detective Ray Hermosillo began a discreet surveillance on her to see exactly what she had been up to.

THIRTY-ONE

A BEACH WEDDING

On Sunday, November 3, Lori and Chad flew to Kauai and checked into a luxury suite at the Kauai Beach Resort. They went online and contacted a Hawaiian wedding-package company to inquire about a romantic beach wedding for November 5, just two weeks after Tammy's death.

The next morning they arrived at the company's office and met with the owner, Basil Hearn [not his real name], who was also a licensed Hawaiian minister.

"They were just so eager to meet and get it nailed down," said the Reverend Hearn. "One of them mentioned [November 5] being Guy Fawkes Day, and I thought that was sort of humorous."

Lori opted for a simple beach ceremony, saying they would recite their own vows to each other. They said they were in a hurry to be legally married as soon as possible.

When Hearn asked how they had met, Lori said Chad was a "brilliant writer," and they had fallen in love at one of his workshops. Chad visibly blushed.

"Lori was definitely much more forward than Chad," the Reverend Hearn remembered. "She really did all the pushing on this. She was definitely wearing the pants that day."

After signing up for a simple $600 wedding package on nearby Anini Beach, the couple left to get their marriage license.

At 1:00 P.M. on Tuesday, November 5, the Reverend Basil Hearn and his photographer, Jonathan Moeller, met Lori and Chad on Anini Beach. The couple both wore loose, flowing white cotton beach-casual wedding attire and were barefoot. Lori had a lacy top with a long, soft, and airy flowing skirt, her long blond hair styled to perfection. Chad sported a crew cut and wore a white hooded linen shirt and matching pants.

They arrived five minutes early and were in a hurry to get it over with. There were no witnesses except for the Universal Life Church minister and his freelance wedding photographer.

"They just breezed right in," said Hearn. "We just had the tiniest bit of small talk before they said, 'Let's do this.'"

Although this was Lori's fifth wedding ceremony, and her second on a Hawaiian beach, she seemed nervous and kept bursting into fits of "giddy laughter."

"They seemed like strange people . . . in their own world together," remembered Moeller. "[Chad] had this professional grin on his face all the time . . . like no one else existed."

The private beach was deserted when the Reverend Hearn blew his special conch shell to launch the ceremony. Moeller clicked away as the minister brought out his ukulele and serenaded Chad and Lori. They danced down the beach to the spot where their vows would be exchanged.

"I asked if they were ready to commit to each other," said the Reverend Hearn, "and if they had any words from the heart they wanted to speak to each other."

Chad asked the minister to step away so Chad and Lori could be alone for a couple of minutes. After finishing their private declarations of love, they exchanged the malachite gemstone wedding rings that Lori had bought on Amazon. And in true Hawaiian tradition, the minister wrapped leis around their wrists to bind them together.

He then pronounced Chad and Lori man and wife, and they shared their first lingering kiss as a married couple with the photographer snapping away.

"She was like a schoolgirl gazing in rapture at him," remembered Hearn. "She was much more the adoring one, and he seemed a little shy and sheepish. There were a couple of times when he really manned up, but most of the time she was the pilot."

A bottle of sparkling cider was opened for the official wedding toast, as champagne was not permitted on the beach. Lori and Chad then posed for romantic wedding photographs with the beautiful Hawaiian beach as a perfect background. In one of them Chad gallantly picked up Lori and held her in his arms as they French-kissed. In another he took the ukulele and pretended to serenade his new bride as she danced girlishly around him.

Although they had paid for a one-hour wedding, they wanted to leave after forty-five minutes.

"That made my eyebrows go up," said Hearn, "because usually brides just want to milk it as much as they can. But they wanted to knock it off early."

Two days later, Lori and Chad turned up at Jeani Martin's house at the northern tip of Kauai, asking if they could rent it. The seventy-year-old explained that it wasn't for rent, confused as to why they had thought it was. Chad explained that God had sent them to her address, so she invited the couple inside anyway.

"They needed someplace to stay the next day or two days at the latest," Martin later told *MailOnline* reporter Martin Gould. "They said their landlord was coming back from the mainland so they had to leave."

Lori said they owned their own house in Princeville, but it was being rented out. She also seemed well acquainted with the island.

"They said they had a blended family and all the kids got on," said Martin. "They would come out to Kauai to visit them."

After Lori and Chad left, Martin felt something was not quite right. So she googled *Chad Daybell* and immediately saw a report about his wife Tammy dying two weeks earlier.

"And I thought, 'There's something wrong with that,'" she said. "'He's not even grieving and he's as happy as he can be. They're kissing and rubbing bodies . . . like two teenagers let loose from their parents. This is just nuts.'"

The next morning, Chad emailed Kauai Dreams Realty, inquiring about a house in Princeville: "We are interested in seeing this property. Would the owners be interested in leasing . . . to a clean couple with no pets or children?"

* * *

That night, Kay Woodcock could not sleep. She went on her computer, accidentally stumbling upon her late brother's Google account. In it she found a stream of emails from Amazon for orders made after Charles's death. She clicked on one and saw an address in Rexburg, Idaho, instantly realizing that that was where Lori and J.J. had moved to.

"That's divine intervention," recalled Kay. "I truly believe that . . . Charles was speaking from beyond the grave."

As she sifted through all the orders, she was shocked to find one for wedding rings made two weeks before Tammy's death. There were also searches for beach-wedding attire.

"[Lori] is not tech savvy at all," said Kay, "so it never, I'm sure, ever crossed her mind that she was leaving a trail behind her."

For the rest of the night Kay, who knew all her brother's passwords, methodically accessed all Lori's internet activity since his death.

Four days later, Melani Boudreaux was arrested when she and Alex turned up at Brandon's parents' house in American Fork, Utah, to get her children. After they refused to leave, her terrified former father-in-law, Carlson Boudreaux, called 911.

When the 911 dispatcher asked what the emergency was, Boudreaux said his son's estranged wife was threatening him.

"I don't want her here!" he yelled. "She's in my garage! I'm not opening the door because it leads to my house. If I open the door, there's going to be a problem. Somebody tried to kill my son three weeks ago."

While he was on the phone to the dispatcher, Melani began banging on the connecting door in the garage, attempting to get in.

"Get out of my house! Get out of my garage! Get away from the door. Now!" Boudreaux screamed at her.

American Fork police arrived and arrested Melani, booking her into the Utah County Jail on charges of criminal trespass and domestic violence. The next day her uncle Alex posted her bail.

By mid-November, Chad and Lori were back in Rexburg as a newly married couple. A nervous Chad called Tammy's sister, Samantha, and her husband, Jason, saying he had something important he needed to tell them. But first he swore them to secrecy.

"[He said,] 'I got married while I was in Hawaii,'" Jason later told *Dateline*. "I sat there for a good five seconds and I said, 'Excuse me, you did *what*?'"

Samantha was shocked, believing the only possible explanation was that grief was clouding his judgment. She asked why he would remarry so soon after Tammy's death.

"He just told us that he's known [Lori] from before," said Samantha, "and she understood what he was going through because she had lost a spouse through a heart attack. Obviously I was really upset."

Chad also introduced his new bride to his parents, explaining that her daughter had died a year earlier and that Lori was an "empty nester."

THIRTY-TWO

"I'M A GOOD PERSON"

On Monday, November 25, Kay Woodcock called the Gilbert Police Department, reporting that she had not had any contact with her grandson J.J. for three months and his mother was not responding to her calls. Gilbert police than contacted Detective Ray Hermosillo of the Rexburg Police Department, who was already investigating Lori, Alex, and Melani as persons of interest in the attempted shooting of Brandon Boudreaux. Hermosillo agreed to carry out a welfare check for J.J.

The next morning, Detectives Hermosillo and Dave Hope arrived at Lori's town house. Alex Cox opened the door, Chad Daybell standing behind him. Detective Hermosillo asked if Lori was home and Alex said she was out. Hermosillo then asked if J.J. was home, explaining he was there to carry out a welfare check for the child.

Alex didn't respond, looking at Chad for some kind of signal. The detective asked again where J.J. was, and this time Alex replied he was with his grandmother Kay Woodcock in Louisiana.

"I told Mr. Cox that that was unlikely," Detective Hermosillo would later testify, "because Kay was the one who originally called in the welfare check."

When Hermosillo asked for Lori's cell phone number, Alex said he did not have it. This seemed odd to the detective, as he knew from his ongoing surveillance that they were close. Asked where they could find Lori, Alex said she was in his town house next door.

As Detective Hope was knocking on Alex's front door and getting no response, Chad Daybell came driving toward them in his black Equinox. Hermosillo flagged him down to question him further.

Chad told the detectives he had last seen J.J. at Alex's town house in October. When asked for Lori's phone number, Chad said he didn't have it, claiming he only knew her through Alex and had only met her a couple of times.

"I found it suspicious," said Hermosillo, "because I knew they were married two weeks prior in Hawaii."

Detective Hope came over to Chad's car, and Hermosillo asked Chad again for Lori's phone number, and this time Chad gave it to him. Asked why he hadn't initially, Chad said he felt that he was being accused of something.

Chad then drove off, and Detective Hermosillo called his superior, Detective Ron Ball, explaining that Alex Cox and Chad Daybell were acting suspiciously and he needed backup.

Soon afterward, Detective Ball and several other officers showed up at Lori's town house and knocked on the door, but there was no answer. They went next door to Melani's unit, but there was no answer there either. Detective Ball told Hermosillo to get a search warrant for Lori's house, and Hope left a message on her voice mail to call the Rexburg Police Department.

Detectives Ron Ball and Dave Stubbs later returned to Lori's town house, and this time she answered the door, saying that her brother Alex was with her.

Before Detective Ball could even explain why they were there, Lori told him she had just spoken to another police officer on the phone.

"Well, this is a big mess," she said with an air of frustration.

"And what did he ask you?" said Detective Ball.

"He was just saying that he wanted to do a welfare check on J.J."

"So J.J. would be where?"

"He's with one of my friends in Arizona."

"Who's the friend he's with?"

"My friend Melanie Gibb." Lori sounded annoyed. "My son has autism. I gave him all the information on the phone."

Detective Ball told her they were concerned because the officers who came earlier had gotten "a bad vibe" after asking Alex and Chad about J.J. They were evasive and their answers were "kind of weird."

"It is very weird," snapped Lori. "I've had to move around a lot. One of my brothers is trying to kill [me], not the brother that was here obviously. He's kind of my protector."

As Lori explained how her brother Adam had been working with her late husband to kill her for her life insurance policy, the detectives raised their eyebrows.

"It's been a horrible year for us," sighed Lori.

She then launched into a venomous attack on Kay Woodcock, saying that her drug-addicted son had had a baby with his girlfriend, another drug addict. As a baby, she explained, J.J. had been taken by Child Protective Services and given to his grandmother Kay.

"She wanted my husband and I to adopt him, which we did," Lori told the detectives. "[He] died earlier this year. He passed away."

Lori said that since Charles's death, Kay had been "really horrible" to her and had fought her for J.J. "She's kind of the paternal threat. Does that make any sense? I'm sorry."

"Okay, thank you," replied Detective Ball. "That's what I needed—the paternal threat."

"So what happened was," Lori continued, apparently pleased by his reaction, "my husband, we were married for fifteen years and had raised all these five kids together, switched his life insurance to *her*, right."

"To who?" asked Ball, sounding confused.

"To his sister, who got a million dollars and we got nothing," Lori fumed, "so I knew she was going to try and sue me for [J.J.]. Because now she has this million dollars, she can hire people who will help him. And I have nothing."

"But you have legal custody."

"He's my son. I adopted him when he was two years [old]. So she does nothing but wants to cause me trouble, so I don't tell people the truth about where we are and what we're doing, because of those reasons. So I look like a suspect but I'm not. I'm a good person, raise all my kids. I've done everything that I'm supposed to do, but everyone is causing me trouble right now."

"We don't want to cause a lot of trouble. How long have you been here?"

"We moved up here in September. My daughter had enrolled in BYU-I [Brigham Young University–Idaho]."

Lori described her life in Idaho as "a nightmare," saying she was moving back to Arizona because J.J. didn't like his new school.

She furiously accused Kay of sending her threatening emails and documenting everything to use against her to get custody of J.J. Detective Ball said he was only concerned about J.J.'s welfare, but understood things better after hearing her side of the story.

"It's awful," said Lori. "I feel like I'm being tracked all the time. Why are the police coming to my door?"

Then Detective Ball casually asked who the other man was that officers had seen earlier with her brother Alex.

Lori acted as if she hardly knew her new husband. "My brother and his friend probably. They're moving Chad."

"Chad from around here?" the detective asked, aware she had just married him. "What's his last name?"

"Daybell. He's an author."

"Doesn't he live out in [Salem]? Isn't that the Chad Daybell that . . . I think his wife passed away recently?"

When Lori didn't answer, Detective Stubbs said the name Chad Daybell sounded familiar as a local author.

"I think I know who he is," said Detective Ball. "Has he got a couple of daughters?"

"I think he has lots of kids," said Lori.

Suddenly she launched into a manic diatribe about going into hiding after discovering emails between her brother Adam and her late husband, Charles, planning to get rid of her.

"Well, that's why I'm moving back," she said. "I'm going to live with my friend Melanie Gibb, [but] don't tell anyone her name. I've been staying over here with my brother because he protects me. He's *very* protective of me."

Unable to reach Melanie, the detectives left a voice mail and went straight back to Lori's.

"Hi, Lori," said Detective Ball. "Sorry to bother you, but we haven't been able to get hold of your friend."

"Melanie. She's probably at *Frozen Two* right now because that's one thing [J.J.] wanted to do."

Detective Ball told Lori to contact Melanie Gibb and ask her to call them as soon as possible.

While the detectives were questioning Lori, a nervous Chad Daybell called Melanie Gibb, who was at David Warwick's house in Pleasant Grove, Utah. Chad warned her to expect a call from Rexburg police and asked her not to pick up the phone. He said the police were over at Lori's house asking where J.J. was, and she had told them he was staying with her.

Melanie was "confused," as Lori had told her that J.J. was with his grandparents in Louisiana. She asked Chad if J.J. was at Kay's house, and he replied no.

About an hour later she got a call from Lori, who seemed "cheery" and "upbeat," saying that everything was fine. She told Melanie to tell the police that she had J.J. and they were at the movies watching *Frozen II.*

"She asked me to pick up my phone," said Gibb, "and take a random picture of kids running around . . . to make it look like it was J.J."

Lori explained that Kay was trying to kidnap J.J. and Lori was protecting him. She had told the police she would be in Arizona at Thanksgiving to bring J.J. home.

"[I was] very confused," Gibb later testified. "I had a very bad feeling in my stomach."

Soon afterward, Gilbert police detective Ryan Pillar called Gibb and she didn't answer.

Later that night Melanie called him back and lied: "I told him that I had been with J.J., and he would soon be back with Lori."

At 9:30 P.M., Detective Pillar drove over to Melanie Gibb's house in Gilbert, Arizona, but she was not there. He called her again, and this time she admitted that J.J. was not with her and that she hadn't seen him since September.

After the Rexburg detectives left, Lori and Chad were in a panic. The police were asking too many questions about J.J. that they couldn't answer. They decided to flee Rexburg and hide out in Hawaii until things calmed down.

Lori started packing up some of her clothes, and a neighbor saw her and Alex loading up his truck with large bags. When asked if they were moving, Lori said they were going on a trip.

Around midnight Lori and Chad drove out of Rexburg and headed west into the night.

The next morning, Rexburg police obtained search warrants from a Madison County judge for Lori's, Alex's, and Melani's town houses. The warrants stated that investigators were looking for "any evidence that the boy was residing in any of these residences and/or evidence of foul play or the commission of a crime." They were also authorized to take fingerprints and collect blood, hair, and hygiene products for DNA.

When they arrived at Lori's house, there was no sign of her. Almost all her clothes were gone, although her furniture was still there.

Detectives searched her house and photographed it from every angle. They found a bottle of J.J.'s prescription tranquilizer, risperidone, dated January 2019 and still containing seventeen pills. They also searched Alex's town house, which was abandoned.

Later that day they searched the storage unit, finding photo albums of Tylee and J.J., as well as their clothes, bikes, and a scooter. There were also two quilts with pictures of J.J. and Tylee that Lori had sewn into them.

That night, two detectives arrived at Colby Ryan's house, asking where his mother and siblings were.

"I just started flipping out," said Colby, "like, 'What are you talking about?'"

After they left, he called his mom and asked what was going on, and why the police were looking for Tylee and J.J. "And she basically just said, 'I've got it, I'll take care of it. I love you.' That was the last time I spoke with my mom."

THIRTY-THREE

NO TASK WOULD BE TOO DIFFICULT FOR ALEX

Chad and Lori Daybell spent Thanksgiving in Southern California, visiting the Knott's Berry Farm amusement park in Buena Park. They made plans to stay in Kauai until things cooled down and they could return. But their cult's mission would continue without them, as Chad's forecast of end-times was now just eight months away.

The next phase of the cult called for two marriages in Las Vegas over the Thanksgiving weekend. Alex Cox would wed fifty-five-year-old Zulema Pastenes, a longtime friend who was close to Lori and Chad. And Melani Boudreaux would marry a Rexburg man, Ian Pawlowski, whom she had met on an LDS dating site only a few days earlier.

She had already introduced Pawlowski to her aunt Lori and Chad Daybell, who had both vetted him and given their approval.

"They said they were planning on taking off . . . to Hawaii," Pawlowski said, "and that I'd be taking the reins concerning care of Melani."

On Friday, November 29, the two couples drove to Las Vegas for the weddings. Melani, whose divorce to Brandon had only been finalized ten days earlier, would be given away by her uncle Alex.

They all arrived at A Chapel of Love on South First Street for Alex's wedding to Zulema. A couple of blocks away from the strip, the no-frills venue advertises itself as offering "Affordable Las Vegas Weddings." The basic $100 ceremony was conducted by the Reverend Carlos Vallesillas and lasted just three and a half minutes.

"He just wanted a simple, short-and-sweet get married and be out of there," said the Reverend Vallesillas.

On the marriage certificate Cox inexplicably changed his name from Alexander Lamar Cox to Alexander Lamar Pastenes.

"That was the first time I'd ever seen a groom take a bride's last name," said the chapel owner, Sebastian Salas, who booked the wedding. "Zulema was the one that coordinated and paid for everything. Alex was quiet and wasn't too eager to add anything onto his package, like flowers for his bride or even have a picture taken of the wedding."

The next day, Melani and Ian Pawlowski were wed at the same venue, in a more elaborate ceremony.

The bride wore a white chiffon wedding dress and carried a bouquet of flowers as she was led into the marriage office by her beaming uncle. With Alex and Zulema looking on, Ian and Melani took their wedding vows and were declared husband and wife.

On their wedding night, Melani began to initiate Ian into the cult and reveal some of its secrets. Previously she had only told him bits and pieces of her radical spiritual beliefs, which she had learned from Chad and Lori.

Pawlowski had thought the beliefs "fun and exciting" and hadn't taken them too seriously. "It felt like many of them were ripped out of a Dungeons & Dragons manual. Between the stats, accounts of dark and light weapons . . . it sounded like someone had created a tabletop [Book of Mormon game] based on the Bible."

That night Melani shared the cult's beliefs to a frightening new level.

"She explained zombies," Pawlowski later wrote, "and her fears about what Chad and Lori stated concerning the original spirits being caught in limbo until the body's death."

Melani said that in June her ex-husband, Brandon, had been possessed by a demon. She had been told through a revelation that something would have to happen to him, so he could progress and the Lord's plan could continue.

"She shared the idea," wrote Pawlowski, "that Chad and Lori could have directed Al to take a shot at Brandon."

Melani then said that Chad and Lori had told her that J.J. and Tylee had become zombies, expressing concern that her uncle Alex may have been told to "take care" of them.

"She explained that Al had great faith," he wrote, "and never wavered in his trust to the Lord. No task would be too difficult or great for him."

That same night, David Warwick called Chad Daybell, demanding to know where J.J. and Tylee were. Chad refused to tell him, saying it would endanger everybody.

"And I said, 'How is me knowing where J.J. is going to threaten my safety?'" he remembered. "And he just said, 'I just can't tell you, Dave.'"

Then Melanie Gibb called Alex, asking why Chad and Lori were being so secretive about J.J.'s whereabouts.

"And he said I did not want to know," said Gibb, "and they won't be found."

The next morning, Chad and Lori flew out of Los Angeles to Kauai on American Airlines. Lori brought along J.J.'s and Tylee's birth certificates, as well as Tylee's cell phone and bank card, which she was now regularly using. She was also still collecting J.J.'s $4,800 a month Social Security benefits.

Chad opened up a bank account at the First Hawaiian Bank, transferring more than $150,000 from Tammy's life insurance payout into it. It would easily keep the newlyweds living first-class for the next few months.

After hearing Melani's alarming story about zombies and her concerns that Chad, Lori, and Alex might actually have acted on these beliefs, Ian Pawlowski was terrified. He feared that he had just married into a dangerously sinister cult.

He texted his ex-wife, Natalie, and gave her Melani's full name, asking her to check out his new bride and see what she could find. Natalie googled Melani and learned about her recent divorce from Brandon Boudreaux. Natalie found his phone number and called him.

Brandon informed her that Melani was deeply involved in a murderous cult led by Chad Daybell and Lori Vallow. He said they had tried to kill him and he had narrowly escaped with his life, although they had succeeded in killing Lori's ex-husband, Charles Vallow.

Natalie was terrified and told her ex-husband that she was going to the police in case their four kids were in danger. Ian agreed to accompany her.

On December 3, Melani arrived back in Rexburg to find police had gone into her town house, searching for any sign of J.J. She later claimed that they seized her computer, iPad, and other electronic equipment.

She immediately went to the Rexburg Police Department, where Detective Ray Hermosillo and several other officers interviewed her for the next five hours.

"I was asking Miss Boudreaux how we could get ahold of Mr. Daybell or Lori Vallow," Hermosillo later testified. "I did ask about [J.J. and] Tylee."

After the interview, Melani told Ian that the police officers were possessed with the dark spirits of two of the original twelve disciples of Cain. One day later, Melani pled no contest to criminal trespass of her former in-law's property, after American Fork City Police dropped the domestic violence charge. She was placed on unsupervised probation for a year and fined $733. A 180-day jail term was suspended.

Ian was now having to sneak around Melani so she didn't discover that he was relaying information back to his ex-wife. He feared that Melani was now isolating him by not letting him talk to his family. She also insisted on driving him to and from work.

"[She] makes him listen to weird podcasts," Natalie emailed Brandon Boudreaux on December 4. "She tells him that there are light and dark weapons . . . and that in a past life she was the niece of Jesus."

Natalie told Brandon that she was "legitimately scared" for her and her kids' lives, saying if Melani found out Ian was going to the police, Natalie would be blamed.

"If she is convinced that I am a demon and God tells her to kill me," she told Brandon, "I could end up a missing person case."

After Lori and Chad disappeared from Rexburg, Detective Ball called in the Phoenix FBI to help search for J.J. and Tylee. Agents began listening to Preparing a People podcasts to get better acquainted with the leading characters in this increasingly bizarre missing children's case. When they learned about all the mysterious deaths surrounding Lori and Chad, they set up a joint task force with the Rexburg, Chandler, and Gilbert Police Departments.

Over the next several days law enforcement served search warrants on the L.I.F.E. school and Gilbert Pediatrics for all of J.J.'s and Tylee's records. They also began investigating any state assistance that Lori had received for her special needs child.

Melanie Gibb called the Rexburg Police Department, admitting that she had lied at Chad's and Lori's behest. She said they had both called her on November 26, asking her to tell police that J.J. was with her in Arizona. Detective Ball later wrote that Gibb's lie had delayed the investigation to find J.J. as detectives tracked down a false lead.

On December 5, Ian Pawlowski and his ex-wife, Natalie, were interviewed at the Rexburg police station by Detectives Hermosillo and Hope and an FBI special agent. Ian told them that Chad, Lori, and Alex may have planned the attempt on Brandon Boudreaux's life, and that he believed J.J. and Tylee were in serious danger.

"I shared that Melani had concerns about them," remembered Pawlowski. "The kids' lives could be forfeit[ed] based on the idea that they're not really Tylee and J.J. anymore."

Ian also told them that Chad had warned that there would soon be terrible earthquakes in Salt Lake City, and that Alex and Zulema had remained behind in Las Vegas to prepare for them.

In another solo interview with Detective Ron Ball and an FBI special agent named Travis, Pawlowski had agreed to do anything he could to help law enforcement find J.J. and Tylee. After some initial concern that he might be spying for Chad and Lori, Ian convinced them that he was only there for his kids and to protect Melani.

Travis asked if he'd be willing to spy on Melani, secretly recording any phone calls she made to Chad and Lori that could lead to the children. Pawlowski agreed and was given a secret thumb-drive recording device to put on his key chain.

"I thought that would be an easy way out," he explained. "Chad and

Lori will probably call and talk to Melani [and] we'll get this recorded. They'll slip up and say where the kids are . . . and I can take my new wife and we'll live happily ever after."

For the next two weeks, Pawlowski went undercover for the FBI, encouraging Melani to open up further about Chad and Lori and their cult, as well as recording any phone calls to them in Hawaii. He was also in daily contact with another FBI special agent who would debrief him.

Now realizing how dangerous the cult might be, as well as Melani's involvement in it, Ian Pawlowski prepared a detailed breakdown of everything she had ever told him about the cult and Chad's teachings, if it was ever needed as protection.

He also included Chad's manifesto of his beliefs, explaining multiple probations, zombies, translated beings, and teleportation.

In it, Chad explained that a minimum of nine mortal lives were required to become exalted, but more were needed to become a God such as he was. He believed multiple sealings allowed mates to choose whether to have one "true spouse," or many.

Translated beings, such as himself and Lori, were immortal and did not need sleep or food. Although they could be injured, they had accelerated healing powers, so wounds were never fatal. He outlined that there were fifty "dark translated beings," naming Rexburg Detectives Hope and Hermosillo as two of them. He wrote that they were working under the direction of Satan, Lucifer, and Cain.

Perhaps even more chilling was his definition of zombies as spirits trapped in limbo and unable to progress to a new mortal life.

"The only way forward is to await the death of their current possessed body," he wrote, alluding to Chad's warped rationale for murder.

Translated beings also possessed powers of teleportation, allowing them to teleport anywhere to perform the Lord's assigned duties.

His manifesto also outlined the Church of the Firstborn and the 144,000 and its role in the Second Coming, which he and Lori believed the Lord had appointed them to lead.

"The mysteries of God are revealed to those who have become part of it," he wrote. "Prophet of the Mormon church presides over the general congregation, while others are called specifically to run the church of the firstborn."

Under a final section he called "Spiritual Gifts/Powers," Chad bizarrely wrote that wizards, sorcerers, and witches actually existed, as did the spells and curses in J. K. Rowling's *Harry Potter* books, which required "great focused will to use."

THIRTY-FOUR

"HE IS SAFE AND HAPPY"

The first week of December, Lori and Chad Daybell signed a long-term lease for a house in the stunningly beautiful Villas on the Prince in Kauai. The luxury gated complex is situated right at the entrance of Princeville, with its own pool and a private path to the Prince Golf Course. Just a twenty-minute walk from Anini Beach, where the two were married, it was directly across the road from where Lori and Charles Vallow had once lived.

Soon after they signed the $4,000-a-month lease for 4141 Queen Emma's Drive, large boxes started arriving from Rexburg, Idaho, and piled up on their porch. Furniture soon followed.

Neighbor Steve Latham was asked by the realtor to bring the boxes inside until the new tenants came, which he did.

When the Daybells finally arrived, they introduced themselves to Latham, thanking him for bringing everything inside the house. Although polite, the newly married couple were not overly friendly. They made small talk, avoiding any questions about why they were there and where they came from.

"Usually when you meet people that are moving here, they're very excited about being on this beautiful island," said Latham. "They seemed . . . guarded."

Over the next couple of months, the new renters were rarely seen in their newly furnished condo.

"It seemed vacant most of the time," said Latham. "I don't know if they were living there or not."

* * *

After lying to the police about J.J.'s whereabouts, Melanie Gibb started to realize the full implications of what she had done. With all of Chad's and Lori's talk of zombies, Melanie became scared that if anything bad had happened to the kids, she would be seen as an accessory.

After discussing it at length with David Warwick, they decided to record a phone call with Lori and Chad, to try to get them to incriminate themselves.

"There was something going on that was awfully wrong," explained Gibb. "[I wanted] to show my innocence."

At 3:45 P.M. on December 8, Melanie called Chad on speakerphone, with Warwick recording the twenty-one-minute call. They still had no idea that Lori and Chad were in Hawaii.

"I was wondering, where are you guys?" Melanie asked after saying hello.

"We're just hanging out . . . near Idaho," lied Chad.

"I see. I just want to ask you a question, if you don't mind, Lori?"

"By all means," she replied.

"Remember we talked about J.J. going to Kay's house, and you told me that he went there, and now he's not there. I was wondering, What happened?"

Lori said she had had to move him elsewhere because Kay had threatened to kidnap him.

"Is there a reason I should be in danger to know where he is?" Melanie asked.

"There are people after me, but if you know, it puts you in danger."

"Right, so you're worried, okay?"

"We keep him protected," said Lori, with an edge to her voice.

"We keep you protected," added Chad.

"I appreciate that," said Melanie. "I was wondering why you told the police he was with me. Is J.J. safe?"

"He is safe and happy," replied Lori.

Melanie then asked why Alex had told her that she didn't want to know where J.J. was, and that he would never be found.

"I don't even know why he would say that," answered Lori defensively.

"I don't even want Al to know. I don't want anybody to know . . . so that he can be safe."

Then Gibb asked when they were coming back to continue their sacred mission.

"I will do whatever the Lord needs me to do," replied Lori obliquely.

"I just wondered if I was ever going to see you again?"

"Absolutely you will." Lori then accused Kay of working with the police "in some dark capacity" against Lori, and sending threatening emails and texts.

"I'm just worried for you guys," said Melanie, "because [J.J.'s] missing."

"I know exactly where he is," snapped Lori. "He's perfectly fine and safe."

Melanie then shared a scripture from the Book of Mormon, saying it paralleled the present situation. She cited the evil, adulterous king Noah, who presided over a wicked kingdom and broke every commandment.

"When we open the door to Satan," warned Gibb, "he comes in and then he attacks."

"I agree with you one hundred percent. We have not opened the door to darkness, Mel. I promise you that I have done nothing wrong in this case, but sometimes you have to hide in the cavity of the rock for your own life's safety. There is a lot of darkness on the earth."

Lori suddenly became suspicious, asking if the call was being recorded for the police to use against her. "I don't know what your intention is. I love you with all my heart and have forever."

Melanie countered that if Lori and Chad really loved her, they would not have told the police she had J.J. "That's not what a friend does. That just makes me look weird. You have to think of my welfare if you love me."

Lori insisted that she was only following God's instructions and would never harm anyone.

"I believe that you have been deceived by Satan," Gibb told her. "I mean Tammy dies, and then your husband dies, and then [J.J.'s] missing. It doesn't sound like God's plan to me. It gives me a gut feeling—it feels weird. It doesn't feel right."

"You know me, Mel. This does not sound like you. It sounds like you've been influenced by somebody dark, who wants you to believe dark things . . . and have fear in the celestial world."

Chad said that Tammy's sister, Samantha, was spreading wild conspiracy theories about his involvement in Tammy's death, and he hoped Melanie had not fallen for that "dark scheme" against him.

"It's just not true," he reassured Melanie. "My own children were there. They testified that Tammy had been getting weaker and sick. I begged her to go to the doctor. Her heart was failing her [and] she was physically falling apart. She need[ed] doctors and she just passed away. That's how it happened. These conspiracy theories just make me sick to my stomach. Absolutely sick."

He explained that Tammy's dying at a young age had been foretold. He had always known that his life would have two segments, but had no idea Lori would be in his second. He assured Melanie that Tammy was now on a special mission and had already visited him and their children since passing.

"Melanie," he said firmly, "you just have to have faith, and this is not some kind of master plan. There's no way Lori and I could ever come up with this."

Apparently unaware that Warwick was also listening, Lori accused him of planting doubts in Melanie's mind, saying she now regretted giving Melanie access to their highly privileged level of spiritual teachings. "I wish you didn't have as much knowledge as you have because you will be accountable for the knowledge that you do have now."

Melanie then called them Korihors, a Book of Mormon reference to the Antichrist. She accused them of acting purely on lust.

"Is that me?" replied Lori angrily. "Carnal and natural desires?"

"Well, you've got a lot of natural desires. We all know that."

"That is what you think of me—Korihor? Are you kidding me right now?"

Melanie doubled down, comparing them to the Antichrist in the Scriptures who had opened "dark portals" by disobeying God.

"[The Lord] has my back," replied Lori defiantly.

"Well, if he has your back, you would not be where you are and we could find J.J. Where is he? That's not the Lord's work."

"I could tell you . . . where J.J. is right now," Lori retorted, attempting to turn things around, "and that would not be good for J.J. So I'm sorry that you don't want me to protect my children. I can tell you're just adversarial now. I love you. I'm sorry you feel that way."

Lori then accused her onetime best friend of working with Charles Vallow's sister against her. "I never had any idea that you would be the person of all people to trap me. I cannot believe it."

"I'm very troubled," said Melanie. "You being with Chad before he's even divorced is unusual behavior for a person that's seen Jesus Christ."

"Really? Do you know what the future behavior would be if you're seeing Jesus Christ? He is protecting me, and he will protect me against this accusation. And we will both stand there with him and he'll tell me if I was lying or not."

Lori hung up. It was the last time the two ever spoke.

The next day Melanie Gibb called Detective Ryan Pillar, saying she had important new information for him. She went to the Gilbert police station and handed him a thumb drive of her damning phone call with Lori and Chad.

After listening to Chad's strange, defensive comments about Tammy's death, Detective Pillar called Fremont County sheriff Len Humphries, suggesting he take a closer look at exactly how she had died.

Sheriff Humphries got a court order to exhume Tammy's body so a proper autopsy could quietly be performed.

At 6:00 A.M. on Wednesday, December 11, about a dozen people gathered at Tammy's grave, including county attorneys, two detectives from the Rexburg Police Department, Utah and Idaho sheriffs, and a funeral director.

Ironically, the exhumation was organized by the Springville city administrative manager Rod Oldroyd, who had once been Chad and Tammy's boss.

"It was kept quiet," said Oldroyd. "It wasn't a media circus."

Tammy's body was taken to the Utah Medical Examiner's Office to be autopsied and photographed, and she was back in the ground by two thirty that same afternoon.

THIRTY-FIVE

FALLING APART

After a brief honeymoon in Las Vegas, Alex Cox moved into Zulema Pastenes's house in Gilbert, Arizona, to prepare for the upcoming earthquakes. Her daughter Cara disapproved of the relationship and moved out. Later, Cara would tell police that Zulema, Alex, and his sister Lori were all "Preppers," actively preparing for the end of the world.

Since Alex had been questioned about J.J.'s whereabouts and Lori and Chad had fled Idaho, the pressure on him was mounting. The cult now lay in ruins, and Melanie Gibb had warned him she was going to the police with what she knew.

Alex must have known it was only a matter of time before he faced even more searching questions from law enforcement about Tylee and J.J.

On December 7, he drove to Los Algodones, Mexico, to buy prescription drugs. It is believed that he had decided to make the ultimate sacrifice and commit suicide to protect Lori and Chad so they could continue their divine mission. Later, others close to Alex questioned whether he had developed a guilty conscience and couldn't live with the horrors of what he'd done.

At 8:00 A.M. on Thursday, December 12, one day after Tammy's body was exhumed, Zulema went to work, leaving Alex alone in the house with her twenty-five-year-old son, Joseph. She later told police that Alex had been complaining of shortness of breath since his four-hundred-mile day-trip to Mexico.

Alex was due to meet his niece Melani halfway between Rexburg and

Gilbert to collect his possessions from his now-abandoned town house. But at the last minute he canceled, saying he wasn't feeling well.

Just before 1:00 P.M., Zulema texted Alex and got a brief response.

Soon afterward Alex called a friend, asking for a blessing over the phone. After talking to Alex the friend became so concerned that he called Zulema and told her to go straight home. She called her new husband, who struggled to speak, saying she was coming home.

She asked her son to check on Alex. He went into the bathroom and found his new stepfather lying unconscious on the floor in his own feces, gasping for breath.

At 3:20 P.M., Joseph dialed 911.

"Okay, what is the emergency?" asked the dispatcher.

"Um, I have an older male here. He's just passed out here in my bathroom."

"Is he breathing normally? . . . Hello?"

"I hope so," Joseph finally replied.

The operator told Joseph to turn Alex onto his back and do chest compressions.

"I'll try."

Joseph asked Alex to turn over on his back but got no response. Joseph told the operator that Alex was now making a high-pitched *whoo* sound as he exhaled.

"He's not breathing," said Joseph. "He's too big."

A hysterical Zulema then burst into the bathroom, screaming.

"Okay, ma'am," said the dispatcher, "the paramedics are pulling up. But in the mean[time] . . . we need to get him flat on his back and we need to give him chest compressions, okay?"

"I've got it," said Zulema. "Yeah, I know how to do CPR."

Zulema managed to get Alex on his back and straddled him, beginning chest compressions as paramedics arrived.

But it was too late to save Alex, lying dead on the bathroom floor at age fifty-one, pink foam coming out of his mouth.

When the emergency call went out on the police radio network, Gilbert police instantly recognized the name Alex Cox; he was on their radar in several other investigations. Officers were dispatched to Zulema's house to investigate.

They arrived as Alex's body was being carried out of the house by Gilbert Fire Department medics to go to Banner Gateway hospital. Zulema went with them.

Officer Jason Biggs met a distressed Zulema in the hospital trauma room, where she was anxiously sitting next to her husband's body. Initially she refused to be interviewed but finally agreed to talk to the officer in an adjoining room.

"Zulema asked me why she was being questioned," Officer Biggs later wrote in his report, "and if she was considered a suspect in the death of her husband. I assured her she was not a suspect."

Zulema said she had married Alex two weeks ago after knowing him for a year. He had recently complained of trouble breathing. When the officer asked about Alex's sister Lori, Zulema seemed vague and evasive. She claimed not to know where Lori lived and said the last time she had tried texting her, the number had been disconnected. Zulema said she had only met Lori a few times in Arizona.

"She had not seen Lori since she moved [to Idaho] a few months ago," reported Officer Biggs. "She did not think Lori was married."

Alex Cox was officially pronounced dead at 4:19 P.M. Gilbert police quickly got a search warrant for Zulema's house, looking for any clues to J.J.'s whereabouts and Charles Vallow's death. Detective Ryan Pillar, who had interviewed Melanie Gibbs several days earlier, was assigned to the case.

As her residence was searched, Detective Pillar interviewed Zulema outside in his unmarked police vehicle. After receiving a phone call, she informed Pillar that she wanted a lawyer present before she said anything further.

She got out of the police car and walked into her house, with Detective Pillar following.

The search of the house and Alex's vehicle continued, and seized items were brought back to the Gilbert police station to be analyzed.

On December 14, an autopsy on Alex Cox's body was performed by the Maricopa County medical examiner, Lesley E. Wallis, with Detective Pillar and an FBI special agent present.

"There were no obvious signs of trauma to his person," wrote Pillar, "or outstanding evidence discovered during the exam."

Two days later, the medical examiner ruled that Alex Cox had died of natural causes. Blood clots had been found in his lungs, and he suffered from severe atherosclerotic and hypertensive cardiovascular disease, leading to high blood pressure caused by plaque buildup in his arteries.

Barry and Janis Cox, who had no idea that their oldest son had even gotten married, arranged for him to be cremated and held a small memorial service.

On December 19, Ian Pawlowski broke down and told Melani that he had been spying on her for the FBI. He confessed to recording her telephone conversations with Chad and Lori to help gather evidence against them. After several weeks of snooping around for law enforcement he could no longer handle the stress and told the FBI that he would longer help them.

Pawlowski had compiled a detailed dossier of everything he had told the FBI, along with Chad Daybell's spiritual manifesto. He gave it to his ex-wife, Natalie, who handed it over to Brandon Boudreaux to use in his bitter custody battle with Melani.

Melani forgave her new husband immediately, saying she could see why he had done it.

"As big of a betrayal as it sounds and felt in the moment, too," she said, "I have to look at the entirety of it. And he's recording my conversations [between Chad and Lori] and there's nothing there. I don't hold any resentment for what Ian did."

THIRTY-SIX

GOING PUBLIC

On Friday, December 20, Rexburg police and the FBI went public with their search for J.J. and Tylee, linking it to Tammy Daybell's newly opened death investigation. They issued a dramatic two-page press release with the headline "Missing Endangered Children," ensuring that the story would make front-page news all over America.

It revealed that Tammy's remains had been exhumed and an autopsy conducted, calling her death "suspicious." This was news to Tammy's children, who had not been informed of the autopsy.

But the release mainly focused on Tylee and J.J., who hadn't been seen since September 2019, and their mother's mysterious disappearance after a welfare check in late November.

"Investigators . . . spoke with Lori Vallow and her new husband Chad Daybell," the release read, "who indicated Joshua was staying with a family friend in Arizona. Investigators left and learned later that day that Joshua had not been staying with the friend."

The release went on to say that family members were concerned about J.J. and his seventeen-year-old sister, Tylee Ryan, who had also disappeared and had not been reported missing.

"Attempts to obtain the cooperation of Lori Vallow and Chad Daybell in locating the children have been unsuccessful."

Rexburg police also released photos of J.J. and Tylee, along with their physical descriptions, adding that the seven-year-old might be in need of medical attention. They also issued headshots of Lori and Chad, making them America's most wanted couple.

* * *

On Saturday morning, the *Idaho State Journal* printed a front-page story with the headline "Alarming Missing Persons Case Unfolding in East Idaho."

"The suspicious death of a popular librarian at Central Elementary School in Sugar City," it began, "and the ensuing disappearance of her husband's new stepchildren has caused law enforcement and the FBI [to] ask the public's help in searching for [them]."

Fremont County sheriff Len Humphries named Chad Daybell and Lori Vallow as persons of interest in the widening investigation.

"We're working very hard to find more information," said the sheriff, "and to follow up everything that we can."

A few hours later, Brandon Boudreaux and Kay Woodcock, who were now working together to find the couple, posted on Facebook about the attempt on Brandon's life and all the mysterious deaths surrounding Lori Vallow. They forwarded the post to the media to help them start piecing together the real story of Chad and Lori's dangerous cult.

"I know firsthand how scary these people can be," Brandon wrote. "But I want to be a person who stands and fights for truth and justice [and] I can no longer sit by when by sharing I might help someone who knows something to come forward."

In interviews to the *East Idaho News* and other media outlets, Kay and Brandon condemned Preparing a People as a "dangerous organization," accusing it of being responsible for Lori's and Melani's religious radicalization.

"I don't want to attack anyone's beliefs," said Boudreaux, "but when you look at the fruit that comes from this group and its beliefs . . . it certainly, from my mind, doesn't come from God."

Three thousand miles away in Kauai, Lori and Chad read the headlines with horror. Over the Christmas holiday they hired the Rexburg law firm of Rigby, Andrus & Rigby to represent them. One month to the day after fleeing Rexburg, their newly appointed attorney, Sean Bartholick, issued a terse statement to the media:

"Chad Daybell was a loving husband and has the support of his children in this matter. Lori Daybell is a devoted mother and resents assertions to the contrary. We look forward to addressing allegations once they have moved beyond speculation and rumor."

Bartholick also informed the Fremont Sheriff's Office that any further communication with Chad should go through him.

A few hours later, Michael and Nancy James of Preparing a People issued a "Statement on Recent Events" on their website. They denied that PaP was a cult, distancing themselves from Chad and Lori by removing all podcasts and references to them from their website.

"We consider Chad Daybell a good friend," it read, "but have since learned of things we had no idea about. In light of current concerning media reports and ongoing criminal investigations . . . we feel it inappropriate to not [sic] promote any media content that may feature or contain references to either Chad Daybell or Lori Vallow."

The next morning, Rexburg police captain Gary Hagen told reporters that his tiny department had been fielding tips from all over the country since the story broke. But he admitted they were no nearer to finding the children than they were two weeks ago. A team of eight officers were following up all credible tips, but they needed to speak to Lori and Chad.

"We just strongly feel," Hagen said, "that if the mom and dad . . . knew that the kids were safe, they would show proof of it. But we have yet to see anything."

On December 30, Rexburg police issued another press release, with an update on the missing children. It thanked the media for all their help in publicizing the story and appealed for Lori and Chad to do the right thing. It described Lori's apparent lack of concern as "astonishing."

"We strongly believe that Joshua and Tylee's lives are in danger," it stated. "Lori Vallow/Daybell, the adopted mother of Joshua and biological mother of Tylee, has completely refused to assist this investigation."

It added that law enforcement had information that Lori either knew where her children were now or knew what had happened to them, but had refused to cooperate.

THIRTY-SEVEN

WHERE ARE THE CHILDREN?

On Friday, January 3, 2020, special agents from the FBI's Evidence Response Team, assisted by officers from the Rexburg Police Department and the Fremont Sheriff's Office, raided Chad Daybell's property, while his sons Seth and Garth waited outside. The officers spent the entire day executing a search warrant for probable cause, looking for any clues regarding the whereabouts of Tylee and J.J. and Tammy's untimely death.

The officers paid special attention to a shed at the back of the property, using metal detectors, rakes, and other probes to closely examine the yard. They seized forty-three items, including computers, cell phones, and journals, as well as hair and bodily fluids for DNA testing.

Emma Daybell drove by and pulled faces at the reporters gathered outside the property.

That night, Colby Ryan told ABC News that his mother had not told him where his siblings were: "I'm just in the dark as anyone else, and that's a really hard position to be in when those are your siblings. I just hope and pray that everybody is safe."

Two days later, Larry and Kay Woodcock flew in from Louisiana to be interviewed by Rexburg police and the FBI. The couple had been doing as much press as possible to spread the word about J.J. and Tylee.

The case had now gained national attention, with widespread coverage of the lost children and their mother's abject refusal to help find them.

"The mysterious disappearance of two children from Rexburg has left family and authorities pleading for their safe return," trumpeted CNN. "J.J.'s grandmother says she prays that the children are alive."

"Some days we hardly function because we're fearing the worst," Kay told a reporter.

On Monday morning, the Woodcocks held a press conference, announcing a $20,000 reward for information that led to finding the children. They had also set up a special website, Find J.J. and Tylee, to collate information.

"I get extremely emotional when I talk about J.J.," said Larry. "J.J. is my heart and I'm hoping that this will allow one person to simply say, 'I know where he's at,' so we can bring J.J. and Tylee back."

Larry also appealed to Lori to start cooperating with the authorities to find her missing children. "Please give them back to us," he said, becoming emotional. "J.J. was just developing his own little personality. And with the special needs that he has . . . since he was born, it's amazing to be around this young boy."

Larry pleaded for the public to step up and call the authorities or contact the new website if they knew something.

A television reporter apologized before asking if the Woodcocks thought J.J. and Tylee were still alive.

"Nobody has said anything to the contrary," replied Larry, "and we want and believe that they are alive. And that's the reason for the reward. It's the reason that we don't say the D-word . . . because we hope and pray that these kids are alive."

Another reporter asked if there was any hint of Chad and Lori's whereabouts.

"No, ma'am," said Larry. "It's my understanding that when some people want to go underground, that they do it. I don't know how to do it."

"How was Lori with those kids?" asked another reporter. "Did you ever witness her mothering instincts?"

"You couldn't ask for a better mother," said Larry. "She loved J.J. She loved Charles, and I don't know what caused this conversion. You don't go from being the mother of the year of a special needs [boy] to the person that won't even tell you where they are. That just doesn't happen."

*   *   *

Meanwhile in Kauai, Lori and Chad carefully monitored the escalating coverage. They regularly attended the local Mormon temple, where they told ward leaders they were victims of bad press and merely protecting J.J. and Tylee from evil forces.

"[She was] telling people there's a lot of media hype around her right now, and [she was] waiting for that to die," said April Raymond.

On January 10, Chad's younger brother Matt Daybell and his wife, Heather, issued a joint statement, appealing to Chad to cooperate with law enforcement's search for the children. Matt emphasized that their statement did not represent the rest of the Daybell family.

"I have not seen nor directly spoken to Chad since Tammy's memorial here in Rexburg on October 23," the statement began.

Matt had texted Chad after his "shock and dismay" at learning about Chad's "quick marriage" to Lori Vallow, calling Tammy's death "suspicious."

"We are deeply saddened at the recent events that have played out the last several months," the statement said. "I plead again for Chad to come forward and cooperate with the investigation, so that this very difficult situation might be resolved."

On January 16, the State of Idaho filed a Child Protection Action in Madison County, ordering Lori Vallow to produce J.J. and Tylee within five days to the Rexburg Police Department or the Department of Health and Welfare. But Lori and Chad had to be found before it could be served.

Soon afterward detectives discovered that the fugitive couple had bought plane tickets to Kauai. Using cell phone tracking data, they zeroed in on the couple's new rental on Queen Emma's Drive.

Eight days after the protection order was filed, Detectives Ball and Hermosillo flew to Kauai to assist in serving it. Working with the FBI and Kauai Police Department, they began surveillance on Chad and Lori's luxury condo.

On Saturday, January 25, Kauai detectives officially served Chad and Lori with the child protection order, compelling Lori to physically produce Tylee and J.J. in Rexburg within five days or be in contempt.

The next day Kauai police pulled Lori and Chad over on their way to the Kauai Beach Resort, serving them with search warrants for their SUV and rental property. During a search of the condo, they discovered J.J.'s iPad and school registration and Tylee's ATM card, as well as both children's birth certificates. But there was no sign that either of them had ever lived there.

The damning *East Idaho News* footage of Chad and Lori avoiding reporter Nate Eaton's barrage of questions about the children, followed by Lori's flippant "That's great" comment, was seen all over the world. Millions were stunned by Lori's heartless indifference to her children's fate.

Colby watched it with shock.

"She just seemed so dismissive," he later told Justin Lum of Fox 10. "And just to see her walking by and not answering questions . . . struck a deep chord [of anger] in me. When I saw her and Chad there, I lost it."

Adam Cox felt sick to his stomach when he saw the video. "Lori and Chad were on the beach being married and carrying on. I just thought, 'What is happening? How are they able to do this? The kids are missing. It's not right.'"

Melanie Gibb, now in hiding, saw them on the news and was horrified. "I didn't think it looked good. It just made her look more guilty . . . both of them."

April Raymond did not recognize her old friend and feared what had happened to the children. "It was just such an empty answer, and her reaction and her behavior did not match the gravity of the situation. People all over the world were losing sleep over Tylee and J.J. . . . and their own mother was so dismissive and flippant at the mention of them."

On January 27, Kauai police issued a press release to announce they were now assisting Rexburg detectives in the search for Tylee and J.J. It emphasized that at the moment there were no local charges or warrants of arrest for either Chad or Lori.

"It's our sincere hope," said Kauai police chief Todd G. Raybuck, "that the children have a safe return."

But all the police and media scrutiny did not stop Chad and Lori from enjoying their beach vacation. The day after the couple were stopped by police, reporters from *Dateline NBC*, who were on the island preparing a story about them, got a tip that the couple were staying at the Kauai Beach Resort and planning to flee to Mexico.

Reporters staked out both the hotel entrances for nine hours, before catching Lori and Chad leaving the front lobby dressed for the beach.

"Just wondering where you guys are heading to?" asked one reporter. "You guys heading back to Idaho?"

"No comment," said Lori, sweeping past their cameras like a movie star.

On Thursday, January 30, reporters and TV crews from all over the world gathered in Rexburg as the 5:00 P.M. deadline for Lori to produce Tylee and J.J. approached. Earlier that day, Kay and Larry Woodcock had filed for emergency guardianship of their grandson, calling his mother "neglectful."

"She has lied to police," read the filing. "It is believed that the Minor Child is in danger while being in the care of his mother."

It asked the Madison County court to serve the order once Lori produced J.J., so his grandparents could care for him instead of his being placed into foster care.

Five P.M. came and went with no sign of Lori Vallow. Instead of returning to snowbound Rexburg, she stayed in sunny Kauai and lawyered up with two local attorneys. She was now in contempt of the Madison County court, and prosecutors were able to seek her extradition back to Idaho to face charges.

An emotional Kay Woodcock held a press conference. Larry was back at the hotel, feeling unwell due to all of the stress.

"Lori hasn't come to Rexburg," Kay told reporters. "The kids haven't been delivered. What kind of mother does that? The only word coming in my mind right now is *monster*. She's a black widow."

Kay said she and Larry had been hopeful that Lori would meet the deadline and produce J.J. and Tylee. Now Kay was mostly disappointed. "I'm not at all surprised though. Lori's not going to make this easy. She's got an endgame in her head, and although this is not a game, she obviously thinks it is."

"Are you feeling less optimistic about the outcome?" asked a reporter.

"A lot less optimistic at this moment. Everybody asks Larry and I how we are getting through all of this the last few months. And it's because we stay optimistic, because we aren't accepting the worst-case scenario. I don't think we ever will until we know one hundred percent."

At the end of the press conference, Kay was asked if she had a message for her former sister-in-law.

"Lori," Kay said into the camera, "show me the kids! Show me the kids! Show me the kids!"

Later that night, Chad called his longtime friend and AVOW website founder, Christopher M. Parrett, to defend himself and Lori against all the accusations. After putting down the phone, Parrett declared that Chad and Lori were completely innocent.

"Chad and Lori called me tonight, and we spoke for almost a full hour," he wrote on his widely read Mormon Prepper website. "Finally they were able to lay out the ENTIRE SAGA from their side of the story. From the beginning all the way to today. **And I'm here to tell you I feel <u>TOTALLY VINDICATED</u> in standing up for Chad.**"

Parrett wrote that he and his wife, Sue, fully understood everything that had happened with the kids, Tammy's death, Chad's marriage to Lori, and the move to Hawaii. "It took them 54 minutes just to walk us through the whole ordeal. Those of you who chose to think the worst of our friend and THROW HIM UNDER THE BUS and believed all the LIES that have been posted on Social Media and in the Lamestream news will have some crow to eat after their story is released."

The couple's staunchest defender said that the court of public opinion was once again wrong, promising the real story would emerge soon. Parrett also attacked Kay Woodcock, claiming her main motive was money:

"This is a **<u>NASTY UGLY CUSTODY CASE</u>** involving major sums of money with everything being driven by 'Grandma.' And yes, there is SO MUCH MORE going on just beneath the surface that hasn't been put out yet. And yes, Chad IS WRITING a new book about this whole drama!!

"To those of you who chose to stand with Chad, he expresses his HEARTFELT APPRECIATION. In Lori and Chad's words, 'The chaff have been separated from the wheat in this sifting.' They KNOW with a certainty who their real friends are."

The AVOW founder finished by saying that once Tammy's autopsy results were released, he would share further details of Chad and Lori's real story.

Lori officially had her Mormon Church membership records transferred to Kauai to join the congregation. She and Chad met again with the ward leaders, repeating that it was all lies. They apologized for all the reporters trailing in their wake, saying they didn't want to cause any trouble.

On February 10, Chad and Lori issued a statement on the AVOW website, explaining why they had refused to talk to the media and address all the accusations.

"Lori and I have been absolutely silent for three months," wrote Chad. "I am constrained by my lawyers from saying more until the legal mess is complete, but be assured I will be back."

On February 14, *Dateline NBC* aired a two-hour special entitled "Where Are the Children?" It featured exclusive new footage of Lori and Chad enjoying the beach at the Kauai Beach Resort.

East Idaho News reporters Nate Eaton and Eric Grossarth had been recruited as *Dateline* correspondents. It was the first of four specials, and *Dateline* would eventually produce a podcast on the case with NBC News investigator Keith Morrison.

"The bodies are piling up," he told listeners. "Nobody has seen the two children. The police have asked us to be very careful. Where are J.J. and Tylee?"

PART FOUR

END-TIMES

THIRTY-EIGHT

THE ARREST

On Thursday, February 20, at 2:20 P.M., Lori Vallow was arrested by Kauai police at her Villas on the Prince condo. Rexburg detectives Ball and Hermosillo were there to observe.

She was charged with two counts of felony desertion of a child, misdemeanor charges of resisting and obstructing an officer, solicitation of a crime, and contempt. She was booked into a cell at the Kauai Police Department on $5 million bail, pending her extradition back to Idaho. Lori now faced a maximum sentence of fourteen years in prison.

After her arrest, Kauai police chief Todd Raybuck thanked the public for the "massive outpouring of concern" for J.J. and Tylee.

"We also want to thank everyone for their patience," read his statement, "while investigators worked diligently to comprehensively gather everything they needed in order to obtain this arrest warrant."

Lori's arrest made the evening news on all major television networks, as well as the Friday morning shows.

"Missing since September," reported *CBS This Morning*. "*Bizarre* doesn't even begin to describe this story."

On Friday morning, Lori appeared in front of Judge Kathleen Watanabe for her arraignment. Lori was wearing a black dress and stood next to her attorney, Daniel Hempey. In the front row of the public gallery Chad Daybell sat nervously, wearing a plain white shirt and a purple tie.

"Will Miss Vallow be waiving her right to extradition?" asked the judge.

"No, Your Honor," replied Hempey. "She is exercising her right to an extradition hearing."

He asked the judge to lower Lori's $5 million bail to $10,000, claiming it was far too excessive for a couple of felonies and misdemeanors. He labeled the arrest a "made-for-media event" at the taxpayers' expense, claiming Lori had offered to surrender to police three weeks earlier and did not even have a passport.

"And given her residency here," said Hempey, "they didn't even need to arrest her."

Kauai County prosecutor Justin Kollar opposed bail. He called Lori a serious flight risk who would attempt to obstruct justice and engage in illegal activity.

"She has no ties to this island," he told the judge, "other than a rented condominium in Princeville. She has apparently resources to travel and leave."

Judge Watanabe ruled to let the $5 million bail remain, and Lori was transported to the Kauai police detention facility until a March 2 extradition hearing.

The next day, Prosecutor Kollar held a press conference, explaining the next move in the extradition process. He said the upcoming hearing was just a formality to establish that the Lori Vallow now in custody was the same person named in the Idaho warrant.

"Of course we are also hoping against hope," he said, "that Tylee and J.J. are out there somewhere and will be reunited with their other family members at some point."

A reporter asked Police Chief Raybuck whether Chad Daybell, who had canceled his condo lease after Lori's arrest, was free to leave Kauai.

"At this time there are no criminal charges pending," said Chief Raybuck. "He is able to move about as he wishes."

Chad was in daily phone contact with Lori and visited the Kauai detention center as often as he could. During their one-hour visits they read the Scriptures and discussed their next move.

He calmly reassured his wife that it was all part of his celestial plan for riding out the end-times. Through his visions he saw that earthquakes, war, and chaos would soon begin, heralding the end of the world on July 22—now less than five months away.

*　*　*

On February 25, Madison County prosecutor Rob Wood filed a fourteen-page Probable Cause Affidavit against Lori. Compiled by Detective Ron Ball, it methodically laid out everything law enforcement had done so far to locate J.J. and Tylee. It also revealed how Lori had lied to Rexburg police about J.J. being with Melanie Gibb and then telling her friend to mislead the authorities.

That same day, Idaho governor Brad Little said he was hoping to expedite the extradition process to bring Lori back to Idaho as quickly as possible to face charges.

"I hope there is justice and I hope the children are found," he said.

On February 26, Lori was led into the courtroom in handcuffs wearing a bright orange prison jumpsuit and sandals displaying bright-green-painted toenails. Judge Watanabe had given permission for NBC News, A+E Networks, and other media organizations to film the much-anticipated bail reduction hearing.

This time Lori was represented by attorney Craig De Costa, who told the judge that his client also had an Idaho lawyer fighting the Madison County court order to produce her children in Rexburg.

"That order was unlawful and should be quashed," he explained. "It pretty much said, 'Bring your children so that we, the government, can take the children and put them in foster care.' And that's the reason she's fighting that order."

As Lori smiled behind him, De Costa denied the prosecutor's assertion that his client was a flight risk. "Mrs. Daybell and her husband moved to Kauai. It was a previously planned move and it's something that makes sense because . . . in the past six years her longest residence has actually been in Kauai."

De Costa claimed that far from hiding from law enforcement, Lori had known she was under police surveillance for weeks and could have fled at any time. He appealed to Judge Watanabe to set reasonable bail and to ignore all the hype and sensationalism surrounding his client.

Prosecutor Justin Kollar told the judge about the defendant's long history of defying court orders during her years-long custody battle with Joe Ryan.

"She has a history of disappearing when the child's custody is at issue," Kollar said, as Lori whispered into her attorney's ear. "I'm talking about the 2009 and 2011 reports in which she was civilly found in contempt and charged with judicial interference."

Ideally she should not be granted bail, he told the judge, but if so, $5 million would be appropriate.

"This case is extraordinary," said the prosecutor, "especially given the fact that the very same day investigators went to her house in Rexburg, she dug out for Hawaii. It certainly raises eyebrows with the State that the move appears to have been planned before her husband passed away."

On hearing this, Lori turned around and glared at the prosecutor.

"Miss Daybell is certainly a flight risk and had resided in numerous states in recent years," Kollar continued, "She is in open defiance of court orders [and] has a history of digging out when the chips are down, Your Honor."

De Costa pointed out that although his client had been tried for criminal contempt in the Ryan custody dispute, she was never convicted.

After to listening to both sides, Judge Watanabe confirmed Lori's bail at $5 million, asking if there was anything further.

"Yes, Your Honor," said De Costa. "At this time Miss Daybell has executed a waiver of extradition. She would like to expedite her return [to Idaho] so she can defend herself against these false allegations."

On Saturday, February 29, Chad Daybell flew back to Idaho while Lori remained in the Kauai detention center.

He arrived at the airport for departure wearing a baseball hat, carrying a large backpack, and wheeling a suitcase. After dropping off his rental car he was confronted by an ABC News reporter, who asked about J.J. and Tylee.

"The kids are safe," replied Chad pleasantly, as he strolled into the terminal to board the plane home.

The following Wednesday morning, Lori Vallow Daybell made her final appearance in the Kauai court in orange prison garb and wearing leg irons. FBI special agents and two Rexburg police detectives were busy making final arrangements to bring her back to Madison County.

"She's due to be picked up sometime this afternoon or evening by the transport team from Idaho," Prosecutor Kollar told Judge Watanabe. "They are here on island."

Craig De Costa invoked his client's Fifth Amendment rights, saying she should not be questioned during the long flight back to Idaho without a lawyer present.

On Thursday morning, as a handcuffed Lori Vallow boarded a commercial flight back to Idaho, the FBI released the last known photographs of Tylee with her uncle Alex, taken six months earlier at Yellowstone National Park. They appealed to anyone who might have taken photos of the children on September 8, 2019, to upload them to a special FBI website.

After a brief layover in Los Angeles, Lori and the detectives flew to Boise, where they boarded a State of Idaho airplane for the short flight to Rexburg. When they landed, *East Idaho News* reporter Nate Eaton was waiting, firing off more questions to Lori about her children.

Lori was then taken to Madison County Jail, where more than a dozen TV camera crews broadcast her arrival live.

Lori was treated like a celebrity by the other inmates. Everyone knew about her missing children and wanted a glimpse of her.

"I'm sitting in the pod and in walks two or three guards with [Lori]," remembered an inmate. "She walked in with her stripes but she also had a bulletproof vest on."

Lori was given her own private cell and allowed out into the pod to relax, watch television, read books, and make phone calls. She appeared to relish all the media attention and carefully monitored coverage of her case on the news.

"She was totally aware of all of it," said the inmate. "She knew she was the main story, and she liked it."

THIRTY-NINE

"FRANKLY HEARTBREAKING"

At 2:00 P.M. on Friday, Lori Vallow was arraigned in Madison County Magistrate Court. Outside were hundreds of people, many wearing sweatshirts and hoodies emblazoned with the words WHERE ARE THE KIDS? Others carried placards reading WELCOME BACK LORI and JUSTICE FOR TYLEE AND J.J.

Inside the courtroom, Larry and Kay Woodcock sat anxiously in the third row of the public gallery, behind the prosecution table, wearing leis. They had been waiting for months to see Lori, but now found it "nerve-racking" to be in her presence. Colby was there with his wife, Kelsee, eager to see his mother for the first time in more than seven months.

There was a collective gasp and all eyes turned toward the door as Chad Daybell walked in wearing a dark suit.

"The lightning bolts were coming out of my head," remembered Larry.

Two deputies escorted Lori into the courtroom in handcuffs. She was wearing a loose-fitting orange-and-white-striped prison uniform with a bulletproof vest underneath. Although her blond hair was scraggly, her fellow inmates had given her a makeover for her first Idaho court appearance, which would be broadcast live from coast to coast. She sported bright red lipstick made from Jolly Rancher candies, as well as eyebrow liner made from pencils.

As Lori took her place at the defense table, she smiled at her three newly hired attorneys, Edwina Elcox, Mark Means, and Brian Webb. Her original Rexburg lawyer, Sean Bartholick, was now representing Chad Daybell. Across the courtroom at the prosecutor's table sat Madison County prosecuting attorney Rob Wood, and his deputy Spencer Rammell.

Before the hearing began, Madison County magistrate judge Faren Eddins warned that any disruptive behavior would result in immediate removal from the courtroom.

"In the court pleadings it designates 'Miss Vallow aka Miss Daybell,'" said the judge. "How would your client like to be referred to by the court?"

Elcox asked Lori, who smiled, glancing at Chad in the public gallery.

"Mrs. Daybell, please, Your Honor," replied Elcox.

After Lori agreed that she understood her legal rights, Judge Eddins read out the two felony counts against her: desertion of Tylee and J.J. and the three misdemeanor ones of obstructing officers and giving false information.

After the defendant said she understood all the charges against her, Judge Eddins set a two-day preliminary hearing for mid-March.

Defense attorney Elcox asked Judge Eddins to lower the current $5 million bail to $10,000, noting that her client was presumed innocent: "A five-million-dollar bond is unreasonable. It's astronomically excessive and is the functional equivalent of holding Lori without bond. This is a violation of Lori's constitutional rights."

Elcox also accused the government of coming up with charges to satisfy all the media attention the case had generated, demanding that "public opinion and rampant speculation" not dictate how the case proceeded. She claimed that the heavy media attention on Lori guaranteed that she was not a flight risk.

"She has TV cameras in her face," said Elcox. "She has people following her. It is a built-in pretrial monitoring to a level I have never seen before, [and] more effective than any sort of surveillance that law enforcement could put on. She is intent on defending against these allegations and proving that she is innocent."

Prosecutor Rob Wood argued against lowering the bond, saying Lori's behavior over the last year had been concerning: "Since this last summer, the defendant has lived in Arizona, Idaho, and Hawaii. And quite frankly the circumstances under which she left Arizona, which was soon after the killing of her estranged husband by her brother, and the circumstances under which she left Idaho, which was the same night Rexburg police did a welfare check on her, give the State serious concern that she is a flight risk."

Since last summer, Wood told the judge, there had been "a clear and alarming pattern" in the defendant's life, resulting in three still-active investigations of suspicious deaths.

"We're not saying she's been charged in those," said Wood, "however, she is related to each of those deaths and it is alarming to the State."

Wood said the most "aggravating" factor in not lowering bail was her still-missing children. "That's quite frankly heartbreaking and is the reason why there's so much media attention. And the defendant has not only misled law enforcement in their efforts to find the children, but she has completely and utterly refused to aid in any attempts to find [them], even before charges were filed."

Judge Eddins decided to reduce bail to $1 million, saying if Lori did manage to post bond, she would have to wear an ankle monitor around the clock and appear at all future court hearings. Lori was escorted out of the courtroom, grinning at Chad, who looked on sheepishly from the public gallery.

After the hearing, Chad Daybell snuck out of the courthouse through a back door, dodging reporters' questions. But out front the Woodcocks and Colby Ryan held an impromptu press conference. Lori's son, who had traveled all the way from Arizona for the hearing, pleaded with his mother to tell him where his siblings were.

"My first question is going to be 'Where are Tylee and J.J.?'" he said. "This can't be a hard answer."

Over the next week, Lori met with several bail bond companies about raising her $1 million bail, but they all decided she was too big a risk with such a high-profile case. Although she and Chad could easily raise the $100,000 needed to put down, the bond companies feared that if she ran away again, they would be left to pay the rest.

Chad texted Summer Shiflet that Lori wanted to speak to her. He added that Lori had not told him where J.J. and Tylee were.

Summer called her older sister at the detention center. Lori assured her that the children were safe, and she was just protecting them from bad people.

"And she said, 'You know me and I've always taken care of my kids,'" said Summer. "It removed any doubt in my mind that she's done anything wrong."

After her arraignment, Lori fired two of her three attorneys. From then on she would be solely represented by Mark Means, whose law office in Meridian, Idaho, was 315 miles west of Rexburg. He also represented Chad Daybell.

Although apparently lacking in any criminal-defense experience, Means was a tenacious pit bull. His firm's motto, as stated on its website, is "Don't get 'thrown under the bus.' Contact us today to protect your rights!"

Reportedly, Lori had told her new attorney that he had been her son in a previous probation.

Means immediately filed a motion to remove Judge Eddins from the case and postpone the preliminary hearing. At a hearing held over the phone on March 13, Judge Eddins removed himself and the case was assigned to Magistrate Judge Michelle Mallard.

Three days later, Mark Means issued a terse statement to the media declaring Lori's innocence. It said there was no room for "conjecture, innuendos, and/or speculation" in her constitutionally guaranteed legal process.

"As with any citizen of our Country," it read, "Mrs. Daybell is entitled to all the privileges and rights that accompany our cornerstone belief of innocents, until proven beyond a reasonable doubt otherwise. It is this innocence that Mrs. Daybell assertively maintains regarding all charges. In the coming days we look forward to the opportunity . . . to prove Mrs. Daybell's innocence."

That same day, Madison County prosecutors turned over more than sixteen hundred pages of discovery to the defense, including videos of the Yellowstone National Park visit just before Lori's children went missing.

* * *

By mid-March, the COVID-19 pandemic was sweeping across Idaho and would slow down the wheels of justice for Lori Vallow Daybell. The Idaho court system instituted strict new regulations for hearings, which would mainly be held remotely via Zoom.

The Madison County Jail now screened all inmates for the virus, and attorneys could only communicate with their clients through a video call at the jail. No special arrangements were being made for the jail's most famous inmate.

"Her presence doesn't change our preparation in any way," said a spokesman for the jail. "She gets treated the same as any other inmate we have."

Under the jail's new rules for the pandemic, defense attorney Mark Means would now meet his client in the public visitor room, with a glass partition between them. They could only communicate through a special telephone system, and any document that Lori needed to see had to be handed to a deputy, who hand-delivered it to her.

In an April 2 motion, Means described the new procedures as "unlawful" and violating his client's rights.

In his response, Madison County prosecutor Rob Wood said the current restrictions at the jail addressed the COVID-19 pandemic: "The safety of both the inmates and employees is of the utmost importance to Madison County, the Sheriff's Department and the Prosecutor's Office."

Chandler police had now reopened the investigation into Charles Vallow's shooting death and were targeting his widow. But the shooter, Alex Cox, being dead presented many problems for lead detective Nathan Moffat.

"We continue to work on Charles [Vallow's] case," he emailed a reporter on March 24, "and are confident we are getting closer to getting Lori indicted for her involvement in [his] death."

A week later on April 1, Chandler police investigators sent their case against Lori Vallow to the Maricopa County Attorney's Office, recommending she be charged with conspiracy to commit first-degree murder.

The worldwide publicity surrounding the missing children shone a glaring spotlight on the sleepy city of Rexburg, and every one of Rexburg's twenty-eight thousand residents felt personally involved. Although Tylee and J.J. had only moved there a couple of weeks before their disappearance, the city embraced them as their own. Everywhere were purple and blue ribbons and posters of the children, and Larry and Kay Woodcock were feted like royalty.

A local advertising firm had donated two huge billboards in prime locations along US Highway 20, the main route from Rexburg to Yellowstone National Park, and US Highway 26 in Idaho Falls. Both billboards had large photos of the children with information about the $20,000 reward, as well as listing a special hotline number and the new website FindJJandTylee.com.

"We're doing this as a public service," said a representative from the advertising company. "People need to get the word out."

The first week of April, a headstone was finally placed over Tammy Daybell's grave at the Evergreen Cemetery in Springville. It depicted a large duck, Tammy's favorite animal, followed by five little ducklings, representing her children.

The headstone was etched with TAMMY WAS A BELOVED WIFE AND MOTHER, DEVOTED DAUGHTER AND SISTER AND FRIEND TO ALL ANIMALS.

Six months after Tammy's suspicious death, little progress had been made in the murder investigation. Initially a coroner had ruled that she had died of natural causes, but after the exhumation in December authorities were calling it "suspicious."

Fremont County prosecutor Marcia Murdoch had requested assistance from two other local county prosecutors, but they had both declined. Finally, in desperation, she had appealed to the Idaho Attorney General's Office for help, saying she didn't have the necessary resources or experience to handle such a complex investigation.

The Idaho attorney general had agreed to officially take over the investigation of Chad and Lori for conspiracy, attempted murder, and/or murder.

Since Chad Daybell's return from Kauai, he had been living with his sons Garth and Seth at the Salem house where Tammy died. Whenever he went out his front door, he would see the pet cemetery and yard area where J.J.'s and Tylee's bodies were buried. It did not seem to bother him in the least.

At the end of April, Melani Pawlowski turned thirty-one and went on Facebook to angrily deny she was in a dangerous cult. She deplored all the bad publicity that her aunt Lori's high-profile case had generated and addressed several recent newspaper stories linking Alex Cox to the death of her mother, Stacey, in 1998.

"My world has been turned upside down," she wrote, "as my family and friends turned their backs on me when things in the media got confusing. While I was also unjustly taken away from my mother at age 6 and told all manner of lies about her, I stand here today grateful knowing that no one and no lie can take me away from the bond of my mother who has laid to rest since I was 9."

On Friday, May 1, Lori Vallow Daybell was back in the Madison County court for a bail reduction hearing. It was her first court appearance since the State of Idaho resumed hearings in person after a long hiatus. Two previous bond reduction hearings had been canceled because of the pandemic, and this one was being livestreamed over the official Madison County court YouTube channel.

Magistrate Judge Michelle Mallard was now presiding, and everyone in court wore a mask. At the defense table, Lori sat in her pink-and-white-striped jail suit, with matching pink sandals and a light blue mask. By her side was Mark Means, wearing a large scarf wrapped cowboy-style around his nose and mouth.

He immediately went on the attack, accusing Madison County Jail officers of illegally recording several telephone calls he had made to Lori during visits. In an affidavit filed in court, Lieutenant Jared Willmore of the detention center had admitted that two of the calls were accidentally recorded, but immediately deleted as soon as the recordings were discovered.

"I was specifically told multiple times that my communication with my client," Means said, "would be confidential and not recorded."

Means demanded to know whether detectives had listened to the calls before erasing them and how many others had been recorded.

"There were hours of times that I spoke with my client," Means told the judge. "We discussed detailed facts of the case that are incredibly sensitive. When an agent of the state goes in and deletes these recordings, I do not have the opportunity to say, 'Oh my gosh! What was on those recordings?'"

Means again asked Judge Mallard to lower Lori's bail to $10,000, so they could work on her defense together without being hampered by the detention center's COVID-19 regulations.

"I cannot in good faith communicate with my client through a telephonic system," Means told the judge, "in preparation for what is probably one of the largest cases to ever come through Madison County."

Means claimed Lori, like everyone else, had been economically affected by the pandemic. "My client is obviously unemployed at this time. Her husband is a publisher, but people aren't buying books. My client is not . . . a rich woman."

In response, Prosecutor Rob Wood accused the defense of deliberately misleading the court to get the defendant released on bail: "This is an attempt to divert the court and the public from the actual facts of the case. It's a way to try and get the client out on an issue that doesn't exist."

Wood also pointed out that before her arrest, the defendant and her husband were living the good life in one of the most expensive places in the world.

At the end of the lively two-hour hearing, Judge Mallard refused to lower the defendant's bond, finding no evidence that Lori had been treated any differently from her fellow inmates.

"I really don't see an impact on Ms. Daybell's constitutional rights with the jail process," said the judge. "There are other people in jail right now that have defenses that they need to go through with their attorneys. I'm confident that that can be worked around."

Outside the courthouse, Mark Means told reporters it was unlikely that Lori would be able to post bond: "There is not a lot of goodwill for her as she's sitting in the Madison County detention center. There are not a lot of people that are willing to step up and . . . put their name down on a cosign to help acquire a million dollars for the bond."

Means refused to comment on reporters' questions about why his client still refused to reveal where her children were.

A week later, Janis Cox and Summer Shiflet broke their silence with an exclusive sit-down interview with Phoenix's CBS-5. They said their only goal was to tell the truth about Lori, complaining that the media had falsely portrayed her as "a monster" and a "heartless villain."

Summer said, "And that couldn't be further from the truth. I'm really hoping that by us speaking out that people might soften their hearts . . . and see she's really a loving, sweet, warm person. She's more beautiful on the inside than she is on the outside."

Janis admitted to not knowing her two grandchildren's whereabouts, but trusted Lori was protecting them from harm, for reasons she could not even discuss with Janis. She speculated that Lori might be hiding them in a bunker somewhere for their safety.

They were then asked if Lori was involved in the death of her late husband Charles Vallow.

"Not even a little bit," replied Summer. "I know for a fact that she did not conspire to kill Charles in any way, shape, or form."

When asked about allegations of Alex being the family hit man, his mother laughed. "I can't help but laugh. Alex is the most laid-back person. He's been funny his whole life. He was very protective of Colby and Tylee. He said, 'I tasered a pedophile. . . . I'm willing to admit it.' He's always owned up to anything he's done wrong."

At the end of the interview, Janis was asked about Lori and Chad being on a beach in Kauai while there was a nationwide hunt for the children.

"It didn't look good, we agree," she said, "but we knew they weren't missing to her. That's a whole difference if your children are missing . . . or if they're not missing to her."

FORTY

HUMAN REMAINS

For months the FBI had been sifting through dozens of cell phones and other devices belonging to everybody connected to the case. Then an FBI agent discovered an intriguing text exchange on Tammy Daybell's cell phone from September 9, 2019, the day after the last known sighting of Tylee at Yellowstone National Park.

The text, sent by Chad at 11:53 A.M., informed Tammy that he had had an "interesting morning," shooting and burning a raccoon.

"He is now in our pet cemetery," Chad had quipped. "Fun times!"

On Monday, June 1, 2020, the FBI forwarded the text to Detective Ron Ball of the Rexburg Police Department, who was immediately suspicious. He knew raccoons are nocturnal animals and don't come out in daylight. Additionally, a Daybell neighbor, Matt Price, had told police that he had heard the gunshot and asked Garth Daybell about it, who'd said his father had shot a raccoon. Price also said that the Daybells had rarely used the firepit prior to that day, but since then there had been frequent bonfires on the property.

The next day, Detective Bruce Mattingly of the Fremont County Sheriff's Office called Tammy's sister, Samantha, inquiring about the pet cemetery near the firepit. Samantha said several of Chad and Tammy's pets were buried there.

Meanwhile, Detective Ball asked the FBI's Cellular Analysis Survey Team (CAST) to analyze when Alex Cox had been on the Daybell property based on his cell phone tracking data pinging off local cell towers.

The CAST team discovered that Cox had visited Chad's property on four separate occasions in September 2019. And he had spent most of the morning on the day of the raccoon text by the firepit.

Then on September 23, the morning after Melanie Gibb and David Warwick had seen Alex carrying J.J. over to his town house—the last known sighting of the boy—Alex had spent seventeen minutes on Chad's property by the pond.

Confident of a breakthrough in the case, the FBI's Salt Lake City–based Evidence Response Team spent the next week carefully devising a search strategy to return to the Daybell property and start looking for bodies.

Behind the scenes, Prosecutor Rob Wood had secretly been negotiating a plea deal with Lori. He had been optimistic that she would soon start cooperating, but Chad Daybell had talked her out of it.

"Which is too bad," Wood later said. "It would have been better for her to tell us."

Cult expert Rick Ross said that Chad was still manipulating his new wife, even while she was behind bars, with his daily calls and scripture readings.

"He could just speak endless[ly] about the end-times and was projecting a date—July twenty-second, 2020," explained Ross. "Basically he continued the marination of her mind."

At 7:00 A.M. on Tuesday, June 9, Detectives Ray Hermosillo and Dave Stubbs arrived at Chad Daybell's Salem property armed with a search warrant. They were accompanied by officers from the FBI's elite Evidence Response Team (ERT), the Rexburg Police Department, and the Fremont County Sheriff's Office. They knocked on the door and were let in by Garth and Seth Daybell, who led the detectives to their father's room.

As soon as Chad was informed they had a search warrant to dig up his backyard, he called his attorney, Mark Means. Chad was given the option of either staying on his property with an officer during the search or leaving.

"Mr. Daybell left and went and sat in his vehicle," Detective Hermosillo later testified, "which was parked in the driveway."

All the roads leading up to the Daybell property were sealed off as officers set up tents in a nearby field to serve as a command post.

A tense Chad Daybell waited in his gray SUV across the street, by his daughter Emma's house. He watched as a small army of FBI specialists began hauling heavy equipment onto his property.

At 7:45 A.M., an FBI victim's advocate called Larry and Kay Woodcock to inform them that Chad Daybell's property was about to be searched for human remains.

Around 9:00 A.M., the ERT began marking off parts of the backyard into grids and setting up blue canopies and tarps.

By now almost one hundred law enforcement officers were on the property, each with his or her own designated tasks. Five cadaver dogs were led through the entire four-acre property, looking for any clandestine graves. Officers also conducted a systematic line search, pacing up and down the backyard with rakes on the hunt for any ground disturbances.

Using satellite imagery, an FBI artist made sketches to pinpoint where each of the pings from Alex Cox's phone had been, while another team focused on finding the pet cemetery Chad's texts had mentioned.

They soon discovered it, ringed by a circle of bricks with a statue of a dog nearby, and concentrated on how best to excavate the suspected grave site.

A separate ERT was also working over by the east side of the pond, where Alex's phone had pinged for seventeen minutes on September 23. Cadaver dogs soon zeroed in on a small area by the pond underneath a tree, which had a slightly raised berm, two feet by four feet, surrounded by longer and thicker weeds.

It was photographed before special equipment was brought in, including a 3D laser scanner and a total-station optical instrument, to take exact measurements.

The Evidence Response Team began methodically excavating the possible clandestine grave site layer by layer. They removed the sod and upper vegetation to reveal three large white stones. As they dug deeper, they could see the three stones had carefully been placed side by side, and roots from the surrounding tree had been cut to make way for them.

Underneath the stones were thin wooden boards. Each stage of the excavation of the eighteen-inch-deep, shallow grave was carefully photographed and measured as evidence.

"So this is telling a story," Agent Steve Daniels later testified. "Someone's placed these boards over this grave site."

After removing the boards, the searchers saw what appeared to be a black garbage bag tightly wrapped around an oval-shaped object. There was also the distinct odor of a decomposing human body.

"I got in there with my hands," said Agent Daniels, "and I was just scraping off dirt [from] around that oval object that just felt like a skull."

He then took a razor blade and cut a small hole in the garbage bag, revealing a white plastic bag underneath. He gently pulled the black bag off the round object, so as not to disturb forensic evidence, leaving the white one exposed.

"As I cut through the white plastic with the razor blade," explained Agent Daniels, "possible human hair started coming onto my hands. And that was the point where we determined this is human remains."

The team continued their excavation until they uncovered a small body wrapped in the black plastic bag, totally covered in tightly wrapped gray duct tape. Boise State University anthropology professor Cheryl Anderson examined the remains and confirmed they were human.

At around 11:00 A.M., the coroner arrived and removed J.J.'s body from the shallow grave, placing it in a body bag to be transported to the morgue at Madison Memorial Hospital.

Chad Daybell had been watching the search intensely from his SUV, parked on the edge of his property. Detective Hermosillo checked in several times to see if Chad needed anything.

"He had the phone in his right hand," said the detective, "and was continually looking over his right shoulder. He would talk on the phone for a second and then continue looking back pretty intently."

As it became obvious that something important had been found by the pond, Chad nervously got out of his vehicle for a better view.

"He took off his hat and ran his fingers through his hair," said Hermosillo. "[He] looked down towards the ground, put his hat back on, and went back inside the vehicle."

At 11:03 A.M., Chad received a call from Lori at the Madison County Jail, which was recorded. From his dejected voice it was obvious that Chad knew it was all over and that J.J.'s and Tylee's bodies would soon be found.

"Hi, babe," she said.

"Hello," replied Chad sadly.

"Are you okay?"

"No," he sighed, "they're searching the property. So Mark Means will be talking to you."

Lori asked if officers were back at the house seizing stuff again.

Chad said they were out in his yard. "There's a search warrant, and they're looking for the kids."

After a long silence Lori replied, "Okay."

"I'm glad you called. So, we'll see what transpires."

"Okay, what can I do for you—pray?"

"No, I'm sorry. I'm feeling pretty calm. I would call Mark [Means] though. We need . . . can you just talk with him?"

"Have you talked to him already?"

"I've been trying to call him."

"So he knows what they're doing?"

Chad received another call. "I've [got] a call from somebody else who I need to talk to, honey. I love you so much."

"Okay, I love you. Should I try to call you later?"

"Ummm," sighed Chad. "I don't know. I don't know. You can try, yeah, I'll answer if I can."

"Okay."

"I love you and we'll talk soon."

"Okay, baby," replied Lori. "I love you."

"Okay. Love you. Goodbye."

A few minutes later, Chad tried to make a run for it. He started his SUV, hit the accelerator, and drove off. But officers gave chase, flagging him down within a mile of his home.

At 11:30 A.M., Chad Daybell was arrested, handcuffed, and taken into custody. His SUV was towed away to be processed.

* * *

Around 1:00 P.M., the FBI Evidence Response Team moved on to the pet cemetery. They began by removing the top layer of vegetation to try to get a better idea of what was buried there, using hand tools to uncover the remains of a dog and a cat.

A backhoe was brought in to excavate a ten-foot-by-ten-foot area of interest, approximately two feet deep. It unearthed two potential vertebrae, but Professor Anderson was unable to determine whether they were animal or human.

"I caught an odor [of] possibly being decomposing human remains," Special Agent Daniels later testified. "I made the decision [that] we're going to stop using the tractor and have the team focus on hand tools."

His team started digging on the north side of Chad Daybell's pet cemetery until they spotted bones sticking out of the ground and uncovered flesh farther down. They kept digging and found a few more pieces of bone and then a piece of pelvic bone.

Professor Anderson positively identified the bone as human, and the excavation was halted for the day.

"We knew at that point we had found human remains," said Agent Daniels. "That became burial site number two. The pieces that were recovered appeared to have been burned, and some of them were pink still."

It was obvious from the mass of burned flesh and charred bones that someone had dismembered the poor victim. The recovered body parts were put in a body bag, sealed by the coroner, and taken off to the morgue.

The Daybell property was secured for the day, with police officers on guard, until work could resume the next morning.

At 3:37 P.M., Rexburg police and the Fremont County Sheriff's Office held an on-site press conference for the news crews that had gathered on the perimeters of the Daybell property. There was an air of excitement that finally there had been a breakthrough in the case.

Rexburg police assistant chief Gary Hagen confirmed that investigators had found human remains on the Daybell property. He refused to answer any questions about the investigation until they had more details.

"I do want to add," he told reporters, "that Chad Daybell, who resides at that residence, has been taken into custody for questioning."

At 5:21 P.M., Daybell was officially booked into Fremont County Jail and charged with two felony counts of concealment or destruction of evidence.

Later that night, Rexburg police and the Fremont Sheriff's Office held another press conference. Starting with the search warrant being served on Chad Daybell, Assistant Chief Hagen outlined the day's events:

"During the search of the property, investigators discovered what appeared to be unidentified human remains, and an autopsy will be conducted. Chad Daybell was taken into custody [and] will have his initial hearing tomorrow morning at eleven A.M. at the Fremont County Courthouse."

Hagen then thanked the media and the public for all their help since J.J. and Tylee had gone missing. "I want to stress to everybody that this is an active and ongoing case, and as soon as we have more answers, we'll be able to hold another press conference."

Daybell's lawyer, Mark Means, refused to comment on the arrest.

Chad Daybell's arrest and the discovery of human remains on his property made headlines around the world. There were photographs of him in handcuffs taken by a passerby, along with his glum mug shot, released by the Rexburg Police Department.

"Former Grave Digger Husband of 'Cult Mom' Lori Vallow," read the lengthy headline in England's *Daily Mail*, "Is Charged with One Count of Destruction or Concealment of Evidence and Booked into Jail After Human Remains Are Found at His Idaho Home in Search for Her Missing Kids."

The *New York Times* also carried the story: "The stepfather of two Idaho children who have been missing for months was arrested on a felony charge of concealing evidence on Tuesday after investigators found unidentified human remains on his property."

The next morning, as Kay and Larry Woodcock boarded a plane from Louisiana to Idaho, the FBI's Evidence Response Team resumed its excavation of the pet cemetery and nearby firepit. But the numerous pieces of burned flesh and bones presented a real challenge.

"The difficulty I think for us was the way these human remains were found," explained the ERT leader, Agent Steve Daniels. "For lack of a better term [it was] a mass of dismembered human remains partially burnt."

Most of the body parts were an unrecognizable mass of tissue and organic matter, so the team excavated around them layer by layer. At the very bottom of the pit was a melted green bucket over a partial human skull, alongside a mandible containing some teeth.

"The team did the best they could," said Daniels, "to excavate around this and tell that story."

The next problem was how to remove the fragile mass of human remains from the burial site for autopsy. When they first tried to lift it all up, it just fell apart. So the team members had to pick up the dismembered pieces one at a time, placing them into a body bag as the coroner and the anthropologist did an inventory.

After the pieces were removed, the ERT continued excavating the grave, looking for small pieces of bone and other evidence for forensic examination. They methodically sifted through the earth with their hands until they were satisfied they had removed all the human remains.

A backhoe was then used to go even deeper and wider to ensure they had found everything.

At 11:00 A.M., Chad Daybell appeared via Zoom from the Fremont County Jail for his initial court appearance in front of Magistrate Judge Faren Eddins. He was wearing a black-and-white-striped jail jumpsuit and handcuffs. Next to him was his newly hired defense attorney, John Prior.

Daybell had been charged with two felony counts of concealment or destruction of evidence and faced up to five years' imprisonment and a $10,000 fine on each charge. After going through the criminal complaint, Judge Eddins advised the defendant of his rights. Prior waived his client's right to a speedy preliminary hearing within fourteen days.

Rob Wood, now officially appointed special prosecutor to oversee both Chad's and Lori's cases, asked Judge Eddins to set bail at $1 million.

"These are human remains," Wood told the judge. "And although these remains have not yet been positively identified, we are aware [they] are the remains of children, which we believe is an aggravating factor. And the manner and concealment of one of these bodies, the state finds to be particularly egregious."

The prosecutor said the defendant had a "strong incentive to flee" as the investigation into the deaths of the children was just beginning.

John Prior in turn argued for $100,000 bail, denying his client was a flight risk: "He has significant family in the community. He has kids that live here. He owns property here. Mr. Daybell has every intention of staying in the community [to] address these charges."

Judge Eddins set bail at $1 million, saying he had taken into account that the evidence allegedly being concealed was the remains of two people.

A few hours later, Larry and Kay Woodcock confirmed that the authorities had told them that the humans remains belonged to Tylee and J.J.

"We are filled with unfathomable sadness that these two bright stars were stolen from us," read their statement, "and only hope that they died without pain or suffering."

Lori's family also issued a statement to the press: "The Cox Family— Janis and Barry, Summer, Melani and Ian—is deeply saddened by the recent findings in the investigation into the whereabouts of J.J. and Tylee. The family has maintained a strong hope and belief that they were alive and well. With that hope and belief apparently shattered, they struggle to find comfort and hope in this potential new reality."

The only comment from Chad Daybell's family was a statement from his estranged brother Matt and wife Heather, extending their sympathies to Larry and Kay Woodcock and J.J. and Tylee's extended families.

"We are devastated by today's news," it read, "and the apparent role that Chad has played in what has transpired."

FORTY-ONE

THE END-TIMES FAIL TO MATERIALIZE

The following day, autopsies were held on both sets of human remains at the Ada County Coroner's Office in Boise, Idaho. They were performed by Medical Examiner Dr. Garth Warren and observed by Rexburg detectives Ron Ball and Ray Hermosillo.

Dr. Warren started with J.J.'s body, which was still in the dirty black garbage bag and covered in duct tape. He cut through the black plastic bag and then the white one, with the red drawstring, covering the head.

"I observed a small child in red pajamas," Detective Hermosillo later testified. "Black socks that had the word *Skechers* in orange across the toes. A white-and-blue blanket had been placed on top of him."

When the medical examiner removed the bags, the witnesses were astonished at the amount of heavy-duty duct tape tightly wrapped around J.J.'s head, hands, and ankles. Dr. Warren had to use a sharp medical instrument to cut it all off. Additional duct tape was stretched across J.J.'s mouth.

When the face was finally exposed, Hermosillo recognized J.J., with the same distinctive haircut the detective had seen in the Yellowstone National Park photos.

"His hands were folded about chest high," said Detective Hermosillo. "He had [several layers of] duct tape continuously wrapped from [his left] elbow, all the way around his arms, over his hands, all the way up to his right elbow. And the best way that I can describe it is, he had a ball of duct tape over where his hands would be."

In the afternoon, Dr. Warren began the autopsy on what remained of Tylee's body.

"I observed the same melted green bucket," said Detective Hermosillo, "with the charred flesh and charred bone that was located on Mr. Daybell's property, that was now sitting on the table in the medical examiner's office."

It was impossible to identify the remains as they were too damaged by fire, with no recognizable features. Deputy Coroner Dr. Glen Smith, who is also an orthodontist, was finally able to match the mandible that was found with a dental X-ray of Tylee's jaw. There was also enough DNA from the partially burned flesh for samples to be taken.

Chad Daybell's property had become a shrine to Tylee and J.J. Bouquets of flowers, teddy bears, signs, and BRING JJ AND TYLEE HOME T-shirts lined the fence. A neighbor was flying a flag of the two children's smiling faces.

It was Kay and Larry Woodcock's first stop after landing in Idaho. Colby and Kelsee Ryan also came, attaching a sign to the fence addressed to his siblings:

"To my beautiful little brother and sister. We will never forget you. This is not the end. You will have justice and we will meet again in paradise."

On Friday night, hundreds of people attended a candlelight vigil for the children at Porter Park in Rexburg. They wore masks due to the pandemic and purple and blue clothing, Tylee and J.J.'s respective favorite colors. A large purple-and-blue arch had been set up on one side of the field.

The vigil started with a poem, "Their Journey Has Just Begun," followed by a rendition of the Sarah McLachlan song "Angel." Someone recited a moving speech for the children, then everyone lit a candle before a moment of silence and the closing prayer.

The Woodcocks were unable to attend as Larry was feeling unwell, but they watched it on a local TV station. April Raymond, who had now moved to Utah, drove in with a group of friends who had known the Vallows in Hawaii.

"It was very touching," she remembered, "to see a community come together that really didn't know these kids personally."

*   *   *

On Monday, June 29, investigators executed a third search warrant on Chad Daybell's home. They spent almost two hours searching the house, as well as a barn and other parts of the property, leaving with several large brown evidence bags.

A few hours later, Lori Vallow Daybell was charged in Fremont County with two identical counts as her husband: conspiracy to commit destruction, alteration, or concealment of evidence.

On Tuesday afternoon, a masked Lori Vallow Daybell, wearing a light blue shirt, and her attorney, Mark Means, appeared via Zoom at a Fremont County hearing in front of Magistrate Judge Faren Eddins. It came after a sixteen-page probable-cause affidavit had been unsealed, making public explosive new details of the case, including the gruesome condition of the children's bodies. It also revealed Chad's belief in zombies, which Lori thought her children had become.

Special Prosecutor Wood joined the fifteen-minute Zoom hearing from his office. An emotional Colby and Kelsee Ryan were also in attendance and visible on-screen to the defendant.

As Judge Eddins summarized the new charges against her, Lori wiped a tear from her eye whenever Tylee's name was mentioned. When asked if she understood each of the charges and her legal rights, she answered, "Yes."

Judge Eddins set August 10 and 11 for a preliminary hearing, exactly a week after Chad's, and set her bond at $1 million.

The next afternoon, Chad Daybell appeared on a remote hearing, facing two new charges of conspiracy to commit destruction, alteration, or concealment of evidence. These were in addition to the previous two counts of destruction, alteration, or concealment of evidence. If found guilty on all the charges, he now faced up to twenty years behind bars and a $40,000 fine.

As Judge Eddins summarized each of the four counts, asking if Chad understood them, an emotionless Chad answered, "Yes." Leaving his bond at $1 million, the judge then recessed until the scheduled August 3 preliminary hearing.

On July 2, the two felony counts of desertion and nonsupport of her children against Lori in Madison County were dismissed, three weeks after J.J.'s and Tylee's bodies were recovered. Lori still faced two misdemeanor counts of resisting and obstructing officers, as well as for soliciting Melanie Gibb to lie to the police about J.J.'s whereabouts.

The next day, AVOW founder Christopher Parrett, once Chad and Lori's most vocal supporter, publicly apologized for defending them. He was now working closely with law enforcement to help build the case against Chad and Lori.

"In keeping with my pledge to 'Eat Crow' over my misplaced trust and faith in Chad," he posted on the AVOW site, "I contacted the police/FBI and extended an invitation [to] have a long in-depth discussion about Chad Daybell."

Parrett had spent three hours with law enforcement at his home office that morning, writing that he hoped that his "unique information and insights" would help their case.

"I will do everything in my power," he told his followers, "to help them bring this horrible series of events to a timely conclusion."

On July 14, Mark Means entered a not guilty plea on behalf of Lori Vallow on all three misdemeanor charges in Madison County. He demanded an eventual jury trial and that her $1 million bond be reduced now that the two desertion charges had been dismissed.

Three days later, Lori appeared with Means for a remote bail reduction hearing in front of Madison County magistrate judge Michelle Mallard. The defendant wore a blue mask and an orange-and-white-striped jail outfit.

Judge Mallard set a four-day trial, to begin on January 25, 2021.

After a short recess, Means asked the judge to lower Lori's bond, saying, "My client has been a model inmate. These charges are not of a violent nature, and there is no previous criminal record in any other jurisdiction that we're aware of."

Special Prosecutor Wood argued that although only facing misdemeanor charges in Madison County, the defendant was also being held on $1 million bail for far more serious ones in Fremont County.

Judge Mallard lowered the bond to $150,000, saying that it was an "inescapable" fact that the three misdemeanor charges were related to the whereabouts of Lori's deceased minor children.

Chad Daybell's predicted date for the end of the world, July 22, 2020, came and went without incident. His apocalyptic visions of two earthquakes hitting the Wasatch Front in Utah, followed by war and other tribulations, failed to materialize. Now, instead of him and Lori majestically leading the chosen 144,000 toward the Second Coming of Jesus Christ, they were both behind bars and abandoned by all their once-devoted followers.

Many were now asking why no murder charges had yet been brought against the doomsday-obsessed couple for their respective dead spouses and J.J. and Tylee. The toxicology results from Tammy's and the children's autopsies had still not been completed, but behind the scenes, investigators were working day and night.

The biggest problem was that prosecutors believed that the now-deceased Alex Cox, described as a coconspirator, had actually committed the murders, masterminded by the two defendants. The prosecutors were biding their time, wary of filing murder charges until they had a cast-iron murder-and-conspiracy case.

With each of the defendants being held on $1 million bail, they were not going anywhere.

At 9:10 A.M. on Monday, August 3, Chad Daybell was brought into the Fremont County Courthouse for his preliminary hearing in front of Magistrate Judge Faren Eddins. The two-day hearing was being held in person, with masks and social-distancing measures in place and plexiglass dividers surrounding the witness stand.

Special Prosecutor Rob Wood had previously filed a motion to close the preliminary hearing to the public, but Judge Eddins had ruled against him. It would be livestreamed on his official YouTube channel and broadcast by all local media.

The defendant wore a pressed white shirt and blue tie at the defense table with his attorney, John Prior, across from Prosecutors Wood and

Spencer Rammell. In the sparsely filled public gallery sat Kay and Larry Woodcock, who had been warned to expect gruesome details of the recovery of the children's bodies.

The first witness for the prosecution was Lead Detective Ray Hermosillo, who recounted the welfare check he'd completed for J.J. at the urging of his grandparents on November 26, 2019. He and Detective Dave Hope had arrived at Lori Vallow's 565 Pioneer Road home to find Chad Daybell and Alex Cox there.

"I made contact with Alex," testified the bald, goateed detective, "and asked if Lori was home."

When Prosecutor Wood asked how Alex had responded, Prior objected for hearsay.

"Your Honor," said Wood, "this is a statement of a coconspirator coming in. He is an unavailable witness."

Prior argued that there was nothing to suggest that Lori's late brother was a coconspirator in the case.

"The complaint alleges Mr. Daybell, Mrs. Vallow, conspirators known and unknown," said Wood, "and the probable-cause affidavit clearly lists Alex Cox as a coconspirator."

Judge Eddins overruled the defense's objection, and Hermosillo replied that Alex had said Lori was not home.

"I informed Mr. Cox I was there to do a welfare check on J.J.," said the detective. He told the prosecutor that after first refusing to respond, Alex had told him that J.J. was with Kay Woodcock in Louisiana.

"I told Mr. Cox that was unlikely because Kay was the one who originally called in the welfare check."

The detective then asked Cox for his sister's cell phone number. He said he didn't have it but that she was in his neighboring apartment.

On his way next door, the detective had seen Daybell driving toward him and stopped him to ask when he had last seen J.J.

"He stated he saw J.J. in [Alex's] apartment in October," said Hermosillo. "I asked Mr. Daybell for Lori Vallow's phone number and he stated he didn't have it."

"What did you think about that?" asked Wood.

"I again found it suspicious because I knew that they were married two weeks prior to my contact with Mr. Daybell."

Hermosillo had called Rexburg police for backup, as Cox and Daybell were both acting so suspiciously.

"I felt there was something more going on with the whereabouts of J.J.," Hermosillo testified, "so I wanted more officers over there so we could figure out what was going on."

After going to Melani Boudreaux's town house and then back to Lori's without finding anyone in either, it was decided to get a search warrant.

When detectives returned the next day armed with the search warrant, Lori had disappeared. Soon afterward the FBI joined the search for J.J. and Tylee.

"While you were searching for J. J. Vallow," asked Wood, "did Lori Vallow or Chad Daybell . . . ever call the Rexburg police to report missing children?"

"No. In fact we attempted several times to get ahold of Lori, and her cell phone was shut off. We attempted to get hold of Chad and never got any return phone calls. They retained an attorney and refused to answer any questions."

In his cross-examination, John Prior immediately homed in on whether Detective Hermosillo's original contact with his client back in November had been recorded on body cam.

"Is there a reason you didn't record that contact?" asked Prior.

"It's not common practice for detectives to carry body cams."

"And it's important to record an interview with a witness, so that we get the factual statements made by people recorded accurately. Would you agree with that?"

"I would."

"Okay. This was somewhat of an important case, was it not?"

"Not at the time. It was just a welfare check."

In the afternoon session the prosecution called Melanie Gibb to the stand. Chad Daybell looked on anxiously as his former follower was sworn in to testify against him. Wearing a black jacket and matching shirt, Gibb seemed composed and avoided looking at the defendant.

Prosecutor Wood began by asking about her relationship to Chad Daybell.

"The nature of our relationship was talking about some of the books that Chad had written," she replied, "and his relationship with Lori."

Wood then questioned Gibb about the previous September when she and her boyfriend, David Warwick, had stayed at Lori's new home in Rexburg for a conference and podcast recording. He asked how Chad, who was still married to Tammy at the time, had interacted with Lori.

"Affectionately," Gibb replied. "Holding hands, hugging. Light kissing."

"What did [Lori] tell you about that relationship?"

"That they were very much in love with each other and wanted to be together as soon as possible."

"Did you speak to Lori Vallow about the location of Tylee Ryan?"

"She informed me that Tylee was at BYU-Idaho and mentioned something about being with friends."

"During that same period, did you have occasion to see J. J. Vallow?"

"Yes, he was in the family room mostly and then outside some."

Wood asked if Gibb had seen Alex Cox on Sunday night while they were recording the podcast.

"Yes, he brought J.J. into the house during the middle of the podcast."

"How did Alex Cox bring J.J. into the house?"

"He carried him in and he was asleep."

The prosecutor then asked about a conversation with Lori about J.J. going to live with his grandmother.

"[Lori] said that she would express to Kay that she was sick and something was wrong with her, so that J.J. could live with Kay." Later, Gibb had asked Lori how the conversation had gone. "She said it went well. She told Kay that she had breast cancer and that she would need help with J.J. for a period of time."

Wood moved on to November 26, 2019, and the phone call from Chad telling Gibb to lie to the police about J.J. being with her.

"He let me know that the police were over at Lori Vallow's home," Gibb told the judge, "and that they were inquiring about where J.J. was. She was going to tell police that J.J. was with me."

"How did you respond?"

"In shock. I did say, 'J.J.'s not at Kay's house?'"

"How did Mr. Daybell respond?"

"He said, 'No.'"

Several hours later, Lori had called to say everything was fine.

"She was upbeat, cheery, and acting like nothing was wrong," said Gibb.

"After receiving these phone calls, how did that make you feel?"

"Horrible. I felt in shock. I was not okay with it because she had told something to the police that was not true. I had a really bad feeling in my stomach."

Later, she received a call from Officer Ryan Pillar from the Gilbert Police Department and didn't answer because Chad had told her not to. But eventually she returned his call.

"I told him that I had been with J.J., but that he was back with Lori."

"Now Miss Gibb, had you recently had J.J. with you?"

"No."

"So when you told Detective Pillar that you had, was that an accurate statement?"

"No, it was not."

"Is there a reason you told Detective Pillar you had had him?"

"Yes, because Lori was misleading and she was manipulating me to convince me that [they] were in danger. And because of our friendship."

A couple of weeks later, Gibb testified, she was at Warwick's house when they decided to record a phone call with Lori and Chad to share with the police, because they were so worried about J.J.

The entire twenty-one-minute recording was then played for the judge. The defendant closed his eyes, bowed his head, and clenched his hands together as he listened. He looked especially uncomfortable at the part when Melanie asked him about Tammy's recent death and he maintained that she was "physically falling apart."

After the damning recording finished, Judge Eddins recessed for the day.

* * *

On Tuesday morning Melanie Gibb retook the stand to be cross-examined by John Prior. He began by asking about her first meeting with Chad Daybell in July 2017, at a preparedness camp in Ogden, Utah.

"What is a preparedness camp?" he asked.

"It's a camp where people get together where they're learning about how to cook outside or how to filter water or different preparedness skills."

"Preparedness for what?"

"For if there are times where you . . . didn't have electricity and things like that," Gibb answered cautiously.

"I'm just curious as to whether this preparedness camp has any kind of religious undertone as well?"

"Objection," Wood interjected. "Relevance."

Judge Eddins overruled him, allowing Melanie to answer.

"I would like you to explain . . . the religious nature of these preparedness camps?" asked Prior.

"Your client was one of those people that spoke at that and he was expressing his visions and dreams."

Prior then turned to the phone calls where Lori and Chad had asked Gibb to lie about J.J.'s whereabouts, which she had initially complied with.

"So you lied to a police officer?"

"Correct."

He then asked about her meeting with Prosecutor Wood and two Rexburg detectives in June 2020. "And the topic of discussion was Lori Vallow?"

"It was everybody, Lori, Chad, Alex Cox."

"Was there also a discussion about potential difficulties that you might have as a result of lying to the Gilbert PD?"

"No."

"There was never any reference or offer of any deal to testify about anything, and they would forgo going after you for lying to a police officer?"

"No."

Prior then questioned her about Lori and Alex's "close" relationship, and whether he'd given up a job to move to Idaho and be with his sister.

"I don't know if he gave it up. They were good siblings with each other. They got along really well."

"It was a little more than close. They were extremely close, weren't they?"

"I would say yes."

Finally, while Chad took notes on a yellow legal pad, Prior asked about her recording the incriminating phone call: "And you planned this as a means of trying to gain some information to clarify things for yourself."

"Partially correct. I had many objectives in that and one of them was to show my innocence."

"Okay, and one of the other objectives was to impress upon the police that you did nothing wrong?"

"Correct."

The next witness was David Warwick, who told the court that Lori had invited him to stay at her town house during his visit to Rexburg for a conference. Prosecutor Wood asked about the morning of September 23, 2019, when Warwick and Gibb had left Rexburg and J.J. had disappeared:

"Did you talk to Lori about J.J. that morning?"

"I did."

"What did she tell you?"

Warwick replied that Lori had told him that J.J. was "being a zombie" and had climbed on top of the fridge and smashed her picture of Jesus Christ. She had called Alex to come and get him as he was out of control.

On cross-examination, Prior asked if Warwick had observed Alex Cox babysitting J.J.

"He seemed to take care of J.J. really well," answered Warwick. "They seemed to have a good relationship."

"They were very close, would that be fair?"

"They seemed close to me."

The next witness was Lieutenant Jared Whitmore of the Madison County Sheriff's Office. He oversaw the Madison County Jail inmate Telmate phone system, which had recorded Lori's dramatic June 9 call to Chad, just minutes before his arrest.

The brief call was then played in court, as the defendant cowered at the defense table, his eyes tightly shut.

Just after 11:00 A.M., the prosecutor called Special Agent Steve Daniels of the FBI to the stand. For the next few hours, the Evidence Response Team leader described in gruesome detail how they recovered J.J.'s and Tylee's remains. Kay and Larry Woodstock held hands, looking on in rapt attention as the agent went into horrifying details about the deplorable condition the bodies had been found in.

Late Tuesday afternoon, the prosecution rested its case, and Judge Eddins asked the defense if it wished to call any witnesses.

"There'll be no presentation today, Your Honor," replied Prior.

Rob Wood made his closing arguments:

"Based on the state of the bodies of J. J. Vallow and Tylee Ryan, they were victims of a homicide. This court can also take note through the evidence presented that both Chad Daybell and his wife, Lori Daybell, were aware that Lori Vallow Daybell was charged with two felony counts of desertion of a minor child in Madison County. And clearly the location of these bodies was evidence in that felony proceedings.

"These bodies were concealed. One of them was destroyed. They were located on Chad Daybell's property. Alex Cox, whose phone pinged near those locations, became his brother-in-law less than two months later when Chad married Lori Vallow."

Wood noted that for a court to find probable cause on the conspiracy charges, there had to be at least one overt act of agreement between the accused in the charges they faced. "Both Chad Daybell and Lori Vallow attempted to convince Melanie Gibb to either not cooperate with police or to provide false information to the police. At this point they were married.

"Your Honor, for purposes of probable cause the state has met its burden on all four felony counts. We'd ask the court to bind Mr. Daybell [for trial]."

In his closing argument, John Prior argued that the prosecution had failed to provide anything remotely near probable cause to hold his client:

"The testimony, according to this prosecuting attorney, is that Mr. Daybell was married to Miss Vallow. That doesn't provide anything. Marriage is not an overt act towards a conspiracy, and marriage is not an agreement to conceal or to conspire."

Prior told the judge that all the prosecution had was "an obscure text message" about burning a raccoon in the firepit, without any evidence of when this had taken place. "And quite honestly, Judge, they don't even come close on the concealment of Tylee [or] the concealment of J.J., and [for] the conspiracy they lack the agreement.

"I'm respectfully asking the court to dismiss the charges. They haven't met their burden, and I don't believe they have provided anything near the type of evidence that is necessary to overcome that small threshold."

After taking a brief recess, Judge Eddins ruled that the prosecution had met its burden of probable cause on all four counts, binding the defendant over to the higher district court for his arraignment on August 21 in front of Judge Steven Boyce.

A few hours after Chad Daybell was sent for trial, the First Presidency of the Church of Jesus Christ of Latter-day Saints broke its silence. The powerful Mormon ruling body ordered Church members not to get involved "in any type of court case" without first consulting the Church's legal counsel. In an official letter addressed to Church leaders, the three members of the First Presidency reiterated long-standing Church policy, forbidding leaders from participating in criminal cases involving other members.

"However well intentioned," read the letter, "Church leaders sharing information in legal proceedings can sometimes be misinterpreted and even damaging."

A couple of days later, Mark Means waived Lori Vallow Daybell's preliminary hearing, not wanting a repeat performance of Chad's highly damaging one. Lori was automatically bound over to the district court for trial.

The defense attorney then fired off an angry five-page response to the First Presidency letter, accusing the LDS Church of tainting his client's right to a fair trial.

"By issuing this correspondence on the second day of a preliminary hearing," wrote Means, "the LDS Church has told approximately 26% of the residents of the State of Idaho to . . . enter into a code of silence."

Means labeled it as "disturbing, and at worst, criminal," adding that because the LDS Church was so prevalent in Idaho, it affected everybody involved in the case and would taint jury selection.

On August 21, Chad Daybell appeared from Fremont County Jail via Zoom for his arraignment with John Prior. Dressed in a loose-fitting white shirt and red tie, he showed no emotion as Judge Steven Boyce summarized the four felony charges.

At the end of the ten-minute arraignment, Prior entered a plea of not guilty on each count for his client, who now faced up to twenty years in prison and $40,000 in fines.

Judge Boyce scheduled Daybell's three-week trial to start on January 11, 2021.

Three weeks later, Lori Vallow Daybell was arraigned in front of District Judge Dane Watkins. Due to COVID-19 precautions Lori appeared via Zoom with her attorney, Mark Means, who entered not guilty pleas on all four felony charges. Her trial was set for March 22, 2021.

Meanwhile, Special Prosecutor Rob Wood had filed a motion to join Lori's and Chad's cases together, as they faced identical charges. In a supporting memorandum, Wood wrote that the charges against the married defendants involved the willful destruction and concealment of dead bodies to cover up a felony.

"Specifically," read the motion, "the charges relate to the discovery of Lori Daybell's minor children's bodies on her husband Chad Daybell's property and Lori Daybell's alleged conspiracy with Chad Daybell and others (including but not necessarily limited to her brother Alex Cox, now deceased) in committing those acts."

Wood argued that assigning both defendants' cases to separate judges would create "an undue burden" on the State, due to the repetitive work and hearings involved.

"The State understands the high-profile nature of this case," stated the motion, "and the workload it will present to the Court and the judge that presides. The State maintains that judicial economy, efficiency, and consistency will be better served by consolidating the cases."

John Prior also filed a motion to dismiss the entire case against his client, arguing the State had not presented sufficient evidence at Chad's preliminary hearing. In a separate motion he asked for Chad Daybell's trial to be moved out of Fremont County, as it would be impossible to find a "fair and impartial jury" there.

CHAPTER FORTY-TWO

"SUCKED INTO THE VORTEX OF THIS MAN"

On Wednesday, September 30, 2020, Special Prosecutor Rob Wood and his deputy, Mackenzie Cole, flew to Chandler, Arizona, to observe Lori's sister Summer Shiflet's and Zulema Pastenes's interviews by law enforcement. Alex Cox's widow had already been granted an immunity agreement in return for her cooperation.

Wood and Cole arrived at the Chandler Police Department to meet Summer and her attorney, Garrett Smith, prior to her formal interview with police and the FBI. For almost a year Wood had been keeping a tight lid on the case regarding possible murder charges. But he now dropped his guard to openly discuss the State's future tactics, unaware that Summer's attorney was secretly recording the conversation.

"I'm just going to tell you right now," the special prosecutor told Lori's sister, "we are going to be filing conspiracy-to-commit-murder charges against both Chad and Lori. And we're not shy about that."

He brought Summer up-to-date on the State's theory of the case, promising not to pull any punches. "We know that this is not the same Lori everyone else knew. She was primary president, she made quilts for these kids . . . everyone loved her. She loved everyone."

"Great mom," agreed Summer.

"So, I'm going to kind of ask you to consider [if] something happened. I don't know what. I don't know if it was psychological. I don't know if we'll ever know."

He asked if she had ever met Chad, and Summer said she had, only once, at a Preparing a People conference. She and her parents had gone to support Lori, and they met Chad after his brief talk.

But after Lori's arrest and transfer to an Idaho jail, Chad had called her several times. "The first thing he said to me was that . . . 'Lori hasn't told me very much about the kids, so there's not really very much I can tell you about it.'"

"Well," replied Wood, "welcome to Chad Daybell."

"I have my own opinions of him. Don't get me wrong."

"I bet you do. He is highly manipulative."

"Yes. I see that."

"I'm not going to say he's highly intelligent," continued the prosecutor, "but you don't have to be intelligent to be highly manipulative."

Wood told Summer that there was enough evidence against Chad to prosecute him for murder, but the case against Lori was even stronger.

"He did not care who died," said the prosecutor. "He did not care at all. Your sister truly believes that everything she's done, has been done in righteousness."

"I know. I think she one hundred percent believes. I get that she's not fully aware of what she's really done."

"I think she knows what she's done."

"She knew enough to lie to us about it."

The prosecutor then attempted to put Summer at ease before her "hard" interview with law enforcement, reassuring her she was not a person of interest.

Summer asked if there was any further information on Tylee's cause of death.

"She is at the FBI's state-of-the-art crime lab," Wood replied obliquely. "Unfortunately, there's a lot of deceased bodies there that they're going through. We may never know due to the destruction of that body."

"Yeah, the way you guys found them," said Summer emotionally. "I would never have dreamed that she would ever hurt them so."

Wood sympathized, saying he was well aware that he was enlisting Summer's help to build a case against her sister. "But I guess the thing I want you to know is, our whole goal is just justice for these kids."

"I don't take any joy in doing anything that's going to harm her," said Summer. "I don't take joy in her spending her life in prison."

The prosecutor revealed that Lori had made "overtures" to cooperate with law enforcement just before the bodies were found, but Chad had talked her out of it.

"And he uses this kind of, I call it, 'spiritual abuse,'" said Wood. "Spiritual manipulation."

"I hope she does [cooperate]. I pray for that all the time."

Wood said the State's game plan from the beginning had been to put Chad and Lori behind bars on lesser charges while investigators built a rock-solid murder case against them. He noted that Lori's counsel, Mark Means, had "never done any meaningful criminal work" and had never handled a felony before.

"He doesn't know what he's doing," said Wood. "And once we file further charges, she'll be appointed counsel who know what they're doing."

"It's weird to be on the prosecution and defense's side at the same time because I love everybody."

"Just because someone's committed a crime doesn't mean they're a horrible person."

"I'm so torn. It's such a conflicting feeling to know that this person's been good her whole life, and then made this error in judgment and got sucked into the vortex of this man. I feel for her. I just have so much compassion towards her because I know that's not what she would have ever done on her own. And I hate her for that."

Summer asked if Wood was going to seek the death penalty for Lori.

"We sure hope we don't," Wood replied. "A lot of that will depend on her . . . but we haven't made up our minds on that."

"Knowing [Lori], if she comes out of this state and realizes the weight of it, she may prefer that honestly."

A few days later, Summer Shiflet's attorney, Garrett Smith, gave Mark Means a copy of that taped conversation. Means and Chad's attorney, John Prior, immediately filed a motion to have Rob Wood thrown off the case for procedural misconduct.

Emboldened by the embarrassing recording, Means went on Twitter, posting two cryptic Tweets accompanied by a GIF of fleeing rats:

"As I prepare the defense for Lori (Vallow) Daybell, I am learning that persons like Melanie Gibb and her boyfriend David Warwick appear to have been eagerly 'involved' in more than they let on . . . if you know something . . . Say something! We need the persons of knowledge to come forward!"

EPILOGUE

On October 29, Judge Steven Boyce agreed to combine Lori's and Chad's jury trials, under an Idaho criminal rule allowing two people accused of participating in the same crime to be tried together. The judge agreed that a motion for severance could be filed at a later date.

The first week of January 2021, Madison County court magistrate judge Michelle Mallard scheduled a jury trial for Lori Vallow Daybell on the misdemeanor charges of lying to Rexburg police about J.J.'s being with Melanie Gibb.

Several days later, after a lengthy two-day Zoom hearing about removing Rob Wood for procedural misconduct, Judge Boyce decided Wood could remain on the case.

"The court cannot find at this time," said Judge Boyce, "that the interaction between Mr. Wood and [Summer Shiflet] would render Mr. Wood's continued participation in this case unfair, and cannot determine that the prosecutor's pretrial activity will be a material issue. For those reasons then the motion to disqualify Mr. Wood are denied."

But the judge did reprimand the special prosecutor for his criticism of defender Mark Means. The judge said he wasn't going to issue an order for Wood to apologize, but would leave it up to the prosecutor to decide whether he ought to for continued "civility and professionalism" going forward in the case.

On February 4, Fremont County sheriff Len Humphries issued a press release to confirm that Tammy Daybell's autopsy had finally been completed, but the results were not made public as the investigation into her death was ongoing.

After hearing the news, a frustrated Emma Daybell finally broke her silence on Court TV: "This whole situation's been heartbreaking. My dad's in jail, my mom's dead. It feels like we're all alone and I just want to see the document."

On Tuesday, May 25, 2021, on what would have been J.J.'s ninth birthday, Chad and Lori Daybell were indicted on first-degree murder charges for his death, as well as Tylee's and Tammy's. At a press conference, Special Prosecutor Rob Wood and Fremont County prosecutor Lindsey Blake, who had taken over the Tammy Daybell investigation in February, announced that a grand jury had returned nine indictments, finding probable cause that Lori, Chad, and the late Alex Cox had all conspired to murder their three victims.

In addition to the charges they already faced, Lori and Chad were each indicted on first-degree murder for the two children, as well as two counts of conspiracy to commit first-degree murder and grand theft. They were also charged with conspiracy to commit the first-degree murder of Tammy Daybell, with Chad also indicted for her first-degree murder.

Lori was also indicted for grand theft of J.J.'s and Tylee's Social Security benefits, which she continued collecting for months after they died. Chad was indicted for insurance fraud on two life insurance policies on Tammy, which he cashed in immediately after her death.

Both defendants now faced life imprisonment without parole for the murder charges, which also carried the death penalty. Now prosecutors had sixty days to decide whether to pursue that option.

Prosecutor Blake told reporters that convening a grand jury had been delayed for months due to the COVID-19 pandemic. "I want to assure everyone that despite the delays, we have been working diligently to pursue justice for the victims in this case, to ensure we have the evidence required to prove the facts beyond a reasonable doubt in a court of law.

"Members of the grand jury deliberated and determined there is probable cause to believe the Daybells willfully and knowingly conspired to commit several crimes that led to the death of three innocent people."

Although the nine-page indictment did not provide new details on how the three victims had died, it blamed Chad and Lori's religious beliefs. It stated that the couple "did endorse and teach religious beliefs for the purpose of encouraging and/or justifying all the homicides."

The indictment also named Alex Cox, along with other coconspirators, both known and unknown, as members of an ongoing criminal conspiracy that "did willfully and knowingly combine, conspire, confederate, and agree to commit Murder in the First-Degree" of J. J. Vallow, Tylee Ryan, and Tammy Daybell.

In the wake of the indictments, Tammy's parents and siblings released a statement, thanking law enforcement and asking for their grieving family's right to privacy.

"We pray that truth will prevail," it read, "and that all of us left will find a way to pick up the pieces and somehow come out of this crucible together."

Larry and Kay Woodcock applauded prosecutors for finally bringing murder charges against Lori and Chad, telling reporters that they hoped for the death penalty.

"These aren't capital murder charges?" Kay had asked Prosecutor Rob Wood. "We want a capital case."

The following day, Chad and Lori Daybell appeared at separate Zoom hearings for arraignment. Wearing a large mask covering most of her face, Lori stared blankly at the camera, her once immaculate blond hair now dyed dark brown. Her maskless attorney, Mark Means, asked Magistrate Judge Eddins for a continuance to adjourn the case, citing "exigent circumstances," before Lori's new charges could be read out. Special Prosecutor Wood objected, but the judge put the proceedings on hold.

On Thursday morning, Lori Vallow Daybell was found mentally unfit for trial, after a court-ordered clinical psychologist conducted a two-day evaluation and recommended she undergo restorative psychiatric treatment. District Judge Steven Boyce had ordered Lori's psychological evaluation in early March under seal after Means had requested it.

Judge Boyce halted the case until a hearing could be held on the incompetency decision, despite Prosecutor Wood's contesting its findings.

288 · THE DOOMSDAY MOTHER

On June 4, Wood dropped his objection to the psychologist's competency evaluation and the proposed plan of treatment. Under Idaho law, Lori must be able to understand the legal proceedings against her and assist in her own defense.

She was to undergo psychiatric treatment in a mental facility to bring her up to the level of competence and undergo another examination in ninety days. If she was not declared fit, then proceedings would be put on hold for about 180 days as her treatment continues.

On Wednesday, June 23, Judge Steven Boyce set Chad Daybell's murder trial date for November 8, 2021. It is expected to last for five weeks. His attorney, John Prior, soon filed a change-of-venue motion to move the trial out of Fremont County because of all the publicity, which could delay the proceedings.

One week later, two years after Charles Vallow's death, the Maricopa County Attorney's Office announced that a grand jury had indicted Lori Vallow on a single count of conspiracy to commit first-degree murder. The indictment alleges that on July 11, 2019, Lori "agreed with Alex Cox that at least one of them or another would engage in conduct constituting the offense of First Degree Murder."

"Complex, difficult cases of this nature," explained Maricopa County attorney Allister Adel, "take time to properly investigate and solve."

Arizona prosecutors decided not to charge Chad Daybell in connection to Charles Vallow's death as there was "no reasonable likelihood of conviction."

When Larry and Kay Woodcock learned about Lori's murder indictment, they were overjoyed that she would finally have to face justice for Charles's death.

"We are ecstatic," said Larry. "We know it's not going to end soon [and] it's going to take time. We want the i's dotted and the t's crossed."

Before Lori can be extradited to Arizona to face the murder-conspiracy charge regarding Charles Vallow, her complex case in Idaho will first have to be resolved. At the end of July, Idaho prosecutors dropped the destruction, alteration, or concealment of evidence charges against Chad and

Lori, so they could concentrate on the newer murder and conspiracy ones, which carry far more serious penalties.

Then on August 5, after conferring with the immediate family of J.J., Tylee, and Tammy, Special Prosecutor Rob Wood and Fremont County prosecutor Lindsey Blake announced they would seek the death penalty for Chad Daybell. They filed a Notice of Intention in district court citing aggravating circumstances in all three murders, as they were committed for renumeration. They added that the murders of J.J. and Tylee were "especially heinous, atrocious or cruel, manifesting exceptional depravity."

Chad Daybell has pleaded not guilty to all charges against him.

The two prosecutors also released a statement to the media explaining why they sought the death penalty.

"Our process in making this determination was lengthy and comprehensive," it read. "The ultimate decision to seek capital punishment rests with the State, and after completing the entire process, we determined that the nature and magnitude of these crimes warrant the possibility of the highest possible punishment."

One day later, Judge Steven Boyce appointed veteran Idaho public defender Jim Archibald to represent Lori, in the event prosecutors also seek the death penalty for her when she is deemed mentally fit to proceed. Archibald has experience with death penalty cases and will work alongside Mark Means, who is still listed as Lori's lead attorney.

Three weeks after learning that prosecutors sought the death penalty, Chad Daybell waived his rights to a speedy trial. He now probably won't go to trial until sometime in 2022.

A week later, his five children gave an exclusive interview to CBS's *48 Hours,* claiming that their father had been "framed" for Tylee and J.J.'s murder and had definitely not killed their mother. It was the first sign that Chad finally appeared to be turning on Lori. "My father needs someone to be a voice for him," said his eldest daughter, Emma Murray. "None of this would have happened if Lori Vallow had never come into my family's life." They also claimed that if Chad had committed the murders he would not have been "foolish enough" to bury the children in his own backyard in such shallow graves. "He knew how to dig graves," explained Seth Daybell. "This just sounds unbe-lievable to me."

Garth Daybell emphasized that their mother had been in failing health. He had been in his bedroom the night Tammy died when he'd heard "a thump," followed by his father frantically calling for help.

"My dad was just pacing back and forth," Garth told *48 Hours*. "Just saying, 'Why? How could this happen. She can't be dead. Like, how could this be? What do we do?'"

As of press time, Lori is still undergoing treatment in an Idaho State mental facility. She still reads Chad's books and writes to him every day. According to sources, she is often seen on surveillance camera dancing in her cell at night to the music deep in her head.

ACKNOWLEDGMENTS

In my many years of writing true crime books I have never seen another case as terrifying as that of Lori Vallow Daybell. It simply defies logic, lying somewhere between cold-blooded murder and wild religious science fiction—the very embodiment of truth being stranger than fiction.

The idea that a once-loving mother and devout church member could allegedly plan to murder her husband and two children, believing them zombies, is beyond belief.

Since the story first broke in December 2019, this bizarre web of mass murders in preparation for the Second Coming of Jesus Christ has captured the imagination of the world. In its wake have come a stream of TV specials, documentaries, and podcasts, although none have explained how the seemingly mild-mannered end-times author Chad Daybell managed to lead the glamorous grandmother into homicidal madness. But the real question is, what came first, the Lori chicken or the Chad egg?

During my strenuous eighteen months of research, I have spoken to many people closest to Lori and Chad who reveal for the first time what they think really happened. Some can't be named as it is an ongoing case and with good reason they fear for their safety.

I believe it goes back to Lori's childhood and her older brother Alex, as they grew up sharing an eerie codependence. Unfortunately, Alex holds the key to much of what happened and took his evil secrets to the grave.

I would like to thank Larry and Kay Woodcock for their help. We talked on several occasions and they shared their insights and encouragement.

Special thanks also to April Raymond, Lori's best friend in Kauai, for her unique view into the Vallow family. She witnessed firsthand Lori's startling transformation after meeting Chad and experienced her many attempts to recruit April into his evil cult. Much gratitude also to Echo and Vaisia Itaaehau for sharing their fond memories of Tylee and J.J., during happier times when they were all inseparable. I also would like to thank Julie Rowe and Eric Smith, who shared many of Chad's original religious beliefs, before he wandered into the dark side of religious fanaticism.

I also want to thank Shirley Bahlmann, Peggy "Boss" Barney, Tim Bateman, Randy Hollis, Benjamin Hyde, Neal Mestas, Jonathan Moeller, Rich Robertson, Rick Ross, Don Steinmetz, Keith Taniguchi, and Mary Tracy.

As always much gratitude to Charles Spicer and Sarah Grill of St. Martin's Press for their constant help and encouragement, and my agent Jane Dystel, of Dystel, Goderich & Bourret Literary Management, for her unstinting support and morale boosting.

I am also indebted to Gail Freund, Laury Frieber, Berns Rothchild, David Bunde, Melanie Villines, Dave Mack, Monte LaOrange, Dr. Michael Stone, Virginia Randall, Barry and Charlene Eisenkraft, Martin Gould, Emily Freund, Debbie, Douglas, and Taylor Baldwin, Lenny Millen, and Galli Curci.